THE ALASKA GUIDE

THE
ALASKA
GUIDE

Ron Dalby

Fulcrum Publishing
Golden, Colorado

Front cover photograph: Caribou silhouetted against Mt. McKinley in Denali National Park, Alaska. Copyright © 1993 by John Warden, Alaska Stock Images. Back cover photographs: Kissing Puffins copyright © 1992 Alissa Crandall. Mendenhall Glacier, Juneau, Alaska, photo courtesy of the Alaska Division of Tourism. Book design by Richard Firmage Maps by Patty Maher

Library of Congress Cataloging-in-Publication Data
Dalby, Ron
        The Alaska guide / Ron Dalby.
            p.   cm.
        Includes index.
        ISBN 1-55591-131-5
        1. Alaska—Guidebooks. I. Title
F902.3.D34 1994   93–41008
917.9804′5—dc 20   CIP

Printed in the United States of America
        0 9 8 7 6 5 4 3 2 1

Fulcrum Publishing
350 Indiana Street, Suite 350
Golden, Colorado 80401-5093
1-800-992-2908

This book is dedicated to Dean Gottehrer, author, professor and master of the red pencil. Without his encouragement and instruction, this book and others would have remained unwritten.

Contents

Preface

Despite its vastness, Alaska can be a small state. We don't have all that many people up here, nor do we have that many roads or other types of services. Perhaps better than anything else, an anecdote from my research on this book demonstrates what I mean when I say that though we're large, we're small.

As part of my research, my wife and I spent several weeks traveling through southeastern Alaska on the ferries of the Alaska Marine Highway System. As we prepared to board a ferry in Ketchikan, near the southern tip of Alaska's Panhandle, we struck up a conversation with a couple waiting in line behind us. They were from Oregon and on a month-long tour of Alaska. Like us, they were ferry-hopping northward in southeastern Alaska. After reaching Haines, they planned to drive into the main part of the state.

Later that night, en route to Wrangell on the ferry, they asked me about driving up the Dalton Highway (the pipeline Haul Road as it's known locally) to Prudhoe Bay. I told them that the road was technically closed to vacationers about 200 miles from Prudhoe Bay, but I added that the checkpoint had been unmanned for several years and that they could probably drive right through.

For the next 10 days or so we met this couple in one ferry stop or another until finally parting company in Haines for the drive through the Yukon into mainland Alaska. I thought then we had heard the last from them except perhaps for a card at Christmas.

I was, in a word, mistaken. Five days after we parted, I was flying a helicopter for the Alyeska Pipeline Service Company on the North Slope (travel writing doesn't pay all the bills). While doing a morning recon of the pipe, I spotted their car parked near the Haul Road, deep in the Brooks Range—almost the entire north-south length of Alaska from where we first met, something on the order of 1,500 miles in a straight line.

I landed nearby and leaned out of the chopper with a smile on my face. Though I hadn't really expected to see them there, I knew that such things happen with more than normal regularity in Alaska, largely because there are so few roads. They, of course, were somewhat shocked. Out of nowhere, in the middle of nowhere, I dropped out of the sky to say hello. I'm sure that's one story they'll tell for years to come.

When you travel in Alaska, the same kinds of things are possible, particularly if you travel in a vehicle. Distances are vast here, but in most cases where roads exist, there is only one road. It's quite common to meet people early on during an Alaska Highway trip—such as way back in British Columbia—and keep meeting these people again and again in the places you are visiting. And don't be too startled if some Alaskans you meet keep turning up where you least expect to find them.

Acknowledgments

Where does one start when there are hundreds, nay thousands, of people to thank for help willingly offered; help sometimes given by folks who didn't realize that they would in some way contribute to this book.

The people I remember best along the way were the volunteers behind the counters in local visitors centers. I'd usually blow in the door, generally with my wife and one or more teenagers in tow, and begin by taking one of every brochure offered in the room. Then the questions would start, every one of which would be patiently answered with a smile and other gracious gestures including, at times, free coffee and more information than I had bargained for. Those extra scraps of local lore make this book work; without them it would be pretty sterile and much like a thousand other travel guides about a thousand other places.

Also, I thank the staff at Fulcrum who first suggested this book and encouraged me to take on the project. Certainly senior editor Carmel Huestis and marketing director Linda Stark deserve mention by name for their unswerving support and encouragement over the phone. They are backed up by an office full of people who deserve credit as well. From a writer's perspective, Fulcrum is everything one could want in a publishing company.

Last, but by no means least, there's my wife Jennifer, who has not seen the last of my crazy book ideas and the travel schemes and adventures that go with them. When I pause long enough to listen to her, she always has something positive and meaningful to contribute to these projects. It goes without saying that I should pause and listen more often.

Alaska

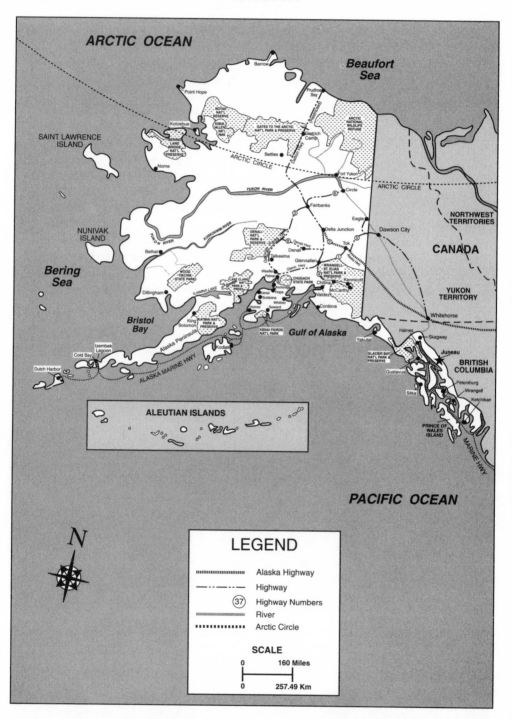

ARCTIC OCEAN

Beaufort Sea

Barrow

Point Hope

Prudhoe Bay

NOTAK NAT'L RESERVE

ARCTIC NATIONAL WILDLIFE REFUGE

KOBUK VALLEY NAT'L PARK

GATES TO THE ARCTIC NAT'L PARK & PRESERVE

Dietrich Camp

Kotzebue

BERING LAND BRIDGE NAT'L PRESERVE

ARCTIC CIRCLE

Bettles

Fort Yukon

ARCTIC CIRCLE

SAINT LAWRENCE ISLAND

Nome

YUKON RIVER

Circle

NORTHWEST TERRITORIES

Fairbanks

CANADA

NUNIVAK ISLAND

KUSKOKWIM RIVER

YUKON RIVER

Eagle

Delta Junction

Dawson City

Bethel

DENALI NAT'L PARK & RESERVE

Denali Hwy

Tok

YUKON TERRITORY

Bering Sea

Denali

Talkeetna

Glennallen

WRANGELL-ST. ELIAS NAT'L PARK & PRESERVE

Glenn Hwy

Wasilla

Palmer

CHUGACH STATE PARK

Kennicott

WOOD-TIKCHIK STATE PARK

LAKE CLARK NAT'L PARK & PRESV.

Kenai

Soldotna

Chitina

McCarthy

Whitehorse

Dillingham

ILIAMNA LAKE

Hope

Homer

Seward

Whittier

Valdez

Cordova

Bristol Bay

King Salomon

KATMAI NAT'L PARK & PRESERVE

KENAI FIORDS NAT'L PARK

Gulf of Alaska

Yakutat

Haines

Skagway

Juneau

Alaska Peninsula

Kodiak

Izembek Lagoon

Cold Bay

GLACIER BAY NAT'L PARK & PRESERVE

BRITISH COLUMBIA

Dutch Harbor

ALASKA MARINE HWY

Gustavus

Petersburg

Wrangell

Sitka

Ketchikan

ALEUTIAN ISLANDS

PRINCE OF WALES ISLAND

MARINE HWY

PACIFIC OCEAN

N

LEGEND

▪▪▪▪▪▪▪▪▪▪▪	Alaska Highway
— · — · —	Highway
(37)	Highway Numbers
▬▬▬▬▬▬	River
●●●●●●●●●●●	Arctic Circle

SCALE

0   160 Miles

0   257.49 Km

INTRODUCTION

BACKGROUND INFORMATION

How big is big? Although it seems like a silly question, imagine Alaska stretching farther from east to west than the contiguous 48 states and farther north to south as well.

Compare Alaska to Texas. Indeed, we've all heard the old saying about cutting Alaska in half and making Texas the third-largest state: but at low tide we could cut Alaska in thirds and make Texas the fourth-largest state. Yes, that much additional land is exposed when the tide slips away from Alaska's shores.

Of course, Alaska has a big coastline and big tides. Alaska boasts more than 40,000 miles of coastline, which is much, much more than all the seacoast in all the other states combined. And it's nothing for the difference between high and low tide to exceed 30 vertical feet; in some flat coastal areas it's miles between the high- and low-tide lines.

Inland is the highest mountain on the continent—Mount McKinley with its 20,320-foot summit reaching almost four miles above sea level. Not only is Alaska the longest and widest, it's the tallest as well.

There's more, obviously. Although some things deserve to be saved for later, one thing can't wait and that's mention of the wilderness for which Alaska is so justly famed. Few travelers journey to Alaska to bask in the neon glow of its cities, though Alaskans are rightfully proud of their hometowns and eager to show them off. Travelers to Alaska are lured by the seemingly endless vistas of mountains, fjords and tundra. They journey north to see the last healthy population of wild grizzly bears in the United States, or the endless herds of caribou crossing alpine valleys, or massive moose browsing in a roadside pond.

About three-quarters of a million people visit Alaska each year, a number that has steadily increased throughout the last two decades and will continue to grow. Most are awed by the experience. Most plan to return. Alaska is not something you can experience totally in a week, a month or a year—or even in a lifetime. There's always another ridge to climb or river to cross. Quite possibly, Alaska is the last U.S. destination that can claim this distinction, a distinction that has changed little in two-and-a-half centuries.

By way of example, Western civilization "discovered" Alaska in 1741. Today that discovery continues. We're still finding out, often to our amazement, just what the land glimpsed from the pitching deck of that fragile, home-built sailing ship contains.

Recommended Reading

The Alaska Almanac: Facts About Alaska. This annually updated book from Alaska Northwest Books (733 W. 4th, Suite 300, Anchorage, AK 99501, 1-800-452-3032) is filled with all sorts of fun-to-know facts and figures about Alaska.

HISTORY

He was a Dane sailing in the employ of a Russian czar. The sheer effort and courage required for his exploits overshadow even the explorations made by his Viking forefathers who beat Columbus to North America by some five centuries.

In Moscow in 1725, Peter the Great commissioned Vitus Bering to journey overland 4,500 miles to the eastern coast of Asia. Once there, in the vicinity of the Kamchatka Peninsula, Bering and his men were to build their own ship, launch it and sail eastward into the North Pacific, searching for the fabled Northwest Passage, unconquered lands and other such riches.

It took Bering three years to reach Kamchatka and build his ship. In 1728 he sailed forth and discovered the Bering Strait between Alaska and Siberia, but somehow didn't see Alaska, though he could only have missed it by a few miles.

Ultimately there would be a second expedition, sailing from Kamchatka in 1741. This time Bering found Alaska, though neither he nor a member of his crew set foot on the mainland. Bering would die heading home from the last expedition and be buried in the Commander Islands between Alaska's Aleutian Islands and the Kurile Islands, currently claimed by the Soviets. (Early in 1992 a Danish archaeologist announced the discovery of Bering's grave and the exhumation of the remains. Plans then were to have the remains of Bering and others of his crew preserved and studied.)

Like Columbus in the Caribbean, Bering and his lieutenants barely touched North America, landing exclusively on islands, primarily in the Aleutians but also Kayak Island near Cordova and Prince of Wales Island in southeastern Alaska. And, like Columbus, Bering never realized the scope of the fabulous riches that he found. His voyages did, however, signal the beginning of Alaska's traditional boom-and-bust economy.

Bering and his crew carried home the first sea otter pelts from Alaskan waters. At the court of Peter the Great in Moscow these lush furs became an immediate hit. Speculators began expeditions to Alaska, most of which went bust for one reason or another. Few people had the fortitude necessary to transport boat-building tools across the vast steppes of Asia or the skills necessary to build a seaworthy boat for the journey to Alaska.

Yet a few did have these skills, or at least a whole lot of luck. And like other adventurers of the age, these weren't necessarily the nicest people who ever sought their fortunes abroad. Alaskan natives, in particular the Aleuts living in the islands closest to Russia, were enslaved, murdered and disenfranchised from their ancestral lands. The sea otters were treated similarly; every year there were fewer and fewer.

Limited improvement in the plight of the natives came with the arrival of Aleksandr Baranov in 1790, the first Russian governor of the Alaskan colony. Baranov first set up shop in Kodiak, and, most important for the Aleuts, he brought along Russian Orthodox priests to introduce their religion to the territory. The combination of limited law and order as well as the coming of religion tamed at least a few of the excesses perpetuated against the Aleuts, though they were still treated as second-class citizens by even the lowliest of the Russians.

But Baranov's priests and laws could not resurrect overhunted populations of sea otters. So Baranov sailed farther east in a effort to find more, eventually moving his capital to Sitka in southeastern Alaska in 1799. Though there were plenty of disagreements with the local Indian clans in southeast Alaska, wholesale genocide was no longer practiced as it had been in the Aleutians in the early years of Russian occupation.

Unlike the peaceable Aleuts, the Tlingits of southeastern Alaska were inclined to fight for their lands, causing a small war three years after Baranov's initial settlement in Sitka. The grounds where this battle was fought can be walked in Sitka National Historic Park.

Ultimately, the Russians took permanent control of Sitka. However, their fortunes began to slip as sea otter populations continued to decline and Russia became more involved in other European affairs. Alaska was eventually offered for sale to the United States.

In the years immediately following the Civil War, U.S. sentiment for buying Alaska was not high. Probably the only one who desired that the United States possess Alaska was William H. Seward, President Andrew Johnson's secretary of the interior. Seward stood up to the insults of "Seward's Folly" and "Seward's Icebox" and prevailed in Congress, ultimately receiving approval to pay $7.2 million to the czar for "Russian America." On October 18, 1867, the American stars and stripes replaced the Russian eagle on the flagstaff in Sitka. Beyond that, nothing much happened.

The United States spent most of the next three decades ignoring Alaska, barely bothering to administer it, much less govern it. A few minor military expeditions penetrated the land, more to survey it than anything else. Gold was discovered in such places as Juneau and Forty Mile, though not in quantities sufficient to create great excitement. Some people expressed interest in laying a telegraph line across Alaska into Siberia and thence across Asia, but the plan never worked out. Mostly Alaska remained the great outback on the northwestern corner of the continent. A few prospectors poked around here and there, but little else went on—until three of those prospectors dipped their pans into a Yukon River tributary just east of the Alaska–Canada border.

George Washington Carmacks, Skookum Jim and Tagish Charlie lifted pans from Rabbit Creek, a Klondike River tributary, with deposits of gold beyond their wildest expectations in early August 1886. A couple of days later they journeyed a few miles downstream to a settlement at Forty Mile on the Yukon River and filed claims with the Canadian government. Within hours, almost every able-bodied man in the Forty Mile region left for the Klondike. Up and down the Klondike River and its tiny tributaries they raced, staking claims for themselves and their friends. By freeze-up seven weeks later, before the rest of the world even realized there was a gold strike in the North, all of the best ground was staked, and the miners settled down in hastily thrown together cabins to wait out the winter in Dawson City, the town they built where the Klondike flowed into the Yukon. Thus began the great Alaska gold rush—in Canada.

But to get to the diggings, would-be argonauts first had to come to Alaska. They began trickling north to Skagway and Street Michael in 1897, after the first load of gold reached Seattle. The trickle became a flood by the spring of 1898.

Skagway, in southeast Alaska, the gateway to the Chilkoot Trail leading to the headwaters of the Yukon River, and Saint Michael, at the mouth of the Yukon River on Alaska's west coast, immediately became bustling cities, transshipping points for would-be miners and their wares. The Chilkoot Trail offered the shortest route to the gold fields, though the most rugged. Going to the mouth of the Yukon, then upstream by boat some 1,500 miles to Dawson was longer, but certainly easier, particularly when one remembers that the Canadian government required all incoming miners to bring at least a ton of food and equipment along with them, enough to last an entire year. Those who hiked inland over Chilkoot Pass had to tote it all on their backs 100 to 150 pounds at a time, then build a boat to float downstream several hundred miles to Dawson.

By the time most of the people arrived in Dawson in 1898, the profitable claims were taken. Certainly there were jobs—digging gold out of the ground for other claim holders and unloading freight from riverboats—but not the kind to make anybody rich. Those who would become rich kept looking.

This search led four Swedes to a black sand beach on the Seward Peninsula in westernmost Alaska in 1898. At a creek flowing into Norton

Sound on the south side of the peninsula, their pans came up brimming with nuggets and dust. Thus Nome was born, a town named by a forgotten mapmaker with bad penmanship. "Cape Name?" written on an early map of Alaska was read by someone as Cape Nome.

Nome offered no natural harbor, no protection from wind and waves for shipping in the Sound, and not even a tree for firewood. The nearest scraggly trees were more than 30 miles to the east. Everything, from coal for heat to food, had to be shipped in and lightered to the beach from ships anchored offshore.

Again, the creeks with profitable concentrations of gold were quickly staked, and most of the 40,000 people in Nome in 1900 were not getting rich. Then someone idly washed a panful of beach sand in the surf and Nome's second gold rush began. The black sands stretching beyond the horizon on both sides of Nome were filled with gold. Within days, sluice boxes sprouted up every few feet as men shoveled the sand through the rockers time and time again.

No sooner had the sand on the beach begun to show signs of wearing out than a geologist realized that over time the coastline at Nome had shifted gradually seaward. There were at least three more ancient beach lines beginning a few dozen yards behind the current shore. Again, the black sands of Nome poured through the sluice boxes, and fortunes were shoveled from the Seward Peninsula.

In its early years, Nome gathered quite a collection of characters while becoming notorious for its lawlessness. Wyatt Earp showed up for a couple of years and ran a saloon and gambling den. Future World War II hero Jimmy Doolittle would spend several of his formative years in Nome just after the turn of the century. The first federal judge sent to Alaska set up shop in Nome and turned out to be an even bigger crook than those he was charged with incarcerating. All contributed to the character of this town, a town twice destroyed by fire and by flood several more times. You can still see that character today when visiting Nome.

Though all this happened less than a century ago, not a trace existed of what are today Alaska's largest cities, Fairbanks and Anchorage. That was about to change.

A fortune seeker introducing himself as Captain E. T. Barnette leased a small river steamer at Saint Michael in the summer of 1901. Barnette believed that an overland trail was going to be pushed into Interior Alaska within a year or two, and he figured to capitalize on this knowledge by opening a trading post where the trail was expected to cross the Tanana River deep in the Interior.

The skipper of the boat that Barnette chartered wasn't so sure. Because the Tanana was a shallow, braided stream, the skipper was uncertain about his ability to reach the area where Barnette wanted to go.

After arguing they compromised; Barnette would pay in advance, and the skipper would take Barnette, his wife, his brother-in-law and their trading supplies as far as possible on the Tanana River. If they could not get as far as Barnette wanted to go, Barnette and his party, along with their gear, would be unloaded as far upstream as the boat was able to get. Like it or not, that would be where Barnette would build his trading post.

As the skipper predicted, he was unable to get within 100 miles of Barnette's goal. With little ceremony, Barnette was dumped off on the Chena River, just above its confluence with the Tanana River, and left to his own devices.

While Barnette was unloading his gear, out of the woods walked Felix Pedro, an Italian prospector who had experienced little success searching for gold but planned to keep trying. Pedro reequipped himself from Barnette's stores and disappeared shortly afterwards to the north.

Barnette and his party quickly built cabins for living and storing the trade goods on the riverbank and settled in for the winter. Once everything was frozen solid, Barnette left his brother-in-law in charge, and he and his wife mushed nearly 400 miles to Valdez to sail outside for the winter.

Pedro returned in the spring for more supplies, though this time he needed a grubstake on credit, having exhausted his funds the year before. Against Barnette's orders, his brother-in-law extended the credit, and Pedro disappeared into the boreal forest north of the river once again. He came out of the woods in July with a poke of gold from a creek a few miles north of the trading post.

Barnette was in Saint Michael when word of the gold strike near his trading post reached him. He had just decided to name the site Fairbanks to please a newfound friend with political influence. Buying all the trade goods he could, Barnette immediately set out for his cabins on the Chena River.

Barnette had experienced several gold rushes in Alaska, but had had little luck in any of them. This time he was basically first on the scene, he knew it, and he knew just how to make that knowledge work for him. Using the names of friends, relatives and anyone else he could think of, Barnette staked claim after claim on the creeks north of Fairbanks. He had no intention of digging gold out of any of them, but knew that if he controlled the ground, he controlled the profits. Thus it became that Barnette and a few others as wise in the ways of the gold fields as Barnette came to have title to almost all of the productive ground in and around Fairbanks.

In the meantime, winter came on as news of the strike made its way around, and miners began mushing toward Fairbanks from all around the north, but in particular from Dawson City. Struggling through the unbelievable cold of an Interior Alaska winter, these men arrived in Fairbanks with few prospects of establishing a paying claim and needing supplies that could only be bought from Barnette. Barnette was well on his way to becoming rich.

A few years later, after a few too many shady deals, Barnette would be forced to disappear from Fairbanks, and nobody is certain to this day were he went. But Fairbanks was part of Alaska to stay, unlike so many other gold-strike towns that lapsed into ghost towns.

After World War I, Fairbanks was the largest city in Alaska, and the territory's economy was really in a slump. One bright spot was the railroad being pushed north from Seward on the Kenai Peninsula to Fairbanks. To house themselves along the way, the construction crews built a tent city that they called Anchorage. It was not yet, however, Anchorage's time—another boom would come first; this boom was fish.

Sea otter, then gold and now salmon. Alaska's major resources were, one by one, leading to economic booms followed by downturns.

Commercial catches of salmon were essentially unregulated in Alaska during the first half of the twentieth century. Huge canneries were built at the mouths of the most productive streams, and cannery boats were sent out with the goal of intercepting every fish that returned to those streams. As the years wore on, more and more canneries were built, and more and more streams came to be all but depleted of spawning salmon. Federal agencies charged with managing the salmon did little to prevent this savaging of a renewable resource. This neglect by federal officials, probably more than anything else, led to the statehood movement in Alaska, a movement that had to wait for World War II and the only boom in Alaska not fueled by natural resources.

This time it was Anchorage's turn. The Army and Army Air Force established major bases in Anchorage, bases forever overshadowing the tiny garrisons that had been established in Eagle and later in Haines during the early days of territorial rule. With those bases came men and materials needed to prosecute a war with Japan. And the war with Japan also brought about a road, the Alaska Highway, or Alcan as it was called in those days. This was the secure overland route the federal government felt it needed in case the Japanese navy succeeded in closing the sea lanes in the North Pacific.

The road led to Fairbanks, but the ships unloading men and materials sent their cargoes to Anchorage. From Anchorage, men and equipment ultimately moved to Kodiak and thence to the Aleutians to fight the Japanese. Concurrent with the battle of Midway in 1942, Japanese invasion forces had occupied Attu and Kiska islands in the Aleutians, the only North American territory captured and held by an invading army during the war.

In a bloody battle, the Japanese were driven out of Attu. Before a similar battle could be fought at Kiska, the Japanese secretly evacuated their troops.

After the war, Anchorage was Alaska's largest city, a status that continues to this day. Yet Alaska's boom-and-bust history doesn't end here; another boom lay just on the horizon—the largest oil field in North America would be discovered on Alaska's Arctic Coast little more than two decades after the war. The only measurable difference this time was that statehood had created a local government to participate in the ruckus caused by this boom. Statehood, as noted earlier, was due in no small way to the ill-conceived manner in which the federal government had managed the last boom relating to an Alaskan resource.

Statehood was not, however, the only force at work in Alaska after World War II. Alaska's Native peoples, descendants of the Aleuts, Eskimos and Indians who greeted the first white explorers, had all but been ignored over two centuries of Russian and U.S. rule. Their voices began to be heard, and before either Alaska or the nation could digest the oil discovered at Prudhoe Bay, the claims of these peoples had to be settled.

In 1971, then President Richard M. Nixon signed into law the Alaska Native Claims Settlement Act, an unprecedented ordinance granting Native Americans from Alaska the opportunity to fully control their own destinies. This act provided roughly $1 billion and title to 100 million acres of land to Alaska's Native peoples. The land and funds were awarded to 13 Native corporations loosely set up along tribal and regional boundaries. Native corporations could select their acreage from the more than 97 percent of Alaska that was then federally owned. Thus, for the first time ever, significant portions of the Alaskan landmass came into private hands.

Once this was done, the state, which owned the land where oil was discovered at Prudhoe Bay, teamed up with the oil companies involved and lobbied Congress for a right-of-way permit for a pipeline. In 1974, Congress approved the building of the trans-Alaska oil pipeline from Prudhoe Bay to tidewater in Valdez some 860 miles away. So began Alaska's most recent boom.

Along the way, though, another major congressional action muddied the waters. In the waning days of his presidency, Jimmy Carter pushed through Congress the Alaska National Interest Lands Claim Act, signing it into law in December 1980. D-2, as it's known in Alaska, placed a California-sized chunk of Alaskan land under varying degrees of federal protection, notably by establishing several new national parks, parks larger in some cases than several other states. Besides the Native Claims Act which created extensive private landholdings in Alaska (including "No Trespassing" signs for the first time), there now exist huge tracts of federally managed land with severe limitations on access for various groups of people.

People who have traditionally lived on these lands are granted hunting, fishing and overland travel rights with little or no impedance. Those wishing to visit from elsewhere often find their movements curtailed or restricted to extremely narrow corridors. There are extensive complaints about allowing privileges to one group and not an other.

This then is the Alaska of the 1990s. It is big, it is still mostly wilderness, and at times it seems that every square inch of it is contested by one special interest group or another.

TEN TOP HISTORIC SITES IN ALASKA

1. **Saxman, just outside of Ketchikan in southeastern Alaska.** Alaska natives left few major sites that are available today for exploration by tourists. This park, primarily relating to Tlinget Indian cultures, offers a look at the totem poles carved by earlier residents and a small glimpse of the culture that was solidly established when Baranov founded Sitka.

2. **Dawson City, Yukon Territory, Canada.** This site is just a few miles outside of Alaska in Canada, yet its importance to Alaska's contemporary history cannot be overstated. One must remember that in 1898 Dawson was a Canadian city populated almost exclusively by U.S. residents. The prospectors who ultimately founded Nome, Fairbanks and other cities in Alaska almost all came first to Dawson.

3. **Nome.** You have to dig a little to find historical Nome. After all, it's burned down twice and washed away several more times in its less-than-100-year history. But the evidence is there from abandoned mining equipment to old gold dredges sitting idle on the edge of town. There's even gold to be found—a few years back a tourist poked his hand under a piece of driftwood on the beach and came up with a gold nugget.

4. **Skagway.** The jump-off point for the Chilkoot Trail, Skagway and neighboring Dyea were rip-roaring frontier towns in the late 1890s. Dyea has pretty much disappeared, but Skagway is still a friendly, exciting place to visit for a taste of the way things were.

5. **Sitka.** Aleksandr Baranov's restored mansion, totem poles and countless other artifacts can be seen at several sites in and around this southeastern Alaska town. The physical setting is truly magnificent.

6. **Kennicott.** Gold wasn't the only mineral attracting investment and excitement. Kennicott and neighboring McCarthy were built, along with a railroad, as part of one of the largest copper-mining operations in the United States. Most of the buildings are still standing.

7. **Eagle.** A small Army post and the headquarters for one of Alaska's most famed early federal judges, James Wickersham, Eagle today has only a few hundred fiercely independent residents, residents who are proud of their town and its history.

8. **Fairbanks.** You'll have to look around and ask a few questions to find the history of Fairbanks, but it's there, from Pedro's discovery site on the Steese Highway north of town to Alaskaland, a theme park preserving many mementos of the gold rush era.

9. **Katella.** Alaska's first producing oil well was pumping on this stretch of remote beach just after the gold rush of 1898. Oil companies are again snooping around this region.

10. **Kodiak.** Russia's first capital city in Alaska was established on this island in 1790. A small museum keeps alive a remembrance of this past and the history of the region's natives who greeted the Russians and suffered mightily because of them.

Recommended Reading

E. T. Barnette and the Founding of Fairbanks, Terrence Cole (Alaska Northwest Books, 2208 NW Market Street, Ste. 300, Seattle, WA 98107, (206) 784-5071), 1981. A great book delving into the crooked speculations of Barnette and his friends as they extorted every cent they could out of the Fairbanks area.

Tracking the Bear, Kathy Hunter, Lazy Mountain Press (P.O. Box 2650, Palmer, AK 99645), 1986. Hunter did an excellent job of tracking down the work of this revenue cutter in western Alaska waters at the turn of the century. Its captain, Mike Healy, was a fiery character, and was for years the only law in western Alaska, both onshore and offshore.

GEOGRAPHY AND GEOLOGY

Of all the states, Alaska is by far the most geologically active. The northern anchor of the Pacific's "Ring of Fire," Alaska has earthquakes and volcanic eruptions quite often. As a general rule, at least one or more volcanoes, mostly in the Aleutian chain, will erupt annually, and earthquakes up to about 6.0 on the Richter scale are so common as to cause little comment. Most of the earthquakes tend to be along faultlines just off Alaska's southern coast, though quite a few each year occur inland near larger cities.

Alaska has two "continental divides," each essentially running east to west. The northernmost of these is the summit of the Brooks Range, arguably the northwesternmost extension of the Rocky Mountains. North of the Brooks Range, water flow to the Arctic Ocean and Beaufort Sea. South of the range, water flow into the Yukon River or other westward-flowing rivers to empty into the Bering Sea between Alaska and Siberia.

The Alaska Range, arcing north around southcentral Alaska, is the other major watershed. North of these mountains, water flows into the Bering Sea in the west. South of the summit, waters flow toward the Gulf of Alaska off Alaska's south coast, the northernmost extension of the Pacific Ocean.

This water has to flow out of Alaska because of another key element of Alaska's physical geography. Permafrost underlies much of mainland Alaska. This is permanently frozen ground under a surface layer of varying thickness. Only the surface layer thaws for a short time during the summer months.

Even at the height of summer, it is possible on most of mainland Alaska to dig down just a few inches to a foot or two at most and find solidly frozen soil. This permafrost affects everything growing or built above it. The thawing and refreezing of parts of the permafrost cause it to shift, making roads buckle and houses tilt. Trees rarely gain significant height in permafrost areas because their root systems cannot reach deep enough to support them in windy conditions. Tree roots on Alaskan trees tend to spread laterally just under the surface instead of probing deep into the earth. Standing trees also tend to lean in every imaginable direction in areas of severe permafrost, giving rise to a condition known locally as "drunken forests."

Water running over permafrost cannot seep into the earth. Thus there are lots of bogs in Alaska—alpine tundra on the side of a mountain is likely to be very wet even on the driest of days. Only rivers and streams can drain water from Alaska.

As might be imagined, permafrost severely limits site options for buildings and roads. For example, a short stretch of Farmer's Loop Road near the entrance to the University of Alaska in Fairbanks is built over a small permafrost bog. In the last couple of decades, an estimated 12 feet of asphalt has been laid over this stretch of road to counter its regularly sinking movement. Several other cold-climate engineering tricks have been tried on this spot, but nothing works for any length of time.

Beyond the still-occurring volcanoes, earthquakes and permafrost shiftings, the other major land-shaping in Alaska was done and is being done by glaciers. Alaska has about 30,000 square miles of active glaciers, including one ice field larger than the state of Rhode Island. These slow rivers of ice are sculpting out huge U-shaped valleys in all of Alaska's mountain ranges just as previous glaciers did. Glaciers and evidence of glaciers abound in almost every region of Alaska.

FLORA AND FAUNA

Like just about everything else in Alaska, the flora and fauna lend themselves to superlatives. For example, birders will find more than 400 species to seek in Alaska. The largest (moose) and smallest (shrew) mammals in North America share the tundra, and all manner of trout, salmon and other fish swim in the depths of inland streams and lakes. Offshore are whales, dolphins, huge halibut, polar bears, seals, sea otters, sea lions and more.

The basic problem with seeing all these critters—or perhaps catching them, when one thinks of the fish—is knowing what kinds of animals to look for in the various types of terrain. More than anything else, the animals you will see in any given location are a function of habitat.

Offshore, things are pretty straightforward. Halibut swim along the bottom in fairly deep water. Various kinds of seals and sea otters prefer coastal areas where they can eat crab, shrimp or salmon.

Onshore, things get more complicated. Alaska's huge landmass creates a wide variety of habitats. Starting from the top, high on mountain ridges is the frightening terrain that is home to Dall sheep and Rocky Mountain goats. The easiest way to tell these two animals apart is to remember that goat horns are black and sheep horns are brown. Also, goats tend to be found around the coastal mountain ranges in Alaska; inland mountain ridges are the province of Dall sheep. Smaller mammals on these ridges include marmots and arctic ground squirrels, the latter called *sik-sik* by Alaskan natives because of the sounds they make.

Somewhat lower than the sheep, on tundra meadows in alpine areas, one can find grizzly bears, caribou and larger bull moose, the latter during the summer. These animals inhabit the vast areas of Alaska's mountain ranges that are above timberline.

At timberline, the makeup of local critters tends to change. Black bears are found in the woods of the Interior more often than grizzlies. In coastal areas, though, the forest can house either black or brown bears, the latter being a variant of grizzly bear. In the woods are also found the smaller bull moose as well as cow moose and their calves.

Besides the bears in coastal forests, there are Sitka black-tailed deer throughout southeastern Alaska, Prince William Sound and Kodiak Island.

Mixed in with all these larger animals are various furbearers, birds and a host of squirrels and other rodents.

Finally, only in arctic coastal areas does one find the great white polar bears. In summer it is exceedingly rare to see one of these bears, as they tend to move offshore onto the pack ice of the polar ice cap. Walruses also inhabit areas used by polar bears, though their range extends much farther south, almost to the Alaska Peninsula near Dillingham.

Fish are scattered throughout Alaskan waters in discernible patterns as well. Rainbow trout, for example, are only native to fresh waters south of the Alaska Range, though they have been successfully introduced to several Interior lakes through various stocking programs.

In the Interior, the primary freshwater fish species are northern pike, lake trout and grayling along with scattered populations of sheefish. Look for lake trout in deep mountain lakes that often don't thaw until July. Grayling can be found in almost any clear stream.

As for plant life, Alaska has relatively few species of trees. Spruce trees, from the massive Sitka spruce in southeastern Alaska to the scraggly black spruce of Interior forests, are most common. Next in order of frequency are birch trees, followed by cottonwoods.

Berry pickers will delight in a wide range of shrubs all over the state, but blueberries are by far the most common. Cranberries, raspberries and others are easily found.

Last, but by no means least, wildflower lovers should time their visits for July. This is the month that the tundra normally blazes with colors, the month the fireweed ripens to a brilliant reddish lavender, and the Indian paintbrush glows bright red at the roadside.

Recommended Reading

Guide to the Birds of Alaska, Alaska Northwest Books (733 W. 4th, Suite 300, Anchorage, AK 99501, 1-800-452-3032). 1990. This recently updated guide is probably the best book available on Alaska's 400-plus species of birds. It is available in almost any bookstore in the state and many gift shops. No serious birder visiting Alaska should be without it.

Alaska's Mammals, Jim Rearden, Alaska Geographic Society (P.O. Box 93370, Anchorage, AK 99509, (907) 562-0164). 1981. Though this book has been around for several years, it was written by one of Alaska's premier outdoorsmen and is definitely not out of date. Many bookstores will have copies available.

Alaska Wild Berry Guide and Cookbook, Alaska Northwest Books (733 W. 4th, Suite 300, Anchorage, AK 99501, 1-800-452-3032). 1983. A great book for identifying berries and suggesting what to do with them after you have picked a pail or two.

Alaska-Yukon Wild Flowers Guide, Alaska Northwest Books (733 W. 4th, Suite 300, Anchorage, AK 99501, 1-800-452-3032). A great book for identifying wild flowers. Lots of color photos.

CLIMATE

This section would better be titled "Climates" with an *s* because Alaska offers at least three major climatic regions.

The first of these is called *marine west coast* by climatologists and includes all of southeastern Alaska, Prince William Sound and on through the Aleutian Islands. This is an exceedingly wet though not a particularly cold climate. Rainfall amounts can and often do exceed 200 inches per year. Ketchikan, as a matter of fact, maintains a "Liquid Sunshine Gauge" on the cruise ship dock so visitors can get an idea of just how much rain falls in a given year. On balance, Ketchikan gets about 165 inches a year— that's an average of about one-half inch of rain per day, every day of the year. Sunny days are highly prized in this part of Alaska.

The bulk of Alaska's mainland comes under a climate generally described as *subarctic*. This tends to be a much drier climate than coastal areas (20 to 30 inches of rain annually), but it is also both warmer in the summer and colder in the winter. The great Interior of Alaska in this climate zone is where one finds the 60- and 70-degrees-below-zero temperatures that make occasional headlines. By the same token, 90-degree days in summer are not at all uncommon.

Alaska's northern and northwesternmost regions exist under a *polar* climate. Summers are cool, just barely above freezing for the most part, winters are cold, though not as cold as Interior Alaska. Rainfall is almost nonexistent, being at most just a few inches a year. Using rainfall as your criteria, polar Alaska would be a desert. However, the limited amount of evaporation because of the cool temperatures and the permafrost underlying the soil combine to keep the land perpetually wet during the short summers.

Of course, nothing is this simple. Take the case of Anchorage, Alaska's most populous city: It lies almost exactly on the line dividing marine west coast and subarctic. Thus winter can be windy and rainy one moment, then frightfully cold and dry the next. Or consider Fairbanks during the winter of 1990–91. Its normally dry climate deserted it that year, and more than 150 inches of snow fell (the average is maybe 50 or 60 inches). Buildings collapsed and city services fell way behind in snow removal efforts.

The message here is to be prepared for anything. Rain forest regions can delight you with wonderful warm sunny days, or it can rain in the normally sunny Interior. To deal with this maze of conditions, dress in layers. If it's warm, you can peel off some clothes; if things cool down, add a sweater or a light jacket. Always keep in mind that a warm hat will go far toward keeping you warm, for people lose body heat faster through their heads than from any other part of their bodies. And never, never be far away from a raincoat.

VISITOR INFORMATION

GENERAL INFORMATION

Virtually every region and city in Alaska frequented by tourists has some kind of a visitors information center. These various centers and chambers of commerce are collected under one heading in Appendix A of this book.

For statewide information, the Alaska Division of Tourism, P.O. Box E-101, Juneau, AK 99811, is a great place to start. Just for asking, they'll send you a lengthy full-color booklet that is essentially a collection of lists—lists of hotels, of restaurants, of air services, whatever. It's well worth having, though you should remember that the only businesses listed in this book are those that pay for their listing in the form of advertising. In other words, these extensive lists are not complete; there are other tourism-related businesses in Alaska.

For information about specific destinations, start with the visitors center or chamber of commerce listed for that town or region. From them learn the names of those attractions appropriate to your travel plans and the names, addresses and telephone numbers of those businesses that can best help you with your vacation plans. Whenever possible, do some comparison shopping and make your initial inquiries to as many separate businesses as possible.

GETTING THERE

Alaska can be any one of three different types of vacations—flying, driving or cruising. Some packages offer a little of each.

Cruising

About one-third of Alaska's visitors select a cruise as their method of visiting part of the state. The most common cruise packages are seven-day, six-night excursions starting and ending in Vancouver, British Columbia. These ships run up through the Inside Passage stopping at three or four cities such as Ketchikan, Sitka, Juneau, Skagway or Petersburg for a few hours. Included may be a sail through Glacier Bay National Park north of Juneau. Rates run about $900 to several thousand dollars per person depending on the on-board accommodations selected. This price covers everything except gratuities and shore excursions. Airfare price breaks to get you to Seattle and Vancouver are frequently offered to those booking cruises.

Driving

Alaska is connected to the rest of North America by the Alaska Highway, the road built to serve the military in World War II. Though not a particularly dangerous drive, the 1,500 miles of road from Dawson Creek, British Columbia, to Fairbanks, Alaska, do pass through some pretty remote and rugged country. Driving to Alaska is a never-to-be-forgotten experience. Allow a minimum of seven days one way from Seattle to Fairbanks. More time is better; there's a lot to see along the way.

Flying

At least five domestic and several foreign carriers serve Alaska. The hub for airlines servicing Alaska is Anchorage, though direct flights are available from Seattle to Juneau and Ketchikan. Points of departure for nonstop flights to Alaska are Seattle (Alaska Airlines, MarkAir, Delta, United and Northwest), Salt Lake City (Delta) and Chicago (United).

Those traveling to and from Alaska on the major airlines generally pay the highest seat-mile rates in the airline industry (we are, after all, a captive audience). You can beat these high rates by watching for special purchase options regularly offered by airlines.

Recommended Reading

The Alaska Highway: An Insider's Guide, Ron Dalby, Fulcrum, 1994. Not only will this book get you to Alaska on the Alaska Highway and its side roads, it will also help you travel throughout the state with its descriptions of every road in Alaska.

GETTING AROUND

Probably nothing makes a vacation to Alaska so different as the lengths one has to go just to get around in Alaska. One does not simply pick a destination, get in a car and go. While this will work for a few places in Alaska, it won't work for most.

For example, it's not an unusual Alaska vacation when over a period of two or three weeks a visitor drives a car, flies in an airliner, rides a marine highway ferry and charters a small floatplane for an excursion into the backcountry. In between there may be trips by train, canoe, bus, cruise ship and sightseeing boat.

Then, too, there are those who plan their Alaska vacation around their favorite mode of backcountry travel—for example, a sea kayaking expedition in Glacier Bay. However, to make that kayaking expedition, paddlers might first fly to Juneau and then take a floatplane or sightseeing boat deep into Glacier Bay National Park to be dropped off.

Rental cars are readily available in the major airline destinations (Fairbanks, Anchorage and Juneau); all the major agencies are represented and reservations can be made through a travel agent. Local operators with vehicles to rent can sometimes be found in smaller towns. It is, for example, possible to rent a vehicle in Cold Bay on the Alaska Peninsula. This may well be the most unforgettable vehicle you will ever rent, but it will probably run well enough to get you around the rather limited local road system.

There are occasional complications with rental cars from the agencies in larger cities. These folks often don't allow you to take their vehicles on certain roads in Alaska. Three roads that are regularly restricted by rental car agencies are the McCarthy Road, the Dalton Highway and the Denali Highway.

For those who like to ride buses, Anchorage, Fairbanks and Juneau do have scheduled bus service around town. There were no regular bus services between Alaskan cities as of early 1992.

Two single-track railroads offer passenger service in Alaska: The Alaska Railroad operating slightly more than 450 miles from Seward to Fairbanks, including Anchorage; and the White Pass and Yukon Route which connects Skagway with Whitehorse, Yukon Territory. You cannot buy a train ticket to Alaska, though; these northern railroads do not connect to the North American rail network.

Taxis are available in almost any town of any size; in rural areas these often will be local folks using their own vehicle to make a couple of bucks.

Charter air services are generally the best and most accepted means of getting to, from and around Alaska's backcountry. These, however, can be expensive. A small plane (Piper Cub) capable of carrying the pilot, one passenger and a limited amount of gear will run about $150 to $175 an hour. The advantage is that this pilot can probably drop you off on a small spot only a few hundred yards long in the middle of nowhere. Larger planes (Cessna 185) holding perhaps three persons and gear plus a pilot rent for $250 an hour and up. Expect to pay more for floatplanes than for wheel planes.

The secret to dealing with charter air services for flights into the backcountry is to get as close to your destination as possible on a commercial airline flight, including the smaller carriers that serve rural Alaska. That makes your time in the air in a charter plane just that much less. And remember, when you charter a plane, you pay for the round-trip. If it takes the pilot half an hour to fly you in and drop you off, you'll pay for a full hour of flight time, the extra time being his half-hour trip back to his base.

INFORMATION FOR THE HANDICAPPED

With a handful of exceptions, Alaska's accessibility for physically handicapped people is limited. As a general rule there is acceptable to good access in all government office buildings, universities and city museums. Beyond that, there may or may not be access; you'll have to check on a destination-by-destination basis. **Access Alaska,** a group serving the needs of handicapped Alaskans, can be of help in planning a trip. Write to them at **3710 Woodland Park Drive, Anchorage, AK 99517,** or call **(907) 248-4777.**

Denali National Park, the Park Service's biggest draw in Alaska, does provide tour buses and other facilities suitable for physically handicapped persons. Most of the other wilderness national parks offer few provisions for handicapped people. However, federal and state regulations are gradually forcing the state and cities to make things accessible to handicapped persons. The results of this, though slow to materialize, are at least fairly steady.

DRINKING LAWS

The legal drinking age in Alaska is 21; be prepared to prove your age with a photo ID such as a driver's license. In an effort to combat alcoholism problems, several rural Alaskan villages have voted themselves dry. In these villages the possession, transportation and consumption of liquor are illegal. Village Public Safety Officers and Alaska State Troopers will enforce these laws. Check carefully before carrying liquor to any rural area.

MONEY

Believe it or not, a regularly asked question in Alaska relates to the type of currency in use. Since Alaska is part of the United States, U.S. currency is the accepted medium of exchange. All major credit cards are accepted in Alaska with VISA and MasterCard being the most widely used.

The one exception to the currency rule is the small town of Hyder wedged against the Canadian border in southeastern Alaska. Hyder is accessible by road from Stewart, British Columbia. As small as it is, Hyder has no banks, thus all banking is done in Stewart. By popular consensus, most of the currency circulating in Hyder is Canadian; it makes it that much simpler to deal with the bank, though it's a lot tougher trying to sort out the conversion rate when you go to the post office and want to buy a 29-cent stamp.

There are still places in Alaska that will take gold dust in lieu of cash, using prevailing daily rates for the value of gold. If you see scales on a shelf near the cash register, ask about using gold instead of cash. The answer might surprise you.

STUDENT AND SENIOR DISCOUNTS

Discounts for seniors are showing up more and more frequently in Alaska; don't be afraid to ask, because this information likely will not be advertised. Discounts for students are almost nonexistent except for occasional special sales during the school year in college towns.

TELEPHONES

One area code, 907, serves all of Alaska, from the cities to the most remote rural areas. Thanks largely to satellite technology, almost every part of Alaska where people live now has telephone service.

In-state directory service can be reached by calling 1-555-1212 in state or by calling (907) 555-1212 from out of state. The standard emergency number is 911. Dialing "0" will normally get you an operator.

TIME ZONES

Geographically, Alaska spans five time zones. In the early 1980s, politicians decided one would suffice. Thus Alaska Standard Time and Alaska Daylight Time were born. The time in Alaska is one hour earlier than the time in California and four hours earlier than New York.

This politically inspired time zone, does make for some interesting sunrise-sunset times. Over near Kotzebue, for example, it's possible to have two sunrises in a single midnight-to-midnight day, because with this revamped time zone midnight on the clock in no way corresponds with true midnight. Thus on one of those short summer nights when the sun only sets for a few minutes, conditions are just right to have two sunrises in a single day—one a few minutes after midnight and a second just a few minutes before the next midnight.

TIPPING

Gratuities for services rendered are appropriate in Alaska just as they are in any other part of the United States. The same percentages generally apply: 15 to 20 percent for meals and to bartenders, 50 cents per bag to bellhops, and so on.

HAZARDS

Because Alaska is largely wilderness, visitors should take several hazards into account when planning activities.

Bears

There are a lot of bears in Alaska, more and more every year according to biologists. And there are more people every year, both residents and visitors. That means it's inevitable that some of those people are going to meet some of those bears. Almost all bear-people confrontations end with no one being hurt; for the most part bears are more scared of you than you are of bears. However, in some circumstances some sort of physical interaction becomes extremely likely. Getting between a sow and cubs is probably the most dangerous situation. Surprising a bear is the next most dangerous.

You can probably avoid both of these hazards by simply making noise while in the wilderness. Talk, laugh or tie a bell to your belt—anything to let the bears know you are around. Also, be sure to keep a clean camp and don't allow any food to be brought into sleeping tents.

If you do come face to face with a bear, don't turn and run as this can trigger an instinct in the bear to give chase. Instead, try to talk in a normal voice as you slowly back away toward safer territory. If there's time, climb a tree, though this doesn't always work because bears can climb, too. If worse comes to worst and you are attacked by a bear, curl up on the ground in a fetal position with your back in the air and lie as still as possible. Bears are rarely interested in people as a meal; they usually just want to eliminate any perceived danger and get out of the area.

A lot of people carry guns in bear territory as protection. By all means feel free to do so, but only if you are thoroughly familiar with firearms and their use. An armed person unfamiliar with guns is generally of more danger to himself and his companions than to any bear he is likely to meet.

Likely areas for bears include berry patches in August when the berries are ripe and along streams and rivers when spawning salmon are present. Do not walk blindly into thick brush in either of these areas.

Recommended Reading

Tales of Alaska's Big Bears, Jim Rearden, Wolfe Publishing (6471 Airpark Drive, Prescott, AZ 86301, (602) 445-7810), 1989. This book balances accounts of bear attacks with large doses of bear biology and fascinating research. Author Rearden is a retired biologist, big game guide and magazine editor; he knows of what he writes when it comes to Alaska's bears.

Hypothermia

Whenever you hear stories of people who die of exposure in the wilderness, it's usually hypothermia, the lowering of the body's core temperature, that kills them. Hypothermia is possible in Alaska even during the height of summer. Wet, hungry and tired people are most likely to be affected by hypothermia. Carry and use raingear, eat regularly while afield and do not overextend yourself.

Shivering is one of the first signs of hypothermia, followed by listlessness and a growing lack of coordination. If anyone in your party shows these symptoms, stop, build a fire, drink warm liquids or snuggle together to rewarm the affected person. Unconsciousness is common in the latter stages of hypothermia, which means immediate medical attention is required.

Boaters in particular should be wary of hypothermia. Almost all of Alaska's lakes and rivers are frozen much of the year, and when thawed rarely warm sufficiently for comfortable swimming. Temperatures of offshore waters rarely rise much above 40 degrees. People thrown into the water in boating accidents are often incapacitated within a few minutes by cold water. In the event of an accident, get ashore as quickly as possible, get out of the wind and try to build a fire. Carrying water-proof matches on your person at all times is always a good idea.

Aviation Accidents

Because so much of Alaska is accessible only by light plane, accidents are not infrequent. Many people do survive the actual crash of a light plane; those who don't make it out alive are those unprepared for survival.

Know your route of flight before you take off; have the pilot go over it with you on a map so you'll at least have some idea of where you are in the event of an accident. Also make certain that the pilot shows you the location of various emergency gear required by law to be aboard the airplane. The most important piece of emergency gear is the emergency locator beacon, a radio on board your plane that should activate in case of a crash. Most of these radios can also be operated manually. Searchers will be en route to the area of an aviation accident within a few hours of these signals being picked up by satellite.

As a general rule, try to travel with your own baggage when on a bush plane flight. These planes generally transport people to remote areas for camping, fishing or hunting activities, so your gear will likely include a sleeping bag, tent and some food—all good things to have should you suddenly find yourself in a survival situation.

If you are stranded by the crash of a light plane, the number one survival rule is STAY WITH THE WRECKAGE. Don't go wandering off unless some physical imperative forces you to move. Searchers will be looking for the airplane; it's a lot easier to spot than a person.

Getting Lost

If you become disoriented or stranded in the wilderness, the best advice is usually to stay put, assuming you left word of where you planned to go and when you planned to return with friends or an agency such as the Coast Guard. If you don't show up on time, these are the people who will start searching for you.

If you feel you must move while lost, the best advice is to walk downhill—downstream if you're along a river. Rivers and streams are the primary means of access in a wilderness. Virtually all settlements are built along rivers and streams for just that reason. If you walk downhill long enough, you will eventually reach a river or a stream. Old cabins that you can use for shelter will most likely be found on stream banks as well. Alaskan etiquette demands that if you use for your survival the supplies someone has cached in a remote cabin you replace these items at your own expense as soon as possible after being rescued.

One tip for finding direction: At high noon in Alaska your shadow points north and the sun is due south of you. Because Alaska is so far north, the sun never rises to a point directly overhead. Except in March and September, sunrises and sunsets cannot be depended upon to show east and west. Depending on your timing in the summer, the sun can rise anywhere on a 60-degree arc between north-northeast and east-northeast and set on a similar arc from west-northwest to north-northwest. Near the equinoxes (March 21 and September 21) the sun does rise in the east and set in the west.

Giardia

Alaska has an abundance of unpolluted, crystal-clear streams. Unfortunately, many of these streams host a parasite naturally transmitted by caribou and beavers, *giardia*. Boil all water for several minutes before drinking or strain it through a filter with a mesh fine enough to filter out these microscopic organisms. *Giardia* usually strikes about 10 days after consumption of the affected water. Its severe flulike symptoms will make you wish desperately that all you had was a case of the flu.

HOW THIS BOOK IS ORGANIZED

Most previous travel guides to Alaska divide the state geographically into five or sometimes six major areas. Though this may be convenient from the standpoint of physical geography, it doesn't always lend itself to realistic travel. *The Alaska Guide* is divided into 10 distinct sections, each section defining a region that is a likely site for a vacation or at least part of a vacation. These distinctions were decided upon after decades of observing the Alaska travel market and how people put their own trips together once they arrive in Alaska.

Matching these sections to your mode of arriving in Alaska will make it easier to use this book.

CRUISE SHIP PASSENGERS

Those cruising to Alaska will find the information they need primarily in section 1, Southeastern Alaska, as this is where the majority of the cruise ships visit. However, there are now several sailings each year to Prince William Sound, section 8, and the Kenai Peninsula, section 5. In these three sections, all ports of call visited by regularly scheduled cruise ships are covered.

ALASKA HIGHWAY TRAVELERS

Those driving to Alaska will probably be most interested in the following sections: 9, The Interior; 2, Anchorage; 5, The Kenai Peninsula; 6, The

Matanuska–Susitna Valley; 7, The Copper River Basin, and 8, Prince William Sound. This assumes a typical driving trip going first to Fairbanks, then south to Anchorage and the Kenai, then through the Copper River region and Valdez on Prince William Sound on your way out of Alaska.

FLY-IN VISITORS

This one's a little tougher to predict, depending on whether you fly into Anchorage, Fairbanks or Juneau. However, several sections of this book cover only those parts of Alaska that you can reach by further air travel. These include section 10, Arctic Alaska; section 4, Western Alaska; and section 3, Southwestern Alaska. As such, these sections can be appropriate for both driving and cruise ship visitors as well. All offer several possibilities for enhancing an Alaskan vacation already rich in vistas seen from the road or from the deck of a ship.

ACCESS

Travel in and around Alaska almost always comes down to a question of access. To this end, the places described in the sections of this book will hold a notation of how one can get there. This is more important than most people think—in the places described in the following pages, all of these means of access will be included:

| bus | bush plane | canoe | car | cruise ship |

| day boat | feet | ferry | jet airliner | raft | train |

FESTIVALS AND EVENTS

It's been said that you can define a people or a culture by the type of things they choose to celebrate or to what (or whom) they dedicate organized events. One look at some of the things on an Alaska list might just give you cause to pause: There's the Talkeetna Moose Dropping Festival and the Talkeetna Wilderness Woman Competition for starters. We're not sure what that says collectively about Talkeetna, but both are lots of fun.

At any rate, there's a whole calendar full of fairs, festivals and other events in Alaska, not all as zanily named as a Moose Dropping Festival, but all fun nonetheless. You'll find nationally renowned cultural events—the Sitka Music Festival in June is one example—celebrations of regional history like Golden Days in Fairbanks, and just-for-fun parties like the Iceworm Festival in Cordova.

This book lists all the various festivals, fairs and other events in the appropriate section corresponding with the city or region where they take place. Dates are approximate because most vary slightly from year to year. Local visitors centers and chambers of commerce can update you on exact dates for any given year by mail or over the phone.

OUTDOOR ACTIVITIES

Nothing defines an Alaskan vacation more than the outdoors, for that is the attraction that pulls most visitors north. Whether one gets his or her dose of the outdoors standing on the deck of a cruise ship or pausing to wipe a sweaty brow while backpacking, the outdoors and all its various activities are the major draws in Alaska.

The following list of activities, while by no means complete, should give you a taste of what awaits in Alaska.

Ballooning

Calm, clear evenings that last all night long are made for hot-air ballooning. However, soaring insurance premiums have forced most of Alaska's balloon operators out of business. There are still a couple of operators hanging on in Anchorage and perhaps one or two in Fairbanks. Inquire locally for the names and telephone numbers of operators.

Biking

Anchorage boasts a tremendous bike path in the form of the Tony Knowles Coastal Trail, 30 or more miles around the entire city and extending quite a ways north and south of town. Any kind of bicycle and any level of skill is appropriate on this wide, paved trail.

Mountain biking is increasing in popularity in Alaska, and there are several suitable trails, particularly in the Chugach National Forest on the Kenai Peninsula south of Anchorage. Interior Alaska trails tend to be too boggy because of underlying permafrost to be very good for biking.

Long-distance bicycle touring buffs trek up the Alaska Highway every year, tour the state's road system, then ride home again. Allow 15 to 20 days one way on the Alaska Highway from Dawson Creek, British Columbia, to Fairbanks. Exceptionally strong riders can probably cover the road one way in 10 to 14 days depending on the weather. Both in northwestern Canada and Alaska, there are long stretches of paved roads with very narrow or nonexistent shoulders. You may have to dismount to avoid traffic along some of these roads.

Canoeing

The ageless romance of northwoods canoeing is alive and well in Alaska; at times it positively thrives. Several great canoe trails are in place and there are virtually limitless opportunities for creating your own itinerary for a canoe trek.

Probably the most popular canoe trails in Alaska are the Swanson River and Swan Lake systems in the Kenai National Wildlife Refuge about 150 road miles south of Anchorage. Both trips wind you deep into a game refuge through a chain of small lakes teeming with trout. Short portages connect most of the lakes.

Other good trips to try include the Gulkana River starting in Paxon Lake and the nearby Tangle Lakes trip that leads into Isabel Pass in the Alaska Range. Both are river trips, and each has a dangerous area of rapids with a marked portage.

Canoes and most of the gear you need can be rented in Alaska, though it's generally cheaper to bring your own if you drive up. If you do the latter, stick to aluminum, fiberglass or one of the high-tech plastics; rivers in Alaska aren't very kind to wooden canoes.

Dogsledding

As Alaska begins attracting winter tourists, various dogsled trekking opportunities have sprung up. Right now most of these are available in the Matanuska–Susitna Valley north of Anchorage and on the Kenai Peninsula. Contact the appropriate visitors centers from the list in Appendix A for the latest information on available trips and tours.

Summer travelers can see a demonstration of dogsledding techniques at Denali National Park. Several times daily a ranger harnesses a dog team to a sled on wheels and demonstrates what it is like to handle the animals and the sleds. Denali National Park is patrolled by rangers driving dog teams in the winter months.

Dogsled Racing

There are essentially two types of sled dog races—sprint and distance. Sprint races generally involve three or four heats over a like number of days. Heats are generally 20 to 30 miles long, and a winning team will cover the distance in less than two hours. The best sprint races each year are normally the Grand Nationals in Anchorage—part of the annual Fur Rondy celebration in mid-February—and the North American in Fairbanks, usually the second weekend of March. Both races start and finish on a downtown street.

Distance races are the long hauls taking several days. Most famous of these is the Iditarod, usually starting the first Saturday in March from downtown Anchorage and ending 11 to 14 days later when a winner crosses under an arch set up on Front Street in Nome about 1,049 miles away. Next best known is the Yukon Quest from Fairbanks to Whitehorse, Yukon, in even-numbered years and from Whitehorse to Fairbanks in odd-numbered years; again, a race of about 1,000 miles, usually in mid-February.

Distance races are usually tougher for spectators because about the only places you can see the action are the start and finish lines. Most of the race takes place in remote, all but inaccessible country.

Fishing

Alaska's tens of thousands of miles of wild streams and rivers, tens of thousands of freshwater lakes and more than 40,000 miles of coastline offer unparalleled opportunities for catching a multitude of species of game fish and succulent table fare. In one sense, this is what Alaska is all about—almost certainly there are fish in Alaskan waters that have never seen a lure and will live out their entire life cycle without ever seeing one. Even popular streams can, during major salmon runs, yield limits of fish to every one of several thousand persons standing shoulder to shoulder along the bank.

Appropriate sections of this guide will suggest several possibilities for fishermen, some relatively accessible, others requiring some extra effort to reach. As a general rule, the harder it is to reach a fishing site, the better the fishing is likely to be. But, like all general rules, there are exceptions; in the Copper River Basin you can park your motor home next to a lake we know, walk 50 feet or so to the dock and cast from shore for rainbows up to two feet long.

A few things about fishing etiquette: We strongly believe that native rainbow trout should only be sought by fishermen willing to practice catch-and-release fishing. Alaska has native rainbows up to 30 pounds, but not very many, and it takes decades to grow a fish that large. Measure and photograph your catch, but by all means handle it carefully and return it safely to the water whence it came.

With an occasional exception, you can keep any salmon you catch up to the specified limits without fear of harming the resource. Exceptions are streams such as the Kenai River where the Alaska Department of Fish and Game may restrict king salmon fishermen to catch-and-release conditions for part of the season to ensure that adequate numbers of fish reach the spawning grounds. With most other salmon runs, more than enough salmon reach the spawning beds, no matter how many sportfishermen catch along the way.

Those catching lake trout and grayling in Interior waters should also consider catch-and-release, though keeping an occasional fish for your supper shouldn't cause any great harm. These species, particularly in readily accessible waters, can quickly be overfished.

Be sure to pick up a copy of Alaska's sportfishing regulations at any outdoor store or fish and game office before going afield. Alaska's fishing laws and regulations can be exceedingly complex; you may need several hours to get through this booklet before you go fishing.

Anyone over 16 must have a fishing license in his or her possession while fishing in Alaskan waters. Exceptions to this rule are certain national parks where no licenses are required. For additional information, contact the **Alaska Department of Fish and Game, 333 Raspberry Road, Anchorage, AK 99518, (907) 344-0541.**

Four-Wheeling

While Alaska would seem to be great country for four-wheel-drive adventures at first glance, the reality is that few marked trails exist and permafrost bogs severely limit overland travel in areas without trails. Four-wheeling in Alaska can cause serious environmental damage during summer months by ripping up the fragile land surface. The best four-wheeling sites are usually small streams with a solid gravel base. By crossing and recrossing these streams, it's often possible to drive quite far off the beaten track. However, it is against the law to drive through any stream in Alaska that hosts spawning salmon, steelhead or arctic char.

There are, however, a few trails mentioned in this book that make for good four-wheeling adventures. For the most part these trails are on Bureau of Land Management (BLM) lands. There are few options for four-wheeling on Alaskan lands managed by the National Park Service, Forest Service and the state. Contact the appropriate agency from the list in Appendix A for information on four-wheeling on public lands.

Golfing

Anchorage, Palmer and Fairbanks offer a few opportunities for "normal" golf. Inquire at local visitors centers.

There are, however, a number of "abnormal" golfing events in Alaska. One of the most fun is the annual Bering Sea Classic in Nome in mid-March, part of the Iditarod Sled Dog Race celebration in Nome. A six- to nine-hole course is laid out on frozen Norton Sound with artificial greens surrounding tuna cans sunk in the ice. Golf balls are painted orange or other bright colors to aid in their being found when they fall into cracks and crevasses in the ice. To aid in defrosting the golfers, several tee shots are made from the seawall behind local watering holes.

If this isn't enough, there's an annual one-hole, par 75 (sort of) tournament in Kodiak. Optional equipment includes chain saws, several spotters to find the ball, machetes and goggles.

Hiking and Backpacking

Few places in the world offer more opportunities for hiking and backpacking than Alaska. Your feet, in fact, are the only means available for exploring vast tracts of the Alaskan landscape—in part because motorized transport is outlawed in many areas, particularly remote national parks. Outside of those areas, nothing yet has been invented that can transport you to some of the wild and beautiful spots that Alaska has to offer.

The **Chugach National Forest (201 E. 9th, Suite 206, Anchorage, AK 99501, (907) 271-2500)** offers some of the best-maintained trails in the state on the Kenai Peninsula south of Anchorage. Various trails are available to challenge those interested in a short stroll for a couple of hours, or extensive backpacking treks, or just about anything in between.

Other trail networks are available in Chugach State Park in Anchorage, in the Matanuska–Susitna Valley about an hour's drive north of Anchorage, and near Fairbanks. Most of the trails in and around Fairbanks are managed by the Bureau of Land Management. In the Mat-Su Valley, the Parks and Recreation Office in the borough office building in Palmer can provide you with a list of more than 140 marked trails.

Besides the few areas mentioned above, there are rather few prepared and marked trails in Alaska. For the most part hiking and backpacking in Alaska mean choosing a place you want to visit, selecting a route from a map, and then striking out overland seeking the best possible walking areas. If you look carefully, you may detect subtle differences in vegetation that suggest an old winter trail from mining days in the early part of this century or some other clues to previously traveled routes. For the most part, though, Alaska is unfettered with trails. Serious backpackers pick a destination and make their own routes.

Although trail etiquette in Alaska is much like it is in other regions, some special things should be considered.

1. *Campfires*: Be extremely careful where you site a fire in Alaska. Tundra and muskeg, the two most frequently found surfaces, are mostly vegetation, and these surfaces will burn. Be certain you are on mineral soil before starting a fire. Usually the best assurance of a safe site for a campfire is on a gravel river bar or an outcropping of rock on a hillside.
2. *Human waste*: Privies are few and far between. Bury waste materials at least a foot down if you are able. Try to avoid soiling frequently used pathways.
3. *Food*: When camping, separate cooking/eating areas from sleeping areas by at least 100 feet whenever possible. Do not take any food into a sleeping tent. If in a timbered area, hang your food bags from a tree at night. Bears are common almost everywhere in Alaska.
4. *Insects*: To minimize disturbances by insects, keep to exposed hillsides and riverbanks whenever possible. There's usually a breeze blowing in these areas, and that will help keep the bugs away.

Weather can always be a problem in Alaska. Keep raingear close at hand while hiking and don't hesitate to use it. Wet clothing leads quickly to hypothermia. Clothing should be adequate to handle below-freezing temperatures at any time of the year, particularly in mountainous regions.

Carry the best maps available when you're hiking in the wilderness. In Anchorage, Fairbanks and Juneau the U.S. Geological Survey offices can help, or you can order the maps in advance from a similar office in your home region.

Hunting

In Alaska, hunting still plays a significant role in the state's tourism industry. In recent years, hunting has become an extremely complex undertaking in Alaska. The federal government regulates what's known as "subsistence" hunting; the state attempts to regulate "sport" hunting around federal and state rules for subsistence; and just about everyone involved in the hunting industry is mad at somebody.

Be that as it may, Alaska offers unparalleled opportunities for big game, small game, waterfowl and upland game hunting. A few key rules should be remembered by those planning an Alaskan hunt:

1. Nonresidents (those who live in any other state except Alaska) must be accompanied by a licensed master or registered guide when hunting Dall sheep, Rocky Mountain goat, grizzly bear or brown bear anywhere within Alaska. The only exception to that rule is a nonresident who is accompanied afield by a relative within the second degree of kindred by blood or marriage—mother, father, sister, brother, son or daughter.
2. Aliens (residents of any country except the United States) must be accompanied by a licensed master or registered guide on any big game hunt within Alaska.
3. With only a couple of clearly stated exceptions, it is illegal to hunt a big game animal in Alaska on the same day that you have flown or ridden in an airplane. (This is locally known as "same day airborne," and it is probably Alaska's biggest poaching problem.)

Prospective hunters can obtain a copy of current regulations by writing to the **Alaska Department of Fish and Game, 333 Raspberry Road, Anchorage, AK 99518.** A copy of the current list of registered and master guides can be obtained by sending $5 to the **Alaska Department of Commerce, 3601 C Street, Suite 722, Anchorage, AK 99503, (907) 562-2728.**

Kayaking

Both river and ocean kayaking are available in Alaska. River kayakers will have all manner of waters to test their mettle; it's really a question of picking just which water and what degree of difficulty one wishes to experience. Ocean kayakers have more than 40,000 miles of coastline available for exploration.

The most popular ocean kayaking trips are in Glacier Bay National Park, Prince William Sound and along the Inside Passage waters of southeastern Alaska. The more adventurous will try the Aleutian Islands or Kodiak Archipelago southwest of Anchorage. Ocean kayakers should be well aware of tidal conditions. Tide books are free for the asking at most outdoor and sporting-goods stores—definitely a "don't-leave-home-without-it" item.

Skiing

Cross-country skiing: Literally all of Alaska lies at the feet of cross-country skiers. Every year a couple of people will try to ski from Anchorage to Nome along the 1,049-mile route of the Iditarod Trail Sled Dog Race; others will trek across the state from north to south as did one recent adventurer who spent a total of 18 months working his way from Barrow in the Arctic to Cold Bay on the Alaska Peninsula.

Most cross-country skiers, however, stick to more staid adventures on prepared trails in or near most of the larger towns or on group outings arranged by various organizations. One of the best of the latter starts from Anchorage every year on a special train arranged with the Alaska Railroad. Carloads of skiers are carried a couple of hours from town to ski all day in untracked wilderness, then party in the train en route back to Anchorage. There is lots of fun and companionship, complete with an "oompah" band on the train.

Downhillers will find two major ski areas, Alyeska south of Anchorage and Eagle Crest near Juneau. Also in Anchorage are a number of smaller sites, but these are the two major alpine ski areas in Alaska. At Alyeska, usable snow is usually present from early October through the end of April.

Snowmobiling

As it is for cross-country skiers, most of Alaska is open to snowmobilers. One needs to be a little careful about avoiding private land (not really a big problem) and certain areas of public land where motorized transport is forbidden. Other than that, just about anywhere is fair game.

There used to be a great snow-machine race from Anchorage to Fairbank. In the early 1970s, the opening of the Parks Highway between Fairbanks and Anchorage pretty much put an end to this race, although for a couple of years it was common on race weekend for drivers on the highway to be passed by snow-machiners heading for Fairbanks.

There is, however, a great race in Alaska for snow-machiners these days, the annual Iron Dog Classic from Nome to Big Lake on the Iditarod Trail, usually in mid-February. Anyone who wants to be a contender in this race has to be able to ride a souped-up machine more than 1,000 miles in less than 48 hours. Contestants are required to travel in pairs.

Inquire locally in individual towns if you are interested in snow-machine trips. There are relatively few machines available for rent, so most aficionados must bring their own.

WHERE TO STAY
ACCOMMODATIONS

A lot of places in Alaska have no hotels or lodges or any kind of rent-by-night accommodations. However, most who visit these regions have made plans in advance and either bring their own tents or arrive in some sort of camper or motor home.

Those places that do provide accommodations can offer a wider range of choices than most people think possible. Luxury hotels are available in the major cities with expensive suites available if that's what you desire and your pocketbook can handle. Then there are some places in remote areas where the sanitary facilities are nothing more than a four-by-four one-holer some 50 feet out the back door. And in some areas, you'll pay a lot of money for a room that includes the use of a one-holer out back.

For the most part, though, the hotels and lodges described in this book will be at least a step or two above completely rustic. Each write-up should provide sufficient information about pricing and available facilities to allow you to decide in advance whether this is a place you would want to stay. We strongly recommend advance reservations confirmed in writing for those planning to visit Alaska during the busy summer season. Hotels and other types of lodgings fill up quickly at the height of the tourist season.

What is expensive lodging in one town may or may not be expensive in another; everything is relative to the local area. For example, $100 a night might get you a comfortable room in an Anchorage hotel with cable television, a private bath and a number of restaurants within easy walking distance. The same money in Bettles might get you only a bed in a bunkhouse with a bathroom down the hall and three meals a day of whatever they happen to be serving in the cafeteria.

Because prices are subject to change with little notice and, unfortunately, with alarming frequency, we've settled on a coding system used throughout the text to rank the accommodations by cost. These are essentially relative values, but they will provide you with some idea of what you might expect to pay for a night's lodging.

$	less than $50 a night
$$	$50 to $100 a night
$$$	$100 to $150 a night
$$$$	more than $150 a night

Bed and breakfasts are becoming increasingly popular in Alaska, and prices can vary wildly. Their big advantages are the wonderful people who operate them and the opportunity to tap their first-hand knowledge of local events and attractions. For more information on B&Bs, contact the **Alaska Bed and Breakfast Association, P.O. Box 1321, 526 Seward Street, Juneau, AK 99801, (907) 586-2959.**

Another uniquely Alaskan type of accommodation is a remote, backcountry lodge. Normally these are in areas offering world-class fishing for several species of game fish, and these are extremely pricey, often $4,000 per week per person. That price includes the bush flights in and out of the lodge, wonderful food, attentive staffs and daily guided fishing expeditions; certainly an unparalleled experience if you can afford it. Most of these lodges are booked one or more years in advance; normally there are fewer than 20 guest rooms or cabins.

Elderhostel programs are increasing annually in Alaska. For those more than 60 years old, these programs offer a modestly priced alternative to the normally high commercial prices for lodging and meals. Participants normally stay in college dormitories or similar digs, and meals are cafeteria style. For additional information on this national organization, contact **Elderhostel, 80 Boylston Street, Boston, MA 02116, (617) 426-8056.**

CAMPING

Whether you prefer "camping" in a deluxe motor home or packing in a pup tent to a mountain peak, Alaska has something—a lot of somethings, in fact—for you. Roads through wilderness areas offer hosts of opportunities for campgrounds to accommodate both RV operators and tenters. Alaska's 590,000-plus square miles of wilderness are great for campers of all kinds.

Essentially, there are two kinds of campgrounds, public and private. Public campgrounds are those built by the appropriate agencies on government-managed lands. In Alaska, these agencies include the National Park Service, the Bureau of Land Management, the National Forest Service, the Alaska Division of Parks and Recreation and a number of city and borough governments. Private campgrounds are those on private land and run as businesses.

As a general rule, private campgrounds cost more for a one-night's stay than public campgrounds, but private campgrounds offer many more amenities such as showers, washers and dryers, electrical and water hook-ups, and sewer dumps for RVs. Public campgrounds will generally provide a suitable parking space for a vehicle, a heavy-duty picnic table and an outhouse. There may or may not be potable water available at public campgrounds. Some of the better public campgrounds will have prepared tent sites for pitching your favorite canvas house. Expect to pay around

$20 per night in a private campground and from $5 to $10 in a public campground. Showers and washers and dryers in private campgrounds are usually coin operated, so you'll need a few bucks worth of quarters to take advantage of these facilities besides the cost of staying overnight.

Off the road, literally all of Alaska that is publicly owned (more than 75 percent of the state) is a possible campsite, though a little common sense is certainly appropriate when selecting a place to set up for the night. RV drivers can take advantage of old gravel pits and turnouts along all of Alaska's highways if the campgrounds are full. In fact, some of the most fun on an Alaska trip are the impromptu parties at some of these sites on long summer evenings. Look for a site that gets you well off the road, park facing whatever scenery you like, kick back and relax.

Those who hike, canoe, raft or fly to off-the-road sites tend to camp along rivers or on small, exposed knolls. The key reason for this is insects, primarily mosquitoes. There's almost always a breeze blowing up- or downstream along a river or creek; in drier areas, open knolls take advantage of any existing breezes. These breezes help keep the bugs away, particularly important in June. Do exercise some caution in siting your tent in remote areas. Bears, for example, generally keep to fairly well-defined trails along stream banks; you won't want to set up your tent in the middle of a bear trail. As well, if the weather is threatening, make sure your tent site is above the high-water line for a creek or river. Being flooded out in the middle of the night is no fun.

A couple of other tips for tent campers—first, make sure your tent is a dark color. The orange or bright red tents that were so popular in the 1970s are lousy in a land where it never gets dark. Inside an orange tent one gets the feeling of trying to go to sleep under a searchlight. Also, if mosquitoes bother you, plan your trip for late in the summer because June is by far the buggiest month. By August, most of the mosquitoes are gone. Finally, carry a piece of plastic sheeting sufficient to cover your entire tent and rain fly. Soaking rains can come at any time, particularly in southeastern Alaska and in Prince William Sound. Nothing dampens your spirits more on a camping trip than a wet tent and a wet sleeping bag. Being able to stretch that plastic over your tent during prolonged wet periods will work wonders for your morale.

The various government agencies managing lands in Alaska are listed in Appendix A. Use this list to write or call for information on areas that interest you.

Recommended Reading

Camping Alaska and Canada's Yukon: The Motorist's Handbook to North Country Campgrounds and Roadways, Mike and Marilyn Miller, Pacific Search Press (Seattle, WA), 1987.

WHERE TO EAT

Oftentimes in Alaska you'll have few—maybe only one—choice when planning to purchase a meal. Not that this is particularly bad, it's just a fact of life in little-populated areas. As we did with accommodations, we've coded by price the restaurants or other eateries described in this guide:

$	less than $10 per person
$$	$10 to $15 per person
$$$	$15 to $20 per person
$$$$	more than $20 per person

These prices for meals do not include the purchase of any alcoholic beverages.

As for restaurants listed in this book, at one time or another we have tried every one listed or have occasionally relied on the observations of trusted friends. No one connected with any of these restaurants knew that we would one day write a book that would include a description of their offerings; we prefer to travel anonymously when dining out. We did not try to describe restaurants where we have not eaten; and we deliberately left out of this writing those restaurants where the food or service was bad.

Red salmon fishing on the Kenai River. (© 1993 Alissa Crandall)

Ron Dalby's Top Ten

MY FAVORITE ALASKA
—— DESTINATIONS AND ACTIVITIES ——

1. *Kennicott.* This abandoned copper-mining facility and company town offers a little of all the best there is in Alaska for visitors: spectacular scenery, history, and some great fishing along the rustic road leading to it. The most thrilling way to get there is by vehicle. About 30 miles south of Glennallen on the Richardson Highway, turn east toward Chitina. Cross the Copper River at Chitina and continue approximately 60 more miles on the old Copper River & Northwestern Railroad roadbed to the bank of the Kennicott River. Pull yourself across the river via the hand tram to McCarthy. From McCarthy it's an easy five-mile walk to Kennicott, or regular bus service is available between the two sites. The best time is mid-June through mid-September.

2. *Skagway.* For those rushing to the Klondike goldfields just before the turn of the century, the "Trail of '98" began in Skagway. Much of downtown is similar in appearance to the way it was then, and it is a National Historic Park. It can be reached by road (99 miles south of the Alaska Highway from Whitehorse on the Klondike Highway), by sea (ferries and cruise ships regularly call in Skagway) or by air (in small craft from Juneau). The best single day to be there in the summer is July 4th; Skagway throws a great Independence Day celebration.

3. *King salmon fishing.* Blind Slough just outside of Petersburg probably offers the best stream fishing for kings in Alaska. Either fly to Petersburg on Alaska Airlines or ride the ferry. Leaving the ferry terminal, turn right and go 14 miles or so to a parking lot on the shoulder of the road. A boardwalk leads about a quarter-mile across the muskeg to the mouth of Blind Slough. Best fishing in the slough is available at low tide. Almost any lure will work. The last week in June and the first week in July are best.

4. *Kenai Fjords Tours cruise of Kenai Fjords National Park near Seward.* A two-and-a-half-hour drive south from Anchorage puts you in Seward, where the boat leaves the dock at 11:30 A.M. A hot lunch is served on board. In six to seven hours afloat you'll see massive glaciers; all manner of marine wildlife, including whales; and spectacular vistas of one of the most rugged coastlines in the world.

5. ***TEMSCO Helicopters Mendenhall Glacier excursion from Juneau.*** A few minutes after leaving the heliport, your pilot lets you out on the surface of the glacier, where you are met by a guide. For the next 20 minutes or so you are led around on the glacier and shown some of its geology. Then you reboard the helicopter for a flight back to Juneau with a long look at the Juneau ice field en route. TEMSCO provides the necessary parkas and boots as part of the package.

6. ***Valdez.*** On the northeast corner of Prince William Sound, Valdez offers a little of everything. Pink salmon are an every-cast proposition from the shoreline of the bay over near the pipeline terminal in July, trolling for silver salmon in August is great fun, halibut charters are available throughout the summer and day cruises take passengers out into the Sound and up close to Columbia Glacier.

7. ***Cold Bay.*** Only a waterfowl hunter or a dedicated bird-watcher could love this wet and windy site at the southern end of the Alaska Peninsula. Go in October when it seems that all the geese in the northern hemisphere gather at nearby Izembek Lagoon in preparation for their migration south. Lots of caribou, brown bear and ptarmigan are in the area, too. Fly from Anchorage on Reeve Aleutian Airways to this destination. Lodging and dining facilities are limited. Cold Bay is also served by the Alaska Marine Highway ferries, which can be boarded in Homer or Kodiak.

8. ***Prince of Wales Island.*** For this heavily rain-forested island, clear-cutting enhanced its potential for visitors. It is possible to drive almost anywhere on the island these days after ferrying over from Ketchikan on the Alaska Marine Highway. Roads are surfaced with gravel and there are very few other tourists to contend with. True, the roads lead mostly from one clear-cut to another, but in between are dense stands of old-growth rain forest. The numerous deer and black bear are fairly easy to spot if you drive around early in the morning or late in the evening. Also, bald eagles by the score nest in treetops and soar overhead. The island's best visitors facilities are in or near Craig on the western side of the island, about 25 miles from the ferry dock at Hollis.

9. ***The Johnson Pass trail on the Kenai Peninsula.*** This USDA Forest Service trail runs about 22 miles from mile 63.7 of the Seward Highway to a point on the same highway near Moose Pass. Two lakes near the top of the pass offer excellent fishing (grayling in Bench Lake and rainbows in Johnson Lake), and the hike is not particularly difficult. July is the best time to go. Look for hoary marmots in the open country at the top of the pass between the two lakes.

10. *The Denali Highway.* This road, about 130 miles long, runs from Paxon on the Richardson Highway west to Cantwell on the Parks Highway near Denali National Park. Most of the route is right at or slightly above timberline, and there are unparalleled views of the open tundra and the peaks of the Alaska Range. A few rustic campgrounds are available, and if you know where to look there is great fishing for grayling and lake trout just off the road. Best to go in August; early in the month the blueberries ripen and there are whole hillsides covered with berry bushes. Late in the month the fall colors arrive, and the tundra briefly blazes with reds and yellows. Timing has to be perfect for the fall colors, though; they're at their peak in this alpine area for only a couple of days.

Johnson Lake, near the top of Johnson Pass on the Kenai Peninsula, offers excellent rainbow trout fishing. (Photo by Ron Dalby)

Southeastern Alaska

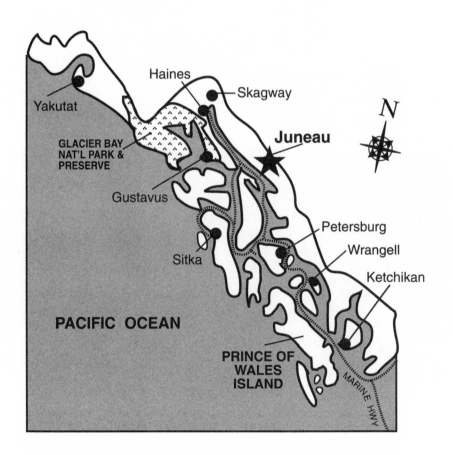

Yakutat

Haines

Skagway

Juneau

GLACIER BAY
NAT'L PARK &
PRESERVE

Gustavus

N

Petersburg

Wrangell

Sitka

Ketchikan

PACIFIC OCEAN

**PRINCE OF
WALES
ISLAND**

MARINE HWY

⁻ SOUTHEASTERN ALASKA ⁻

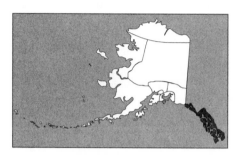

OVERVIEW

Some say southeastern Alaska, also known as the Panhandle, should be a separate state of its own. Physically remote from the bulk of Alaska's landmass, two time zones removed geographically from population centers in Anchorage and Fairbanks (though politicians lumped almost all of Alaska in a single time zone a few years back) and all but inaccessible by road, Southeast remains an enigma to many, but a place of almost unceasing wonder and natural beauty for those who live there and for those who visit.

This is not the Alaska of unrelenting winter cold; it is the Alaska that often seems to offer unrelenting rain—winter, summer, spring or fall. But the sun does shine in Southeast, contrary to oft-repeated rumors, and when it does, weeks of constant rain are instantly forgotten. Nowhere on earth is as magnificent, spectacular and beautiful as southeastern Alaska on a sunny day.

The sea is to Southeast both its highway and its livelihood. Boats— cruise ships, ferries, freighters, tugs, barges, seiners, gill-netters, trollers, trawlers, skiffs and others—are a means of movement, a means of making a living, a means of recreation and a means of visiting this remote region. To drive in Southeast is to first transport your vehicle on a ferry to a town or island having a suitable road system. Not all communities have roads; harbors are much more important, and at least one small community has enacted ordinances banning all forms of motor vehicles.

Yet, if you put your car on a ferry, one of the most thrilling driving vacations in North America awaits you on Prince of Wales Island in southeastern Alaska. Visitors owe this opportunity to the much-maligned timber industry. As various parts of Prince of Wales Island have been logged in the past several decades, the roads built for log trucks were gradually connected into a network that allows hundreds of miles of driving on this island, the third largest under the U.S. flag. Yes, there are clear-cuts, but the road also leads through some of the most splendid old-growth temperate rain forests remaining in North America.

You don't need a car, however, to see some of the most spectacular sights in this part of Alaska. Cruise ships sail almost to the face of monstrous tidewater glaciers, glaciers actively calving icebergs into the sea as spellbound passengers lean over the rails.

Cruise ships, in fact, bring more visitors to southeastern Alaska than any other form of transportation. In an average year, one-quarter to one-third of all visitors to Alaska will reach the state on a cruise ship sailing the Inside Passage waters of the Panhandle. Many will see no more of Alaska than the fjords and islands of Southeast, yet each will have had a spectacular vacation. A cruise through southeastern Alaska compares to no other vacation.

HISTORY

Before the white man and Western civilization, what is now southeastern Alaska was the province of the Tlingit, Haida and Tsimsian tribes. Theirs was a region blessed by a gentler climate than the Interior and north coast occupied by the Athabaskans and Eskimos respectively.

Because of this gentler climate and a more abundant and consistent food supply, life differed here. Wars, infrequent in Eskimo territories, were frequent, and commerce was routine. Anthropologists suggest that the Indians in Southeast had spare time on their hands, unlike their northern cousins who had to work full time just to survive, and thus found ways to fill that time by interacting in various ways with neighboring tribes.

When white people arrived—the Russians in the late eighteenth century—the Tlingits fought for their lands, surprising the Russians, who were by then long conditioned to the more docile Eskimos and Aleuts. Though they ultimately lost the war in the face of Alexandr Baranov's cannons, the Tlingets gained a more important advantage; the Russians did not slaughter Indians wholesale in Southeast as they had done in the Aleutian Islands a few years earlier.

The Russians came because of the sea otter, the lushly furred animal that attracted them to Alaska in the first place. As otters became more scarce in the Aleutian Islands, the Russians ranged farther east and south in search of pelts. As the Russians moved their operations to Southeast, so too did they move their capital from Kodiak to Sitka.

It was in Sitka, in October 1867, that the U.S. stars and stripes replaced the czar's eagle on the flagstaff. A U.S. military governor would reside in Sitka over the next several decades, responsible in name, though hardly in fact, for the administration of Alaska. Most of these men were powerless to act in these early years of U.S. rule, and even if they had wished to, they had not the funds or the means. For many decades after sovereignty Congress and various presidents virtually ignored Alaska's need for equipment and funds.

As the center of the white population gradually shifted away from Sitka to Juneau with the discovery of gold in the 1880s, so too did Alaska's capital eventually move to the city it still occupies.

Yet it was not gold so much that dictated settlement patterns in southeastern Alaska; the silvery flash of salmon determined where men came to live and work in the Panhandle of the late 1800s and early 1900s. Huge canneries were constructed at the mouths of the most productive streams. Though these facilities might only operate at most some three months a year, the money they made encouraged more and more facilities to be built. Some canneries grew into permanent settlements; Petersburg is a prime example. Others were simply abandoned in place after all but wiping out the fish in the stream where they were built.

For the most part, the towns grown up from a few of these canneries gradually got into the logging business as well. Southeast is rich with towering stands of cedar, Sitka spruce and hemlock—some of the finest woods in North America.

At first, Alaska logging was the province of the ultimate in rugged individualists—handloggers. Operating from a small boat and usually alone, these men would cruise the fjords looking for huge trees that could be dropped into or near the water. Finding such a tree, a handlogger would go ashore, set spring boards into the trunks to stand on, and fell the tree. Not all trees dropped directly into the water, some had to be nudged a little more, and these men were expert at applying the force needed to slide a log down a mountainside into the ocean. Once the log was in the water, it was added to the raft of logs already collected and the logger chugged away in his boat searching for more timber to cut or for a buyer.

Handlogging died a slow death in Southeast, ultimately disappearing in the 1950s. By then the USDA Forest Service controlled most of the land and was leasing large tracts of it to large lumber and pulp operations. The corporations were interested more in economics than individualism, and clear-cutting came into fashion as a means of extracting the most logs in the shortest period of time. Visitors sailing the region today will see large stands of old-growth timber interspersed with clear-cuts of varying ages. Timber experts estimate it takes about 80 years for each clear-cut area to produce another marketable crop of logs. The forests arising from the old clear-cuts are referred to as second-growth forests.

However, less and less land is available for clear-cutting these days. Though privately held tracts (mostly by Native corporations formed as a result of the Alaska Native Claims Settlement Act of 1971) can still be cut at the discretion of the owners, the Forest Service is under increasing pressure and regulation to curtail clear-cutting in the Tongass National Forest.

But as logging gradually declines, Alaskans have discovered the selling of a more intangible product—tourism. A lot of people are willing to pay a lot of money to see the virgin rain forests of southeastern Alaska. In a large sense, tourism is the only growth industry in Alaska today. To be sure, there are still oil wells, mines, logging camps, canneries and fur trappers, but each of these resource-extraction industries is receding at present. Only tourism continues to grow, at times it seems unrestrictedly. And fully one-third of Alaska's visitors spend the bulk of their Alaska vacations in the Panhandle, one of the smallest parts of the state in actual land area.

GETTING THERE
AIR TRAVEL

More than anything else, the logistics involved in just getting to southeastern Alaska set the region apart from the rest of the state. As with the other parts of Alaska, scheduled airliners can take you to the larger cities in the region. Alaska Airlines carries most passengers to the Panhandle with regularly scheduled flights to Ketchikan, Sitka, Wrangell, Petersburg, Yakutat and Juneau. Northbound flights originate in Seattle; southbound flights begin in Anchorage. Northwest and Delta also offer a few flights to Juneau and Ketchikan.

However, as efficient and important as the airlines are to southeastern Alaska, most visitors arrive by water.

CRUISE SHIPS

More than 18 ships belonging to seven major cruise lines ply the waters of Alaska's Inside Passage from mid-May through September. These are the luxury liners so well advertised all over the world; each carries from 400 to more than 1,000 passengers on weekly roundtrips from Vancouver, British Columbia.

Why Vancouver and not Seattle? Another one of those federal laws that really only affects Alaska comes into play here. In the 1920s,

Congress passed the Merchant Marine Act, informally known as the Jones Act in honor of its congressional sponsor. Heavily supported by Seattle business interests, the Jones Act mandates that all passenger and freight traffic moving between U.S. ports must be carried on U.S. flagged ships, ships that can only be loaded, unloaded and crewed by U.S. citizens who are members of the appropriate unions.

This gave the port of Seattle a virtual lock on the handling of all freight to and from Alaska, as well as the passenger traffic.

As the years passed, the various merchant marine unions in the United States priced themselves out of more and more business, and by the 1960s there were no more cruise ships flying the U.S. flag. All the liners working Alaskan waters today are foreign-flagged carriers manned, for the most part, by foreign crews. Thus before you can take a cruise to Alaska you must go to Canada, a foreign country, to board your ship. Most Alaskans would dearly love to see the Jones Act overturned or at least modified as a means of creating competition to drive down shipping prices. However, the unions involved are still very strong in the more heavily populated states, and such action is unlikely in the near future.

Nonetheless, a cruise to southeastern Alaska still rates as one of the experiences of a lifetime. From the deck of your liner you can reasonably expect to see whales (orcas and humpbacks), porpoises, sea otters, sea lions, seals, bald eagles and perhaps an occasional bear along the shoreline. Ships nudge in close to calving tidewater glaciers so you can feel the icy breezes and hear the crackling roar moments before an iceberg falls from the face of a slow-moving river of ice. Each ship stops for several hours at various towns, the most frequent stops being Ketchikan, Juneau, Sitka and Skagway. During these stops you'll have opportunities for shore excursions, shopping, flightseeing jaunts, kayak trips and charter fishing expeditions.

A cruise is one of the most relaxing vacations available. Your every wish is catered to instantly. You can participate in shipboard activities and shore excursions as much or as little as you like. Entertainment for almost every taste can be found each night in a number of on-board nightclubs, cabarets, lounges and casinos. Exercise equipment, swimming pools, hot tubs and tennis courts are all available. And, perhaps most important for relaxation, telephones, while available via ship-to-shore radio, are easy to ignore. In short, you can submerge yourself in comfort and safety with hardly a care in the world.

A cruise also includes all you can eat almost anytime day or night, a real danger for those of us with waistline problems. There are, of course, three sit-down meals daily with dinner usually being a fairly dressy affair. Beyond the regular meals, there are snacks and deli items available routinely, lavish midnight buffets, and almost anything else you might desire. You can, as well, get room service if you wish to avoid the dining room and snack bars.

On a cruise, the price of your ticket is determined mostly by the size and location of your stateroom. Prices range from about $900 per person to several thousand dollars for a seven-day, six-night package. This one price includes all your food (all passengers, regardless of their staterooms, eat the same food in the same dining rooms) and your room, plus often a break on airfare to get to Vancouver. Not included are liquor, gratuities and money for the casino. Liquor charges and other on-board purchases from gift shops and the beauty salon are usually handled by signing a chit; at the end of the trip you settle a single bill.

Tipping is expected for good service. Remember to leave appropriate amounts for your cabin attendant, the steward who handles your room service requests, the waiters in the dining room and others as appropriate. For liquor service, it's best to add a tip each time you sign a chit as you'll probably have a different waiter each time. Your table's waiter and the various attendants can be tipped in a lump sum at the end of the voyage.

Besides relaxing and enjoying yourself, about the only required activity you participate in during a cruise is one or perhaps two lifeboat drills. These are usually held the first day out and are designed to provide you the knowledge necessary to deal with a serious problem or accident at sea. Such instances are extremely rare, though in 1980 a cruise ship did catch fire off Alaska's coast. Several days after all the passengers and crew were safely taken off, the ship sank while being towed to port for repairs. Think of the small inconvenience of a lifeboat drill in the same manner as the short speech given by flight attendants on airliners just before takeoff. Both are required by law for your protection.

Because there are so many options in companies, ships, stops, services and prices, the best way to put together a cruise to Alaska is through a travel agent. Almost every city or town in the United States and Canada has one or more agencies that can help you select just the right cruise package for your vacation.

FERRIES

Unique among the states, Alaska owns and operates an extensive network of ships, the Alaska Marine Highway System, under the Department of Transportation. Operating as far south as Bellingham, Washington, to Skagway and Haines in the northern part of the Panhandle and most towns in between, these ferries make regularly scheduled runs carrying freight, passengers and vehicles to destinations in southeastern Alaska.

In a limited sense, the ferries are like cruise ships in that they use many of the same routes and provide maritime access to the wonders of the region. The similarity ends there, however. Ferries are working boats and do not have the huge catering staff featured by cruise ships. If you want a meal on the ferry, you're either going to have to bring a sack lunch or stand in line in the cafeteria and pay cash for it. There's usually a bar on board for alcoholic beverages, but the only entertainment available is a USDA Forest Service ranger giving programs on various facets of the area you're sailing through.

On the larger ferries, cabins are available, though these are pretty plain and provide little more than beds, sheets and blankets. Passengers can pick seats from a choice of several lounges on a first-come, first-served basis; the lounges with the reclining seats are far and away the favorites for overnight voyages.

On the upper deck is a solarium, partially covered but otherwise open to the air. It's common for travelers to set up freestanding tents on this deck for sleeping accommodations or to just stretch out in a sleeping bag in one of the available deck chairs. Late at night during the crowded summer months, the solarium can be a sleeping sea of humanity.

Compared to the cruise ships, the ferries generally attract a younger crowd and, to a certain degree, a more Alaskan crowd. Those who live in Southeast must regularly ride the ferries in the course of their affairs.

Also, as you might guess, the ferries are cheaper for walk-on passengers. Prices don't get up into the cruise ship range until you start bringing vehicles aboard. Still, about $1,000 will let two people and a large camper travel from Prince Rupert, British Columbia, all the way to Haines and make several stops along the way. This price does not include a cabin, any meals and liquor purchased on board.

Perhaps the single biggest advantage to the Marine Highway System is that it allows you to bring your vehicle—camper, motor home, car, truck or whatever—along to some of Alaska's favorite destinations, destinations not connected by road to anyplace else. In southeastern Alaska, only Hyder, Skagway and Haines can be reached by road. Everything in between, and that includes Juneau, Sitka, Wrangell, Petersburg, Prince of Wales Island and Ketchikan, can only be reached by sea or by air.

Ferry travel is less idyllic than cruise ship travel, but just as much fun in its own way. There are almost always kids underfoot, and the only entertainment available is usually the novel in your hand-carried luggage, but you'll still have the opportunity to see much of the same wildlife and scenery as cruise ship passengers, and everyone in the crew speaks English. Finally, things are a lot more informal on the ferries. There's no dressing for dinner or other rituals. The only demands on you are the starting and stopping times at various ports. The thing to remember is that the ferry system was designed to transport people and their goods, not to entertain them.

Travelers planning to use the Alaska Marine Highway during the busy summer months should almost certainly make a reservation. Schedules are normally published in November for the upcoming year, and the ferry office begins taking reservations on December 1. Call **1-800-642-0066** for ferry information from any state except Washington. In Washington, the toll-free number is **1-800-585-8445**. Upon request, you will be sent a colorful booklet outlining schedules by ship and port for the coming year, and once you've made your plans, call the same number to book space. As these telephone lines are constantly busy, you may have to call several times before getting through.

In 1993, the Alaska Marine Highway made a significant change in its booking procedures. No longer will large tour companies be able to book large blocks of space, thus making it almost impossible for do-it-yourselfers to find northbound vehicle and cabin space from Bellingham, Washington, and north. Reservations must now be made in the name of a traveler. Though the ships will still be crowded, there's a much better chance of getting the reservation you want these days.

Another way to ensure getting the space you want is to plan to board the ferry at Prince Rupert, British Columbia, about a day-and-a-half's drive from Seattle over excellent roads. Only two ships a week sail from Bellingham (a few miles north of Seattle), but Prince Rupert generally has two or even three northbound ferries each day.

Here's a tip for potential ferry travelers: Plan to use the smaller ferries whenever possible when sailing between towns in southeastern Alaska. Unlike the mainliners running from either Seattle or Prince Rupert, these smaller ships on the shorter runs are often less crowded. For example, if you are northbound, consider driving to Stewart, British Columbia, which abuts the Alaskan town of Hyder. The ferry from Stewart-Hyder to Ketchikan runs once a week, but often sails almost empty, in contrast to the sailings from Bellingham and Prince Rupert which are almost always jammed to capacity during the summer. From Ketchikan a number of options are available on both the large mainliners and on smaller ships.

Another tip is that it's usually easier to get space on southbound ferries than northbound ferries. So if you plan to take the ferry one way and drive the other way on your trip to and from Alaska, it's usually better to drive north and sail south.

Recommended Reading
Alaska's Southeast, Sara Eppenbach, Globe Pequot Press (3 School Street, Boston, MA 02108, (617) 227-0460), 1988. Recently updated, Eppenbach's book has been the best travel guide exclusively for southeastern Alaska available for the last several years. A longtime resident of the area, Eppenbach makes her home in Juneau and travels regularly throughout the region.

FLORA AND FAUNA

Mountains, glaciers, islands, fjords and precipitation are the dominant factors affecting the plant and animal life of southeastern Alaska. In the case of plant life, precipitation is the overriding factor.

Several places in southeastern Alaska receive more than 200 inches of rain a year. That's an average of more than half an inch of rain per day. Thus the lush, green temperate rain forest dominates the land.

The most visible parts of the rain forest are towering stands of Sitka spruce, hemlock and cedar, with a host of lesser tree species scattered around the region. On the forest floor, a deeply shaded, damp climate encourages ferns, mosses and various fungi. Berry bushes, particularly blueberries, and spiny devil's club are common.

Timberline is about 3,000 feet above sea level, less in some areas. Here the land is more open with various bushes, sedges and grasses. Above these areas are towering cliffs of jagged rock interspersed with mountain meadows.

Starting at higher elevations, the predominant mammals are Rocky Mountain goats, nimble cliff dwellers who seek the most rugged terrain. Between the jagged cliffs and the rain forest, the open areas attract Sitka black-tailed deer during the summer months.

The deer move downslope into the shelter of the rain forest during the winter. The forest shelters bears as well, lots of them, both black and brown. In mainland areas, both types of bears also can be found, though generally not together. On the large islands along the Inside Passage, only one species of bear or the other is present; for example, the ABC islands (Alexander, Baranof and Chichagof) host brown bears, and Prince of Wales Island (and others) host black bears.

A few wolf packs can be found in southeastern Alaska. The best known and most frequently seen are the wolves on Prince of Wales Island.

With the exception of the Chilkat River valley near Haines and the Stikine River valley near Wrangell, southeastern Alaska has no moose. There are no caribou at all in the region.

The Alaska Department of Fish and Game has recently tried to create a herd of elk on selected islands in the southeast, but has had little success.

The best places to see wildlife in southeastern Alaska varys, but here are a few good bets.

Bears: The easiest way to find a bear is to visit the local landfill. Bears, particular black bears, seem to thrive in garbage dumps. Driving the road system on Prince of Wales Island late in the evening or early in the morning is another good way to spot black bears. For brown bears, Pack Creek on Admiralty Island is always a good bet; check with the Forest Service in Juneau for information. During prime viewing times at Pack

Creek, the number of people allowed in by the Forest Service is regulated so as not to overwhelm the bears.

Mountain Goats: The road over White Pass from Whitehorse, Yukon, to Skagway passes through prime goat country. Scan the high, rugged ridges with binoculars.

Whales: The more time you spend on the water or walking along a beach, the better your chances of seeing a whale. Killer whales are seen most frequently, though humpbacks are common.

Deer: Sitka black-tails can be found almost anywhere in southeastern Alaska. Along the roads late in the evening or early in the morning are usually the best bets. Most of the bucks are in the high country during the summer months, so the deer seen from the road are usually does and fawns.

Eagles: They are anywhere at almost any time. Bald eagles rule the skies in southeastern Alaska. It is almost impossible to be anywhere on the Panhandle or along the Inside Passage and not see an eagle. For more eagles than you can count, visit the Chilkat River valley north of Haines during October and November. The late run of salmon in the river attracts eagles from all over the West.

Southeastern Alaska rain forest. (Photo by Ron Dalby)

Ketchikan

The majority of Ketchikan's visitors arrive by cruise ship and spend 6 to 10 hours in the city. Thus visitor activities are geared heavily toward making those few hours as meaningful as possible.

Before docking in Ketchikan, cruise ship passengers have the option of signing up for a variety of different activities, including flightseeing in Misty Fjords, charter fishing for salmon or halibut, and bus tours to various destinations. These same activities can be signed up for on the dock once you arrive, though you'll probably save time by doing it aboard ship before hand.

Should you disdain any of the organized activities, you can easily entertain yourself in Ketchikan. The cruise ships let you off right in the heart of downtown, and the city's visitors center is but a few steps from the gangway. At the visitors center you can pick up various maps, including a map for a first-rate, self-guided walking tour. The tour is entertaining, educational and good exercise, the latter because Ketchikan is built on the side of a mountain overlooking Tongass Narrows. No one walks very far in Ketchikan without going up and down.

One of Ketchikan's more infamous attractions on the walking tour is the restoration of a part of the community built on a boardwalk called Creek Street. This used to be the rowdy part of town, and the favorite saying that evolved over the years was that Creek Street was "… where men and salmon come to spawn." The houses of ill repute are now historical fixtures and no longer offer the former services. The salmon, however, being unencumbered by the laws of man or the finer points of human etiquette, still fill the creek under the boardwalk as they complete their life cycle.

Ketchikan is on an island, specifically Revillagigedo (ra-VEE-a-gi-GEE-doe) Island, named by English captain George Vancouver for an eighteenth-century viceroy of New Spain, the Count of Revillagigedo, Don Juan Vicente de Guemes Pacheco di Padilla y Horcasitas. (Thank goodness Vancouver stuck to the guy's title and not his full name!) Vancouver was exploring what is now southeastern Alaska for the English, and as a gesture of political goodwill was asked to name something prominent for the Count. For obvious reasons, locals tend to shorten the name of their island to Revilla for informal conversations.

Last, but by no means least, it does rain in Ketchikan. So much so that the city maintains a "liquid sunshine gauge" down on the cruise ship dock. Be sure and stop to see how much ahead or behind the average 165 inches of rain annually the city is during your visit. And bring a rain jacket. Wet or dry, Ketchikan's lots of fun, but you'll enjoy it more if you stay dry.

FESTIVALS AND EVENTS

Ketchikan bills itself as the king salmon capital of Alaska; obviously fishing derbies are high on the list of annual events.

There are two king salmon derbies, the largest of which for some 45 years has been the **Annual Ketchikan King Salmon Derby.** Derby dates for this event are usually the last weekend in May and the first two weekends in June—these are all three-day (Friday, Saturday, Sunday) weekends for derby participants. For more information, contact the **Ketchikan Visitors Bureau, (907) 225-6166.**

The second king derby is the **Little League King Salmon Derby,** lasting for the whole season from mid-May through

49

mid-July. Prizes may be smaller here, but it's open for a much longer period. Call **(907) 225-6166** for details.

A third fishing derby is the **Ketchikan Killer Whale Halibut Derby,** which starts in mid-May and runs through Labor Day. This, too, is managed by the city, and the Visitors Bureau number given previously should be used for additional information.

As in all fishing derbies, you must buy a derby ticket before you catch your fish.

Besides the fishing derbies, Ketchikan has two big summer events, a **July 4th celebration** that extends over three days and a **Blueberry Arts Festival** in early August. Both involve a parade and other events and are heavily attended by the whole town.

ACTIVITIES

CRUISING

Most tourists arrive in Ketchikan via some sort of a boat or ship, then often board another watercraft for a close-up look at area attractions. Very popular are cruises in Misty Fjords National Monument. Dale Pihlman, owner of **Outdoor Alaska, (907) 225-6044,** offers several popular Misty Fjord packages including day cruises and drop-offs for kayakers. Prices start at about $135 per person and may include meals, depending on the package selected.

Shorter cruises closer to Ketchikan include a historical waterfront cruise on the M/V *Emerald Fjord*. This, too, is offered by Outdoor Alaska. Departures are coordinated with cruise ship arrivals.

FISHING

Catching salmon and halibut is big business in Ketchikan, and the number of charter boats in the various harbors near town is adequate testimony to this fact. Salmon of one species or another are available throughout the spring, summer and early fall. Halibut can be caught year around, and arrangements can be made for steelhead on Prince of Wales Island.

A good bet for prospective fisherman is to start your search for a charter skipper through **Ketchikan Sportfishing, 1-800-488-8254.** Marge Hanger and her daughter Carol act as booking agents for two dozen or more boats in the Ketchikan area. They can match the smallest or the largest parties with just the right boats for a day of fishing fun.

For those who prefer to search for skippers on their own, here are a few suggestions. Because many of these skippers live on their boats and since telephone shopping can save you a lot of time when looking for a charter boat, particularly on short notice, we've only provided phone numbers. Once you find the skipper and boat you want, he'll give you directions on how to find the slip in the harbor.

Mike Williams—Alaska Scenic Charters, (907) 225-4255.

Barbara and Ken Klein—Ken's Charters, (907) 225-7290.

Tom Ramiskey—Chinook Charters, (907) 225-9225.

Dan McQueen—Salmon Busters, (907) 225-2731.

Sam Barnard—Sea Quest Charters, (907) 225-8688.

Carla Szitas—Carmuk Charters, (907) 225-4199.

Fisherman's Quay—(907) 225-BOAT.

Seamist Charters—(907) 247-2265.

Alaska Adventure Charters—(907) 225-2792.

Northern Lights Charters—(907) 247-8488.

Rogue Charters—(907) 225-5099.

FLIGHTSEEING

Several air services in Ketchikan offer a variety of flying tours through Misty Fjords and other scenic regions. Prices vary according to the flying time involved and the number of people on board. Here's a partial list of air services offering area flightseeing:

KenAir—1-800-478-3243 (Alaska-only toll-free number).

Ketchikan Air Service—(907) 225-6608.

ProMech Air—(907) 225-3845.

Taquan Air—(907) 225-9668.

KAYAKING

Southeast Exposure, (907) 225-8829, offers trips of varying length from a couple of hours along the waterfront to eight-day expeditions. Prices range from about $50 for the waterfront trip to about $1,200 for the longer expeditions. Expeditions include tents, safety equipment and food. They also rent kayaks by the day if you want to explore on your own.

LODGES

The Ketchikan area offers a number of full-service lodges, mostly centered around various kinds of fishing. Some on this list can be reached from town by vehicle, others only by air or by boat. Similar to the charter skippers, we've again only provided phone numbers for the full-service lodges.

Clover Pass Resort—(907) 247-2234.

Sportsman's Cove Lodge—1-800-962-7889.

Stan & Bonnie's Floating Fishing Lodge—(907) 247-8555.

Waterfall Resort—1-800-544-5125.

Whales Resort—(808) 735-2988.

Yes Bay/Mink Bay Lodges—1-800-999-0784.

MUSEUMS

Two splendid museums are available within the city limits. The first is the **Totem Heritage Center** dedicated to the preservation of northwest coast Indian art. This museum offers the only display of original totem poles. There's also a good chance to see contemporary carvers and their apprentices working on new totems outside the building. Admission is $2. **(907) 225-5900.**

The **Tongass Historical Museum** offers more than 20 exhibits relating to Ketchikan's history. Fishing, mining, timber and commerce are all covered. Admission is $1. **(907) 225-5600.**

Both museums are listed as stops on the self-guided walking tour.

OUTFITTING

Various levels of outfitting are available for do-it-yourself trips to some of the more splendid fishing and scenic areas around Ketchikan. Prices vary widely with the services needed and the flying time involved in your adventure. Here are two worth trying:

Alaska Wilderness Outfitting—(907) 225-REEL. Specializing in camping gear packages for Tongass National Forest wilderness cabins. See Tongass details below.

Misty Fjords Air and Outfitting—(907) 225-5155.

TONGASS NATIONAL FOREST

Cabin rentals, hiking trails, wilderness lakes and magnificent fjords all fall within USDA Forest Service management near Ketchikan. Some spectacular adventures are available in conjunction with gear and transportation offered by outfitters. For information, contact the **Tongass National Forest, Ketchikan Regional Office, Federal Building, Mill and Stedman streets, Ketchikan, AK 99901, (907) 225-3101.** Misty Fjords National Monument is also managed by the Ketchikan office of the Tongass National Forest.

TOURING

Sightseeing in Ketchikan, whether on your own or with an organized tour, has a lot to offer. A sampling of attractions includes: **Totem Bight State Historical Park** (totem poles and tribal houses); **City Tour, (907) 225-9465; Dolly's House** (Dolly was one of the more well-known madams on Creek Street), **(907) 225-1992; First City Tours, (907) 247-3672;** and **Saxmon Native Village, Cape Fox Tours, (907) 225-5163.** You can even ride to some of these attractions in a horse-drawn cart available from **Seahorse Ventures, (907) 225-3672.**

WALKING TOUR

Actually, there are three distinct walking tours outlined on a free map available in the **Ketchikan Visitors Bureau** on the cruise ship dock. Stop in, pick up a map, ask a question or two to orient yourself and head off on your own. The longest trip takes about an hour, not counting time spent at various attractions; the shortest trip about 30 minutes.

———————— WHERE TO STAY ————————

ACCOMMODATIONS

Besides the lodges already listed, Ketchikan has a number of hotels ranging from the almost new Cape Fox Westmark to hotels that have been around for decades. Prices for most are in the $$–$$$ range. There are no hotels in Ketchikan that fit the definition of luxury hotel. Most hotels in the Ketchikan area also provide freezers to freeze your catch prior to shipping it home.

$$$
The Cape Fox Westmark

Brand new and built on a bluff overlooking the city, the Cape Fox is worth a stop just to look out the windows. It has a restaurant and lounge, and a tram running down the face of the bluff to downtown Ketchikan. There is lots of parking for guests, unusual in Ketchikan. **(907) 225-8001.**

$$
The Gilmore Hotel

Built of solid concrete in 1927, the Gilmore is now on the national register of historic places. It was completely remodeled in the early 1990s and boasts 42 rooms on two floors. A restaurant and lounge are on the premises. Reservations are strongly recommended for stays during the busy summer season. **(907) 225-9423.**

The Ingersoll Hotel

Right in downtown Ketchikan, on the waterfront, the Ingersoll is another of Ketchikan's older hotels. Downtown Ketchikan's lounges and restaurants are within easy walking distance of the hotel. **(907) 225-2124.**

The Landing

Ketchikan's Best Western Hotel is located near the ferry dock on the north side of town. A restaurant and lounge are available. A courtesy van will take guests downtown or to and from the airport. **1-800-528-1234.**

The New York Hotel and Cafe

The owners describe this as an authentically restored 1920s hotel. Near downtown Ketchikan, there are only eight rooms available. Continental breakfasts are served in your room from 7 to 9 A.M. The cafe offers espresso and light snacks. **(907) 225-0246.**

$–$$
Rain Forest Inn

This is probably Ketchikan's best bargain for travelers on a budget. Private and dormitory-style rooms are available, along with showers and coin-op washers and dryers. Near downtown. **(907) 225-9500.**

Super 8 Motel

This is part of the national chain. It's clean, comfortable and consistent, and a few minutes from downtown. **(907) 225-9088.**

BED AND BREAKFASTS

Ketchikan is home to a thriving—and growing—B&B industry. The list below is by no means complete but should provide several options for those who seek the opportunity to stay with local people. Inquire at the Ketchikan Visitors Bureau for other choices. Because B&Bs generally have limited space available, telephone shopping to find suitable lodging is the best way to go. To that end, we have again provided only phone numbers.

Alaska Home Fishing B&B—1-800-876-0925.

Bucareli Bay B&B—(907) 826-2951.

C-Flee Beachfront Hideaway—(907) 225-9460.

The Classic Stop B&B—(907) 225-3607.

D&W Bed and Breakfast—1-800-551-8654.

Ketchikan Bed and Breakfast—(907) 225-8550.

Main Street B&B—(907) 225-8484.

North Tongass B&B—(907) 247-0879.

Sara Justine's B&B—(907) 225-6567.

Water Street B&B—(907) 247-0200.

CAMPGROUNDS

Options for RVs in Ketchikan are limited. Don Clothier, executive director of Ketchikan's Visitors Bureau, notes that there is little space for them to park and that streets are narrow and hard for big rigs to get around in. Campgrounds can be a real problem as well, especially for those arriving on one of the late-night ferries.

PRIVATE CAMPGROUNDS

Clover Pass Resort, about 10 miles north of town, has about 35 closely spaced RV sites with hookups available. Part of the resort complex, it offers good access to resort fishing and restaurants. **(907) 247-2234.**

Mountain Point RV Park was under construction in 1992 and planned to open in August of that year. No information is available as of this writing other than the telephone number: **(907) 225-6382.**

PUBLIC CAMPGROUNDS

Eight miles north of Ketchikan on a side road leading away from Ward Cove, the USDA Forest Service maintains three campgrounds along about a 2-mile stretch of gravel road. In order, as you proceed up the road, are **Signal Creek** (25 sites), **Three C's** (4 sites) and **Last Chance** (25 sites). Each site has standard Forest Service facilities with picnic tables and outhouses. (At 1 A.M. on a June morning, the author and his wife got the last campsite in Last Chance campground after arriving on the ferry at midnight. The only reason they got this site was a local contact—brother-in-law—who led them straight to the campground ahead of most of the other vehicles on the ferry.)

Settler's Cove, a state campground, is 18.5 miles north of town at the end of the North Tongass Highway. There are 12 campsites.

CAMPING OPTION

For late-night arrivals who don't wish to blunder around looking for a campground that's probably already full anyway, turn left leaving the ferry terminal. Within a couple of miles there's a large pullout overlooking the water that can be used by self-contained RVs. It's pretty easy to find, even in the dark, and there's space for a lot of rigs. Park there for a night and sort out your options after a good night's sleep. This spot is not suitable for tent camping.

WHERE TO EAT

Ketchikan and the surrounding area offers a variety of dining options from the ever-present fast-food franchises to a couple of excellent restaurants. Two of the latter are at **Salmon Falls Resort** and **Clover Pass Resort,** both about a 20-minute drive north of town. The food at both places is reported as excellent, though pricey.

A real treat is lunch at the **Cape Fox Westmark.** The dining room looks out over the town, and it's possible to watch the comings and goings in the harbor while you eat.

Fishing on Red Bay Lake, Prince of Wales Island. (Photo by Ron Dalby)

Prince of Wales Island

Don Clothier, executive director of the Ketchikan Visitors Bureau, describes Prince of Wales Island as the "best-kept secret in Alaska." And he's right. Prince of Wales offers all that lures travelers to Alaska—mountains, fjords, wildlife, fish, wilderness and solitude. It's not built up, it's not publicized, but it's easy to get to if you just know how.

One gets to PWI by going through Ketchikan; there's really no other way. Cruise ships don't stop anywhere on PWI, and no airliners go there—only the smaller air services in Ketchikan and an Alaska Marine Highway ferry from Ketchikan.

But if you plan to go to PWI, a stop at Ketchikan, specifically at the USDA Forest Service office, is a must. The friendly folks behind the counter will help you out with free maps of the road system on PWI and information about campgrounds and the few other facilities available. Grab all of this before you board the ferry or fly over to the island.

It's best to take a vehicle to Prince of Wales. It's a big island with plenty of places to drive, a real change from the rest of southeastern Alaska.

Prince of Wales Island owes its complex road system to the timber industry. Over the years, networks of roads designed to bring logs to market have been built all over the island. These logging-truck roads were eventually connected, and now it is possible to drive almost anywhere on the island. Admittedly, the roads were built to facilitate logging, so they tend to lead from one clear-cut to the next, but in between are stretches of old-growth rain forest, and just a short distance from the road system almost anywhere on the island is even more old-growth forest.

Four towns on the island are accessible by road—Hydaburg, Craig, Klawock and Thorne Bay. The latter is primarily a logging town, though some fishermen base themselves there. Craig is both a lumber shipping point and a fishing town, and it is closely connected to Klawock. At the southern limit of the road system is Hydaburg, a more traditional town populated primarily by Haida Indians.

All the towns offer at least minimal services, including fuel and food. Few truly tourist-related businesses exist though, because the travel industry hasn't yet discovered Prince of Wales Island save for a couple of remote lodges that promote their own brand of fly-in seclusion.

Hiking on barely discernible trails, fishing, beachcombing and wildlife watching are the primary activities on Prince of Wales Island. And, for the most part, you'll be completely alone in them.

On land, fishing includes cutthroat trout, Dolly Varden, rainbows, steelhead and various salmon after they've left the ocean to spawn. Saltwater fishing includes all the five species of salmon, rockfish, halibut and other bottom fish. A few charter boats are available in Craig for those who want to fish salt water.

Wildlife watchers will find plenty of black bears, deer, even wolves. Whales come in close to the beaches on parts of the island. For the truly dedicated, there are even mountain goats on the higher cliffs—you're probably going to have to get out and hike or climb a lot to see goats.

The Forest Service maintains several cabins on Prince of Wales Island. These are available on a first-come, first-served basis for $20 a night; you provide your own sleeping gear, food and transportation. Contact the **Forest Service's regional office in Ketchikan, (907) 225-3101,** for information on renting cabins on Prince of Wales Island or elsewhere in the Ketchikan area.

The cabin at Red Bay Lake is typical of the more than 180 cabins available in the

Tongass National Forest. Two means of access exist for Red Bay Lake—a floatplane rental from either Ketchikan or Craig, or a drive to Red Bay Creek on the north side of Prince of Wales Island and a hike along the creek on a marked trail about 1.5 miles to the lake. At the lake is a Forest Service rowboat; load your gear and row down the lake. After 10 to 15 minutes of rowing, the cabin will be on your left on the lakeshore. There are bunks for four inside the cabin, a wood stove and usually a supply of dry firewood—if you use the firewood, you're expected to replace it before you leave. The lake itself is full of cutthroat and rainbow trout, and red salmon in season. The scenery is spectacular. What more could you ask?

Those who like to hike have all sorts of opportunities on Prince of Wales Island, though it may not appear so at first glance; temperate rain forest seems almost impenetrable, until you get close. The forest floor is surprisingly open in areas of old-growth forest simply because so little light filters down through the trees. Most game trails run through old-growth areas, particularly along creeks and rivers. Find these trails, and you'll be able to walk almost anywhere you want to go, though there will be occasions when you have to wiggle through some dense brush, usually beneath openings in the trees that allow sunlight to reach the forest floor. Also, the higher you go, the less dense the forest.

There are a few marked trails on the island, though most are little used and frequently overgrown with brush. Metal diamonds placed at or slightly above eye level on trees permanently mark the trails in case you lose track of it in new-grown brush.

Hikers should do everything possible to avoid clear-cuts. These are all but impossible to walk through because of the debris left after clear-cutting and the dense brush growing up after the ground was exposed to the sunlight.

Those looking for wildlife should figure that deer will feed on the fringes of clear-cuts and hole up in the old-growth forest. Most of their traveling will be in the uncut rain forest; clear-cuts are hard for deer to walk through, too.

The best place to see a bear is the Hydaburg dump. Drive past the turnoff to the town and keep to your left as you head south. It's only a couple miles from town. Another area frequented by bears is the beach along the road about a mile outside of Craig. Other than those, just driving along the roads late in the evening or early in the morning is your best bet.

Whale watchers should find a stretch of beach with good views in both directions and just sit down to wait. The northern end of the island is good for this activity. Usually the first sign of a whale is when it blows—you'll hear it and turn to look. While waiting for whales, beachcomb or watch for other wildlife. Sea lions can frequently be seen from beaches, and, at low tide, a bear may amble out of the woods to see if the sea left anything behind. In winter months a lot of deer use the beaches as well.

Wrangell

Docking in Wrangell about 9:30 one summer evening, a woman passenger on the ferry *Malaspina* leaned over the rail and remarked, "This is a cute little town. I wonder what it is." She had embarked at Prince Rupert for passage all the way to Haines to continue driving toward Fairbanks in an RV. She hadn't bothered to check where else the boat stopped, and in so doing missed one of the best bets in southeastern Alaska for RVers.

Unlike Ketchikan, Wrangell has the facilities to handle RVs. And, since so few people stop here, it's an excellent place to visit to sample all that's best about southeastern Alaska: friendly people, spectacular scenery, hiking trails, fishing and small-boat cruising in area fjords or up the Stikine River.

HISTORY

Modern-day Wrangell got its start as an outpost of the Russian occupation of Alaska in the first half of the nineteenth century. This fort marked the southernmost limits of the Russian presence in Alaska.

Wrangell really grew, however, in the latter half of the nineteenth century when gold was discovered near Telegraph Creek, British Columbia. Telegraph Creek is on the Stikine River, a few hours by boat upstream from Wrangell. Those rushing to the goldfields passed through Wrangell as the quickest means of reaching Telegraph Creek.

The timber industry later gave more impetus for growth in the twentieth century, though this activity is not nearly as important now as it was a couple of decades ago.

Since a road reached Telegraph Creek in the 1960s, shipment of people and goods up the Stikine has all but disappeared. Now, however, people journey upstream on the Stikine for adventure and recreation. It is one of the most magnificent rivers in North America, and one of only three rivers that slices through the towering Coast Range on the border between Canada and southeastern Alaska.

FESTIVALS AND EVENTS

TENT CITY DAYS

The name stems from Wrangell's gold rush boomtown before the turn of the century. For three big days, the first weekend in February, activities include a tall tales contest, beard judging, long johns contest, children's games and the Shady Lady Fancy Dress Ball.

KING SALMON DERBY

This is a standard fishing derby in the last two weeks of May. Buy a ticket before you fish. Call the visitors center, **(907) 874-3901,** for more information.

SALMON BAKE

This citywide salmon feed is usually on the last Sunday in May.

FOURTH OF JULY

Like many of Alaska's smaller communities, Wrangell goes all out for Independence Day. The celebration is usually three days long, centered on the July 4th weekend, with parades and activities downtown.

ACTIVITIES

CHIEF SHAKES TRIBAL HOUSE

This tribal house replica and the surrounding totems were constructed by the Civilian Conservation Corps in the late 1930s and dedicated to the Stikine Tlingits in 1940. You can walk over a short bridge to the island at any time, but you can enter the tribal house only during specified hours for a $1 fee. The island is about a 10-minute walk from the cruise ship dock, slightly longer from the ferry dock.

CRUISING THE STIKINE RIVER

The Stikine is the swiftest flowing navigable river in North America. Just barely navigable might be a more appropriate description, as one generally needs shallow-draft jetboats to cross the shallows at the river's mouth at most times of the year.

One of the best ways to see the Stikine and its surroundings is from the M/V *Stikine Princess*, a 22-passenger jetboat operated by **TH Charters, P.O. Box 934, Wrangell, AK 99929, (907) 874-3613.** Skipper Todd Harding will outfit you in survival suits for the trip and ensure ahead of time that you're willing to help him shift weight around in the boat as needed in shallow waters. This cruise is an unbelievable one-day adventure through some of the most magnificent scenery in Alaska. You'll see glaciers and wildlife, all up close and personal, and you'll be on the ride of your life. This is a never-to-be-forgotten experience.

Another cruise operator is Eric Yancey of **TK Charters, P.O. Box 2107, Wrangell, AK 99929, (907) 874-2488.** Eric can get you to glaciers and wildlife, as well as handling charter fishing parties.

HIKING

A number of Forest Service trails are available along the road system on Wrangell Island. A particularly good day hike is the Rainbow Falls trail about four miles south of town. This trail offers a moderate climb through the rain forest to an overlook near a high waterfall. It is well maintained and fairly easy to handle. Allow a couple of hours to the overlook and back. Contact the **USDA Forest Service in Wrangell, (907) 874-2323,** for a complete description of the trails available. The Forest Service also offers several cabins in the region on a first-come, first-served reservation basis for $20 a night.

WRANGELL MUSEUM

A $1 charge lets you into the Wrangell Museum downtown. Focused exclusively on the Wrangell-Stikine area, the museum offers an excellent glimpse into the past, all the way back to the time the first Tlingits migrated into the area. Garnets gathered by local Boy Scouts are offered for sale in the museum, as is local artwork.

PETROGLYPH RUBBINGS

Nobody knows who or why, but hundreds of years ago local people etched detailed designs into rocks just below the high-tide line north of town. A 10-minute walk from the ferry dock or a short drive (but parking is very limited) brings you to a narrow access road. At the end of the road, a wooden stairway leads to the beach. Turn right at the bottom of the stairs and walk a few hundred yards. Start looking at the rocks below the high-tide line (check locally for the timing of low tide, the best time for petroglyph hunting). Remember that most of the land above the high-tide line is private property.

Once you find some of the etchings, you'll want to make a rubbing—these things are pretty hard to photograph, being uncolored indentations in flat gray rocks. Take some rice paper (available from Norris Gifts on Front Street) with you to the beach and strip several handfuls of ferns from the dense growth along the access road. Lay the paper flat over the petroglyph you wish to record, wad up a handful of fern leaves and rub vigorously across the paper. It usually works best with two people, one to hold the paper carefully in place and the other to do the rubbing, and it's better if you rub only in one direction. The marks on the rice paper will first appear green, but as the residue dries it will turn brown. This becomes your own personal recording of early Native art.

Take plenty of paper and plenty of ferns to the beach. It's fairly easy to make a mistake, and you'll probably want to record a lot of different designs. This is a great way to spend several hours outdoors.

Don't worry about harming the environment by stripping fern leaves for your artistic medium. These things grow profusely in the rain forest around Wrangell.

Local residents will describe this technique to you and encourage you to help yourself to all the ferns you need.

ROCK HOUNDING

Garnets, in particular, lure rock hounds to Wrangell. However, the best garnet-producing area was deeded to the Boy Scouts of America years ago. There are other options, though, and it's best to inquire locally at the downtown visitors center when you arrive. Or call in advance: **(907) 874-3901.**

For those with limited time in Wrangell, there are usually a couple of youngsters meeting the ferries and cruise ships on the dock with selections of garnets for sale. You can also purchase garnets at the museum.

—————— WHERE TO STAY ——————

ACCOMMODATIONS
$$
The Stikine Inn

It has 34 rooms, telephones, TV in every room and is one block from the ferry terminal. A dining room and bar are part of the facility. **(907) 874-3388.**

Harding's Old Sourdough Lodge

Hotel or bed and breakfast accommo-

dations are available. Courtesy pickup on request. Dining room and lounge. **(907) 874-3613.**

BED AND BREAKFASTS
Clarke Bed & Breakfast—(907) 874-2125 or (907) 874-3863.

Rooney's Roost Bed & Breakfast—(907) 874-2026 or (907) 874-3622.

Petersburg

Alaska's "Little Norway" was founded, appropriately enough, by a Norwegian immigrant fisherman, Peter Buschmann. He began construction of a cannery in 1898. In 1900 he and his 153 employees packed 32,000 cases of salmon.

In the next five years, Buschmann built three more canneries and a sawmill. Petersburg gradually grew up around his businesses. Many if not most of the people who moved to the new town were of Norwegian ancestry. That heritage still is evident throughout. Downtown the most obvious building is the Sons of Norway Hall, built in 1912. In other places, the houses look as if they belong to a community in northern Europe.

This Norse heritage manifests itself in other ways as well. Few people say "Welcome." Instead they say "Velkommen." The annual visitors guide published by the local paper, the *Petersburg Pilot*, is called the "Viking Visitor Guide." You'll also find local businesses like Viking Travel, the Scandia House, Husfliden and Kinder Komfort.

On the weekend nearest to May 17 (Norway's independence day), Petersburg celebrates with the Little Norway Festival. You'll see a replica of a Viking boat sailing in the harbor, many houses are open to visitors, and, according to Petersburg's promotional brochure, this is the time when "Vikings and Valkyries go marauding."

ACTIVITIES

CRUISES

Several operators in Petersburg offer day cruises to see the scenery and wildlife or longer custom tours several days long. Dave and Wanda Helmick, owners of **LeConte Cruises, (907) 772-4790,** offer perhaps the most varied menu. They'll take you fishing, sightseeing, hunting or on a photo safari aboard the 45-foot *Dutch Treat.* Others offering day cruises or longer journeys include

Julie and Scott Hursey—Alaska Passages, (907) 772-3967.

Steve Conner—Real Alaska Adventures, (907) 772-4121.

Ron Compton—Alaska Scenic Waterways, (907) 772-3777.

Ramblin' Marine Charters—(907) 772-3240 or (907) 772-3039.

FISHING

If the town's patriarch found cause to build three canneries in a five-year span, there must be fish nearby, and there are. Actually, one of the best-kept secrets in Alaska sportfishing is just outside of town—Blind Slough.

A 20-minute drive south from the ferry terminal takes you to a turnout and a boardwalk. The boardwalk leads about a quarter-mile to the mouth of Blind Slough, a stream that gets too many returning king salmon almost every summer. Bag limits are generous (four kings a day in 1992), and the fishing in late June and early July is beyond compare. The author spent six hours fishing on July 3, 1992, and hooked a king salmon on every cast. A couple of smaller fish were kept for meals later on and the rest were released. Nowhere else in Alaska is the king salmon fishing this good. At one point, six people fishing the same hole all were fighting kings varying in size from about 25 to 40 pounds. It was an afternoon to remember.

If doing it yourself at Blind Slough doesn't appeal to you, several charter skippers are available:

Dan O'Neil—Secret Cove Charters, (907) 772-3081.

Ed Jones—Sea Trek Charters, (907) 772-4868.

Stan Malcolm—Magic Man Charters, (907) 772-3777.

FLIGHTSEEING

The mainland and islands surrounding Petersburg were made for aerial viewing; it's all but impossible to appreciate the grandeur of the region otherwise. **Kupreanof Flying Service, (907) 772-3396,** can take you to glaciers, fjords and wilderness cabins. Hunters and fishermen can also use their planes as a means of access to remote regions.

WHERE TO STAY

ACCOMMODATIONS
$$
Beachcomber Inn

Four miles south of town, this resortlike accommodation was created from a turn-of-the-century cannery. Charter fishing boats available. Dining room and lounge. **(907) 772-3888.**

Scandia House

Located in downtown Petersburg, Scandia House occupies a structure first built in 1905. American or European-style accommodations. **(907) 772-4281.**

$
Tides Inn

Motel-like accommodations in downtown Petersburg. **(907) 772-4288.**

BED AND BREAKFASTS
Sylvia Broom Nilsen—The Broom Hus, (907) 772-3459.

Jewell Dean Herbrandson—Jewell's by the Sea, (907) 772-3620.

Lorene Palmer—Mountain Point B&B, (907) 772-9382.

Barry & Kathy Bracken—Water's Edge B&B, (907) 772-3736.

Sitka

Several years ago, a few women in Sitka came up with the idea of performing traditional Russian and Ukrainian folk dances for local festivities and for visitors. Local men shrugged off efforts to be recruited and left the women to their own devices. Thus both the men's and women's roles in the dances are performed by women. Now that the group is a major success giving 100 or more performances each year, some men have asked to join. They've been bluntly refused. The group is still completely female, and if a performance is scheduled at any time during your visit to Sitka, don't miss it. Admission is only a couple of bucks to defray the cost of the tape player and the costumes, but the overall effect of every exhibition is positively enchanting.

Sitka's capitalizing on its Russian heritage through dance and the variety of historical buildings and artifacts in the area is deliberate. Here the greatest dramas of the final years of Russian rule in Alaska were played out.

Here, too, is an even longer-lived Native culture that flourished for centuries before the Russians ever arrived. Mingled with evidence of these first white settlers in the area are modern-day Tlingits and their heritage.

On the south side of town in Sitka National Historic Park, built where the Tlingits fought the Russians, there's an interpretive center for Indian and Russian histories of the region, a cultural center for Indian art, a museum and a forested park holding a number of representative Tlingit totems. Wide, graveled pathways lead through the park and across bridges spanning a small river flowing through the area.

The ground was fittingly chosen for this 100-acre park; here the most violent clash between Alaska's Natives and the first white settlers was resolved by Russian cannons. Two powerful cultures fertilized this ground with their blood. Walking through the brooding rain forest, you can sense the emotions of that moment almost two centuries ago when technology became dominant in Alaska.

ACTIVITIES

THE ALASKA RAPTOR REHABILITATION CENTER

Innovative veterinary medicine and a dedicated staff of volunteers have created a unique facility designed to heal injured birds of prey and return them to the wild. A few birds that can never fully recover are housed permanently at the center. Visitors are welcome. Call the **Sitka Convention and Visitors Bureau, (907) 747-5940,** for information and directions.

FISHING

Sitka has some of the finest saltwater fishing in Alaska. Five species of salmon, halibut, ling cod and yellow-eye rockfish are the main attractions. A variety of charter boats are available. But perhaps one of the best ways to experience this classic fishing is with **Alaska Premier Charters and Siganaka Lodge.** Owners Theresa Weiser and Cal Hayashi can take up to 16 guests at a time for fully guided fishing packages from three to six days. They will literally fish you 'til your arms hurt and feed you 'til your clothes don't fit. Call **1-800-770-2628** for more information on rates and dates available. Reservations are a must, and you need to make them plenty early.

HISTORIC SITES

The **Russian Bishop's house,** near the small boat harbor, was recently restored to its early nineteenth-century grandeur by the National Park Service.

St. Michael's Cathedral, in the heart of downtown Sitka, with its onion-shaped domes, is the headquarters for the active Russian Orthodox church in Alaska. Attend a service on Sunday morning if possible. But don't expect pews; with the exception of a few seats for the disabled, worshipers stand amidst the priceless icons decorating the walls.

Castle Hill, near downtown, was originally a Tlingit settlement. Later the Russians built a castlelike building for managers of the Russian American Fur Trading Company. The castle burned in 1894, but the massive stone walls with cannons overlooking the town and the harbor still stand.

MUSEUMS

Besides Sitka National Historic Park and the historic sites noted above, Sitka offers two splendid museums. The best-known collection of Eskimo and Indian artifacts in Alaska is at the **Sheldon Jackson Museum** on the campus of Sheldon Jackson College. The **Isabel Miller Museum** demonstrates a broader picture of Sitka by describing its people and their cultures.

—— WHERE TO STAY ——

ACCOMMODATIONS

$$$

Shee Atika

Located in the heart of downtown Sitka, this is one of Alaska's finest facilities. Lounge, restaurant and meeting rooms. Live entertainment most evenings. **(907) 747-6241.**

$$

Potlatch House

Restaurant and lounge. **(907) 747-8611.**

Super 8

Rooms only. Convenient to local restaurants and other facilities. **(907) 747-8804.**

BED AND BREAKFASTS

Sitka has a growing B&B industry, and these can be a delightful way to get closer to local people and gain an insider's look into the culture of a community. There are several to choose from: **Biorka B&B, (907) 747-3111; Hannah's B&B, (907) 747-8309; Mountain View B&B, (907) 747-8966; Sitka House, (907) 747-4937.**

Juneau

Of all the state capitals in the United States, Juneau is unique in that it cannot be reached by road. The only means of access are by sea and by air. And when the weather closes in, either way can be chancy at best. All too often, people trying to get to Juneau for government meetings wind up waiting out the weather in the Seattle airport.

In the mid-1970s as the first major oil revenues began to flow into Alaska's coffers from the Prudhoe Bay oil fields, Alaskans actually voted to move the capital to a place called Willow about 75 miles north of Anchorage by road. It was a curious selection of a location, unless you understand the Alaskan mentality. Anchorage would have been the obvious choice for a capital city; most state government business, other than the legislative and executive branches, was—and is—conducted there anyway. But, outside of Anchorage, nobody else in Alaska wanted the state's largest city to get a bigger share of the state-government pie. And, of course, no one in Anchorage wanted to see the capital in Fairbanks, the next logical choice.

Ultimately a site selection committee was appointed, operating under various restrictions about not locating the new capital anywhere within so many miles of an existing city. Alaska planned to build a new city in the wilderness to house state government, although the city had to be on the road system and have land nearby suitable for an airport. In due course, Willow was selected.

However, not everybody, and particularly not those in Juneau, wanted to move the capital. Thus came another referendum, this one on the cost of building a new capital city. At the time, in the late 1970s, that cost was estimated at more than $6 billion. Alaskans who had previously voted to move the capital now overwhelmingly voted down the money necessary to move it. There are now two laws on the

books at cross-purposes. The first says we will move the capital to Willow, and the second refuses to allocate the money to move it. Juneau was, is, and will remain Alaska's capital. And, since oil revenues are beginning to decline, it is unlikely now that money could be found to move the capital, even if Alaskan voters changed their minds about spending it.

As this book goes to press, small groups of Alaskans are again circulating petitions to move the capital from Juneau to a location on the road system. These actions were prompted by a plan being promoted in Juneau to fund a bond issue to build a new capital building and lease it to the state. The "capital-movers" figure that the issue will die once and for all if the legislature gets to move into plush new digs in Juneau.

Concerning the location of Juneau, neither timber or fish had anything to do with it, as with most other towns in southeastern Alaska. Juneau came about because of gold discovered in 1880. The population expanded rapidly, drawing people from all over the region and from outside Alaska. In 1906, the territorial government bowed to the inevitable and moved the capital from Sitka to Juneau. Here it stayed despite pressures over the next several decades which saw first Fairbanks and ultimately Anchorage become the largest cities in Alaska, and Alaska's centers of commerce.

Because the business of Juneau is government, there are essentially two tourism seasons here. The largest and most obvious is the summer when anywhere from one to as many as five cruise ships stop in town for several hours, each disgorging between 400 and 1,000 passengers for a rapid-fire swing through the local shops and visitors attractions. Add to these a couple of ferries letting off people every day and several airliner loads of people, and the population rises and falls by the thousands daily.

The second "tourist" season is the annual session of the state legislature from late January through late May. State senators and representatives from all across Alaska and their staffs descend on Juneau for a 120-day session that transforms the town into a maelstrom of publicity, dealmaking, backbiting and even revelry. The annual meeting of the Alaska legislature has been called the "best spectator sport in Alaska." Unlike most of the rest of Alaska's tourism industry, Juneau's hotels, boardinghouses and restaurants have a year-round clientele because of the legislature.

Unless you're really into state politics, summer is still the best time for visitors. The location is superb, a large menu of activities awaits visitors, and the folks are pretty friendly. Outside of government, tourism is Juneau's industry.

ACTIVITIES

BARE-BOAT CHARTER

Here's one you won't find very often in Alaska. Steve and Natalie Bradford offer their 32-foot, twin-diesel yacht for bare-boat charter to those qualified to operate it. With this, you can plot your own custom cruise through the sheltered waters of Alaska's Inside Passage. There are bunks for five on board, one price covers the boat, you provide the fuel and groceries. The price is extremely modest. Call Steve or Natalie at **(907) 586-4255** for details and available dates. For qualified skippers, this is really the way to get to know southeastern Alaska.

A cruise ship on its way to Juneau on the Alaska Marine Highway. (Photo courtesy of the Alaska Division of Tourism)

BEAR WATCHING

Pack Creek on Admiralty Island, a short charter flight from Juneau, offers visitors almost unlimited opportunities to watch brown bears feeding on salmon. Because this activity has become so popular over the last few years, the number of visitors is limited. You'll probably have to await for the results of a lottery to see if you get the dates you want. Call early to get your name in contention for a spot. Contact the USDA Forest Service, **(907) 586-8751,** for information on reservations.

CRUISE SHIPS

Most of Juneau's visitors arrive on a cruise ship, and downtown Juneau's narrow streets cater almost exclusively to these people, who are mostly on foot. Souvenir shops, specialty restaurants, flightseeing trips, glacier tours and even charter fishing trips are just a few steps from the dock. Many of the tours can be arranged by passengers in advance of docking through the Purser's office on board. Whatever you decide to do in Juneau, be sure to allow time for wandering the downtown's narrow streets.

CUSTOM CRUISES

Chris and Al Parce of Douglas (across Gastineau Channel from Juneau) operate the **M/V X-TA-SEA** on custom charters for a maximum of four people in two staterooms. Prepared tours include opportunities for bear watching, whale watching, fishing, crabbing and all-around sightseeing with no crowds and with unmatched comfort. They offer several planned itineraries with built-in flexibility to take advantage of unexpected treats such as pods of whales, or they can tailor a package for what you want to see and do. Few things in Alaska can match the warmth, comfort and awe-inspiring scenery offered by a cruise on the *X-TA-SEA*. Early reservations are a must. Call **(907) 364-2275.**

FISHING

Though Juneau is perhaps not as well known for its fishing as Ketchikan or other communities in southeastern Alaska, there are still plenty of opportunities to tangle with a salmon or a monster halibut. Your best bet for a charter operator is to call Suparna (no first or last name, just Suparna) at **Juneau Sportfishing, (907) 586-1887,** to arrange for a skipper to take you fishing. Suparna has several boats in her stable and should be able to match you with just the right one for what you want to do. Cruise ship passengers can make charter fishing reservations aboard ship before landing in Juneau if they wish.

For those who prefer a lodge-type fishing experience in the Juneau area, one of the best is **Pybus Point Lodge** on Admiralty Island. Your package to Pybus Point includes all lodging, meals, guided fishing and floatplane charter from Juneau to the lodge. Call Alan Veys, **(907) 790-4866,** for additional information and reservations. His combination of great fishing, remote wilderness, spectacular scenery and Alaskan hospitality is close to unbeatable.

FISH HATCHERIES

Four hatcheries dedicated to increasing salmon stocks operate in the Juneau area. The best one to visit, and really the only hatchery in Alaska specifically designed for tourism, is the **Gastineau Hatchery** about 3 miles north of downtown. Huge aquariums are filled with local fish and shellfish, you can watch the salmon entering the hatchery and, if your timing is right, you can observe hatchery workers stripping the eggs and milt necessary to begin raising another crop of salmon. Admission is $2.50 for adults and $1 for kids. During 1992, the Gastineau Hatchery released more than 90 million salmon fry of four different species in various Juneau waters. **(907) 463-4810.**

GLACIER TOURS

Magnificent Mendenhall Glacier hangs over the northern edge of Juneau, and the best way to get close is by helicopter. **TEMSCO Helicopters, (907) 789-9501,** offers a splendid trip several times daily: they fly you up on top of the glacier, let you out for a 20-minute or longer guided walking tour on the ice then fly you back to town on a circuitous route that provides awe-inspiring vistas of the ice field. TEMSCO provides the boots, parkas and whatever else is necessary. You can make your own reservations in advance, or cruise ship passengers can usually sign up for the tour before docking in Juneau. (*Insider's tip*: It's usually cheaper to make your reservation yourself instead of through the cruise lines. Most cruise companies add a significant markup to the price for selling tours aboard ship.)

Besides TEMSCO, **ERA Aviation** offers helicopter glacier tours, and several airplane charter outfits will fly you over the ice field for a bird's-eye view.

If flying to a glacier doesn't suit you, take a bus tour to the **USDA Forest Service's visitors center** near the base of Mendenhall Glacier. The view is tremendous, and rangers are on hand to describe what you're looking at and the recent activity of the glacier. Call **(907) 586-8751** for more details.

HIKING

Trails abound in the Juneau area. Contact the **USDA Forest Service, (907) 586-8751,** for ideas. When hiking, do make noise as you walk and stay in groups. There are a number of black bears in and around Juneau, so avoid surprising one at close range.

MUSEUMS

The **Alaska State Museum,** known informally as Alaska's Attic, is worth several hours of anybody's time. This beautiful facility at 395 Whittier Street offers compelling wildlife dioramas, historical exhibits and countless tidbits of life—and death—in Alaska over the last several centuries. One particularly moving exhibit details the grounding and sinking of the *Princess Sophia* during a storm north of Juneau in 1918. Call **(907) 465-2901** for information on hours and directions if needed.

WILDERNESS CABINS

The USDA Forest Service manages several remote cabins in the Juneau area at $20 a day. You bring all your own sleeping gear and food and you'll have to be flown in at your expense on a small floatplane to reach most of the cabins, but they're well worth your time, for they make for a true wilderness experience. Call the **Forest Service** at **(907) 586-8751** for details. Reservations can be made up to six months in advance and are highly recommended.

———— WHERE TO STAY ————

ACCOMMODATIONS
$$$$

Baranof

One of Alaska's oldest and most famous hotels, the Baranof is on a narrow street in downtown Juneau. Rooms are small and pricey, but quite comfortable and right in the heart of the action downtown. Lounge and restaurant on the premises. **(907) 586-2660.**

$$$

The Alaskan Hotel and Bar

Right downtown with a good dose of Juneau history in its location and decor. Live entertainment. **(907) 586-1000.**

Breakwater Inn

Hotel, restaurant and lounge. Large rooms, kitchenettes. **1-800-544-2250.**

The Prospector Hotel

Next to the Alaska State Museum. Lounge and restaurant. **(907) 586-3737.**

The Silverbow Inn

Heart of downtown Juneau. Restaurant and bakery. **(907) 586-4146.**

BED AND BREAKFASTS

Searching out a suitable bed and breakfast on your own can be frustrating, especially if you're doing it at the last minute. In

Juneau, however, there's a way to avoid the hassle and assure yourself of a good B&B experience. Diane Pearson, who runs her own B&B, **Pearson's Pond** (a truly beautiful facility), can get you a reservation at her own establishment or find you another suitable B&B accommodation if hers is full. Not only can she do this in the Juneau area, but she can handle B&B reservations in almost every community along the Inside Passage from Ketchikan to Haines. Call Diane at **(907) 789-3772** for help in arranging a bed and breakfast in Juneau, or any other city in southeastern Alaska if you're touring the region. B&B tours, such as Diane can arrange, are a great way to see Alaska's Panhandle and get close to some of the people who live there.

Independence Day celebration in Skagway. (Photo by Ron Dalby)

CAMPGROUNDS

Juneau gets considerable RV traffic via the Alaska Marine Highway, and facilities are available to handle those camping in their tin teepees—or tents for that matter.

The largest strictly RV park is the **Auke Bay RV Park** about 1.5 miles south of the ferry dock. Full hookups are available, and there are washers and dryers for your clothes. Turn right leaving the ferry dock and watch for the park; it's pretty easy to spot.

A campground suitable for RVs or tents is the **Mendenhall Lake campground** run by the USDA Forest Service. Potable water and a dump station are available. In this campground 22-foot RVs are about the limit. Also run by the Forest Service is the **Auke Village campground,** which can handle longer RVs. The latter is about 2 miles from the ferry dock; the former is on Montana Creek Road leading to Mendenhall Glacier. Call **(907) 586-8800** for permits for both the Forest Service facilities.

WHERE TO EAT

$$$
The Fiddlehead Restaurant

Juneau's favorite yuppie restaurant, the Fiddlehead offers fare for almost any taste, including vegetarian. Breakfasts are particularly good with the possible exception of the whole-wheat hotcakes. Great, fresh Alaskan seafood. Generally crowded for breakfast and lunch; you may have to wait for a table. **(907) 586-3150.**

$$
Armadillo Tex-Mex Cafe

Excellent Tex-Mex fare, large portions, beer and wine to put out the fire as appropriate. **431 S. Franklin, downtown. (907) 586-1880.**

Gold Creek Salmon Bake

Outdoor salmon bake with salmon and halibut and all-you-can-eat salad bar. On the old mining site at Gold Creek above town. Free bus with 6 P.M. pickup at the Baranof Hotel. Great food! **(907) 586-1424.**

Heritage Coffee Co. & Cafe

Great coffee, cappuccino, espresso, sandwiches and dessert. **174 S. Franklin. (907) 586-1088.**

Gustavus and
Glacier Bay National Park

Tucked away near the top of Alaska's Panhandle, Glacier Bay National Park is at once hard to get to and worth every bit of the effort. Access is generally out of Juneau by either boat or floatplane.

Many of the cruise ships plying southeastern Alaska waters spend an entire day sailing through Glacier Bay. Most visitors who want a longer, more personalized stay in the park travel from Juneau to Gustavus, a small community on the southern edge of the park. A number of options are available in Gustavus to visit this splendid wilderness.

Sea kayaking trips are probably the best way to silently ease into the wilderness of Glacier Bay. **Spirit Walker Expeditions,** based in Gustavus, offers everything from day trips to extended expeditions into the park. Typical of these is a five-day, four-night package of kayaking in search of whales. All meals are furnished in the fully guided trip, and sufficient instruction is provided so even a novice can paddle like a pro and keep up with the group. Each night is spent at a different campsite, sleeping out in the wild. Call Nathan (Nate) Borson, **(907) 697-2266,** for details and reservations. If you really want to touch the wilderness for which Alaska is famous, this is the way to do it.

Should you prefer your wilderness in smaller doses with clean sheets every night,

try the **Gustavus Inn.** For a minimum two-night stay, rates were $120 a night per adult in 1993, which included all meals, airport transfers, use of the inn's bicycles, and transportation to and from an afternoon nature walk. Day boat tours of the park are available from the lodge for an additional charge, as is an overnight boat trip through the park. Fishing charters are also available. Call JoAnn or David Lesh, **(907) 697-2254,** for more details and reservations at the Gustavus Inn.

Another lodge experience in Glacier Bay and an extended small-ship cruise of the park are available from **Alaska's Glacier Bay Tours and Cruises.** This Seattle-based company has summer offices in Juneau, Haines and Skagway for reservations to visit Glacier Bay. Call toll-free **1-800-451-5952** for information and reservations. This company can also help out with special airfares from western cities in the Lower 48.

Spirit Walker Expeditions, Inc. offers sea kayaking—day trips or extended treks. Call **(907) 697-2266.**

For those with only a limited amount of time, day cruises to Glacier Bay from Juneau are available, as are flightseeing trips over the park with various charter airlines. Inquire at any visitor information center in Juneau for more information.

Haines

Until about 15 years ago, Haines was the ultimate northern destination for northbound travelers on the Alaska Marine Highway who had their vehicles along. From Haines you can drive to Haines Junction in Yukon Territory, Canada, to join the Alaska Highway leading toward Fairbanks or Anchorage.

The opening of a road from Whitehorse to Skagway in the late 1970s made the latter the northernmost point on the ferry system. It is, however, a shorter drive by about 75 miles from Haines to Fairbanks than it is from Skagway.

Whether you drive into Haines from the north or arrive from the south by ferry, this city is synonymous with eagles, specifically bald eagles. In the fall of every year, thousands of the huge raptors converge on Haines from all over the continent to feed upon the carcasses of dead salmon from the last major run of fish for the year. A few miles north of Haines it's possible to see a dozen or more bald eagles perched in a single tree intently watching the Chilkat River below for their next meal.

But there's a lot more to Haines than just several thousand eagles. The fishing is great in the surrounding waters, both fresh and salt water. The area is beautiful, with snowcapped mountains reaching right to the edge of the sea in many places. Alaska's history is evident in the remains of the U.S. Army's Fort Seward, constructed just after the turn of the century.

ACTIVITIES

RAFTING

Several operators offer raft trips of varying lengths and varying levels of excitement on the wild rivers reaching the sea near Haines. Try **Alaska Cross-Country Guiding and Rafting, (907) 767-5522,** or **Chilkat Guides, (907) 766-2491,** for a memorable day or even longer excursion.

FISHING

A number of charter outfits can take you into areas where you can wrestle with salmon or halibut. Here's a partial listing to get you started:

Don's Camp—(Chilkat Lake, trout and salmon), **(907) 766-2303.**

First Out, Last In—**(907) 766-2854.**

Gray Fox Charters—**(907) 766-2163.**

McCormick Charters—**(907) 766-2450.**

FLIGHTSEEING

Small airplane charter companies offering aerial viewing and photography of Glacier Bay and the area surrounding Haines include **Haines Airways, (907) 766-2646,** and **L.A.B. Flying Service, (907) 766-2222.**

SOUTHEAST ALASKA STATE FAIR

Because Alaska is so big and so split up geographically, there are state fairs in almost every region. The fair for southeastern Alaska takes place the third week of August in Haines, and it can be the best of the lot.

In a sense, this state fair is much more rural than the big, "official" one in Palmer outside of Anchorage. There tends to be more local color and a lot less commercialism. This fair is pure fun for all ages. Contact the visitors center, **(907) 766-2234** or **1-800-458-3579,** for exact dates.

A homemade raft race down the Chilkat River rapids and the Alaskan Bald Eagle Music Festival are part of the general festivities during the fair.

WALKING TOUR

The best way to get a feel for Fort Seward and the Army's early presence in this part of Alaska is to take the walking tour of the grounds. The tour starts at the former post signal office on Beach Road west of town. From there you generally circle the parade ground and see the various barracks, facilities and officers' quarters that made up the fort. Many of these buildings are used for other purposes today, including the Chilkat Center for the Arts. Call the visitors center, **(907) 766-2234,** for more information, or visit the center downtown and pick up a brochure on the tour that includes a map.

WATER-TAXI

This makes regular daily shuttles along scenic Lynn Canal between Haines and Skagway. A convenient, quick way to move between the two communities, and an eyeful of scenery along the way. **(907) 766-3396.**

WHERE TO STAY

ACCOMMODATIONS
$$–$$$
Captain's Choice Motel
Downtown, convenient to lounges and restaurants. **(907) 766-3111** or **1-800-247-7153.**

Fort Seward Lodge
Originally this building housed the PX and gymnasium for Fort Seward. Ten overnight rooms, dining room and full-service saloon. **(907) 766-2009.**

Thunderbird Motel
Downtown, convenient to restaurants, etc. **(907) 766-2131** or **1-800-327-2556.**

$
Bear Creek Camp & International Hostel
Dormitory lodging, family cabins, kitchens and laundry facilities. **(907) 766-2259.**

BED AND BREAKFASTS
Fort Seward Bed & Breakfast—**(907) 766-2856.**

Officers' Inn Bed & Breakfast—**1-800-542-6363.**

The River House—**(907) 766-2060.**

The Summer Inn—**(907) 766-2970.**

CAMPGROUNDS
As the traditional northern terminus of the Alaska Marine Highway System, Haines has space for RVs and tent campers. The three listed below all have full hookups, tent sites and convenient locations.

Haines Hitch-Up RV Park—**(907) 766-2882.**

Oceanside RV Park—**(907) 766-2444.**

Port Chilkoot Camper Park—**(907) 766-2525** or **1-800-542-6363.**

Skagway

Those of us who can remember studying the Klondike gold rush back in high school almost always conjure up a single image of the event printed in most history textbooks: a long, thin, single file of overburdened men struggling up the steep face of a snow-clad cliff. Those men were toting part of the 2,000 pounds of supplies Canada required them to have when they left Alaska for the Yukon. Each man had to make a minimum of 10 trips up and down that mountain to get his gear to the top of Chilkoot Pass. Before they began their overland treks, these men landed in Skagway.

Now people hike this trail for recreation, and to do so they must still come first to Skagway, then down the road a few miles to the ghost town of Dyea where the actual trail begins. Besides the lighter gear available today and the services that can be called upon in the event of an emergency, civilization has worked another profound change—no longer do prospective hikers have to deal with Soapy Smith and his band of thugs in town.

Soapy and his gang controlled commerce in Skagway just before the turn of the century. They swindled miners out of their grubstakes in various confidence games or just plain stole their supplies. Skagway was pretty lawless in those days, and remained so until a local hero arrived. Frank Reid killed Soapy in a wild-west style gunfight on the dock, but in so doing was mortally wounded himself. Reid hung on for a couple of days before dying and was laid to rest in the same cemetery as his antagonist. After Soapy's death, some semblance of order began to take hold in Skagway, and the gang gradually broke up.

These days Skagway's entire summer seems devoted to reliving the revelry of the "Days of '98." The wooden, false-front buildings remain downtown, as do the boardwalks. The Red Onion Saloon still dispenses copious quantities of spirits, though visits to the upstairs bedrooms are no longer permitted. There are, however, mannequins leering at you from the windows on the second story, just as a reminder that this building was indeed once a profitable bordello.

As to the name Skagway, there's some confusion about the actual Tlingit word from which it was derived, and this confusion subtly illustrates the attitude of the town. First there's "Skagua," meaning home of the north wind, and it is indeed windy in Skagway much of the time. Then there's "Sch-kawai," meaning end of salt water, which is true as well since this is the head of Lynn Canal.

Local groups prefer other definitions of the word: One insists that it is the sound a sled runner makes when it breaks loose from snow and ice, while people in the local pubs declare it an Indian word meaning "lady relieving herself on a rock." Variations on the name theme include "rough water" and "cruel wind." Pick whichever legend you like best, and be prepared for a good-natured argument.

ACTIVITIES

FLIGHTSEEING

Several air services offer flightseeing excursions to areas around Skagway, including glaciers, fjords and other sights. TEMSCO (helicopters), **L.A.B. Flying Service,** and **Skagway Air Service** are best known.

HIKING

This one's obvious. The trailhead for the famed Chilkoot Trail is just a few miles out of town near the long-abandoned site of Dyea. Thousands of visitors come to Skagway every year to partially relive the experience of the early miners who were forced to trudge over Chilkoot Pass if they wanted to reach the goldfields in the Klondike. Be sure to register your plans and your timetable with the National Park Service before setting out. The weather can be vicious up on top, and it always helps searchers to have some idea of where to start looking if you're overdue.

The elevation gain on the Chilkoot Trail is approximately 3,000 feet, mostly in the first 10 miles of this trek of approximately 30 miles. The trail is fairly well maintained but steep in many places. Once you reach the top, you can hike out on the White Pass & Yukon Route railroad bed to the road, or starting in 1994 the train should be available to carry you from Lake Bennett back to Skagway. Expect rain and high winds during your trek up the Chilkoot; count yourself as very fortunate if the weather is otherwise.

But the Chilkoot Trail isn't the only hike around; most of the others are a whole lot less strenuous. Trails lead to Dewey Lake, Reid Falls, Sturgill's Landing, Upper Dewey Lake and other sites. Inquire at the **Skagway Visitors Center** in the old Arctic Brotherhood Hall on Broadway for directions and even more ideas.

HISTORIC SITES

Skagway personifies the gold rush history of Alaska. To that end, much of downtown is considered part of Klondike Gold Rush National Historic Park and is administered by the National Park Service. The decor on Broadway is late nineteenth-century America with false-fronted wooden buildings, many still in operating in their historic roles.

The very best way to get a feel for Skagway is the self-guided walking tour. Begin at the old White Pass & Yukon Route general offices on the corner of Second Avenue and Broadway and work your way up one side of Broadway and back down the other. Pick up a walking tour brochure and map in the WP&YR building, now the National Park Service's visitors center for Skagway. Plan to spend some time on this walking tour, as there are many fascinating places to look into along the way.

JULY 4TH

Many small towns in Alaska offer grand celebrations on Independence Day, and Skagway's is one of the best. The party takes place on Broadway, mostly traditional with a parade and a host of picnic games from egg tosses to tugs-of-war. There's something for all ages going on almost all day long and visitors are welcome to join in the fun. In fact, if you're just standing around watching, you may suddenly find yourself dragged into the fray to be a partner in the three-legged race or some other event. Nobody is shy when the fever of competition strikes.

Skagway's proximity to Whitehorse, Yukon, makes for a wonderful way to celebrate an extended period of national holidays. Canada Day, July 1st, is celebrated in Whitehorse with at least as much fervor as July 4th in Skagway. Many of the locals from both towns celebrate in Whitehorse, then drive the 100 miles down to Skagway to wind up a four-day party marking the independence of both countries.

RAILROAD

"Ride the railway built of gold," claims the brochure of the **White Pass & Yukon Route.** Indeed, it was the quest for the Klondike that brought this railroad into existence. A short, narrow-gauge, single-track route leading 100 or so miles from Skagway to Whitehorse, Yukon, the WP&YR came into being as a means of transporting miners and their supplies to the goldfields. As gold fever gradually died away in the area, it became important for the hauling of freight to Whitehorse where the freight would go on steamboats or barges to points farther downstream in the Yukon and Alaska. In later years, it hauled ore from Canadian mines to tidewater in Skagway for shipment overseas, and tourists with their vehicles from Skagway to the Alaska Highway at Whitehorse.

Then, in 1978, a road was opened between Skagway and Whitehorse. Within a couple of years, trucks were hauling the ore and other freight, people were driving their own vehicles and the WP&YR was essentially out of business.

After being idle from 1982 to 1988, the WP&YR reopened for tourist excursions from Skagway to the top of White Pass and back. The roundtrips offered daily during the summer months are well worth taking. Call **(907) 983-2217** for information and schedules.

——————— WHERE TO STAY ———————

ACCOMMODATIONS
$$–$$$
Golden North Hotel
On Broadway, Alaska's oldest hotel. 32 rooms decorated in the gold-rush motif. Restaurant and lounge. **(907) 983-2451.**

Irene's Inn
Built in 1899, in the center of the downtown historic district. Restaurant and bakery. **(907) 983-2520.**

Westmark Inn
Modern hotel with late nineteenth-century decor. Restaurant and lounge. Handicapped room available. **(907) 983-6000.**

$
Pullen Creek Bunkhouse
Bed and shower for $15, bring your own sleeping bag and towel. **(907) 983-2737.**

Skagway AYH Home Hostel
In historic, restored home. **(907) 983-2131.**

BED AND BREAKFASTS
Gramma's Bed & Breakfast—(907) 983-2312.

Skagway Inn—(907) 983-2289.

CAMPGROUNDS
Hanousek Park—(walking distance to town), **(907) 983-2768**

Hoover's—(one block from downtown), **(907) 983-2454.**

Liarsville—(2.5 miles from town), **(907) 983-2061.**

Pullen Creek RV Park—(next to ferry dock), **(907) 983-2768**

Anchorage

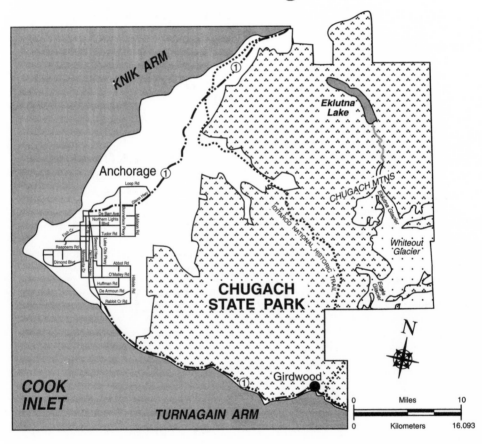

KNIK ARM

Eklutna Lake

Anchorage ①

Loop Rd
Glenn Hwy
De Barr Ave
Northern Lights Blvd
Fish Cr
Tudor Rd
Raspberry Rd
Dimond Blvd
Abbot Rd
O'Malley Rd
Huffman Rd
De Armoun Rd
Rabbit Cr Rd

Boniface Pkwy
Muldoon Rd
Seward Hwy
Lake Otis Pkwy
Hillside Rd

CHUGACH MTNS

Eklutna Glacier

Whiteout Glacier

Eagle Glacier

IDITAROD NATIONAL HISTORIC TRAIL

CHUGACH STATE PARK

COOK INLET

Girdwood ①

TURNAGAIN ARM

N

Miles
0   10
0   16.093
Kilometers

ANCHORAGE

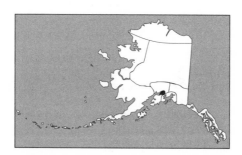

OVERVIEW

Hang around a few old-timers most anywhere in Alaska, and sooner or later you'll hear the old saw, "The only good thing about Anchorage is that it's just 30 minutes away from Alaska."

Part of the reason that this homily hangs around is jealousy—Anchorage is Alaska's business and economic capital, and, because of that, roughly half the state's population lives within 50 miles of the city center. These are not crowded conditions by any conceivable standard in the rest of urban America. In Alaska, however, this is a crowd beyond measure.

This saying, though, hangs around for another reason—a minor dose of contempt. A modern metropolitan area of a quarter-million people just doesn't fit the image most outsiders have of Alaska, and, perhaps more important, the image of roughing it on the Last Frontier that most Alaskans allow to surface in their letters and telephone calls to other parts of the nation.

The flip side of this coin is that Anchorage residents are immensely proud of their city's sophistication and status as the largest in the state. This is most often manifested publicly by the *Anchorage Daily News*, Alaska's largest-circulation newspaper, whose reporters and commentators all too often presume to speak for all of Alaska when in fact they are only writing about Anchorage.

Compared to the rest of Alaska, Anchorage's population tends to be made up of more recent immigrants, those attracted here by the lure of Alaska and more or less forced to settle in Anchorage because this is where the jobs are. By way of example, consider the purchase of a resident fishing license. Under Alaska law you must have lived in Alaska for a minimum of 12 consecutive months before qualifying for the privilege of purchasing such a license. One resident, recently relocated to Anchorage, went in to purchase his license and responded "12 years" to the clerk when she asked how long he had lived in the state. "Wow, you've been here a long time," she replied as she noted his answer in the proper space. In Palmer, 40 or so miles to the northeast, a 12-year residency would make the respondent a virtual newcomer.

More subtly, new arrivals are attracted to Anchorage because this is the part of Alaska that is most like other parts of the United States with which they are familiar.

Perhaps Anchorage's most striking feature is urban sprawl. Of all Alaska's larger towns, Anchorage is really the only one that matured during the automobile age. Fairbanks, Nome, Ketchikan, Juneau and other communities had already established themselves before cars and trucks were part of society's fabric. Though each of these cities, too, have ultimately experienced building conditions directly related to the needs of vehicles, most of it is on the fringes of the original town, not the area of the town that was settled initially and still thrives as the city center.

Anchorage offers all the advantages and disadvantages of cities everywhere in the country. It is at once vibrant and alive and crammed with rush-hour commuters. High-rise offices and elaborate shopping malls compete with escort services and massage parlors. Well-managed lounges and restaurants compete with sleazy bars and strip joints. Finely dressed office workers stride past the homeless and destitute on city streets. Anchorage is, above all else, an American city; as such, it shares the same positive and negative attributes.

Yet there is something a little different and a little special about Anchorage. No other large city in the United States can boast of grizzly bears getting lost and wandering through town. No other metropolis of similar size has a problem with people feeding wild moose in their yards. And where else in America can you find bald eagles soaring and wheeling through the sky between high-rise hotels and office buildings? Like it or not, Anchorage is part of Alaska, and Alaska, as the sum of its parts, includes Anchorage.

HISTORY

Anchorage rests near the head of Cook Inlet on the east side. Captain James Cook, the famed British navigator and explorer, was probably the first white man to see the upper end of Cook Inlet. He was searching for the fabled Northwest Passage when his travels brought him to these waters, only to find frustration because the inlet ends with two landlocked arms, Turnagain Arm, named by Cook because he was constantly tacking his ship to avoid running aground in shallow water, and Knik (pronounced with a hard k) Arm which peters out into low-lying flats near present-day Palmer. Anchorage is on a stretch of flat ground more or less between these two arms of the inlet.

A couple of minor gold strikes in the late 1800s brought a few people to the region, though none of them really settled on the site of Anchorage. It was the nine-year effort to lay a railroad from an ice-free port in Seward on the Kenai Peninsula to Fairbanks in Alaska's Interior that created Anchorage. Beginning in 1914, Anchorage was the midpoint construction headquarters for the Alaska Railroad. Initially, Anchorage was little more than a large tent city along Ship Creek, much, it might be argued, like the early gold rush towns. Within just a few years Anchorage was a thriving railroad town with permanent structures and a city bus tour that lasted almost an hour.

President Warren G. Harding visited Anchorage briefly in 1923, en route to Nenana to participate in the ceremony for the completion of the Alaska Railroad. In Nenana, he hammered in the traditional golden spike and shortly thereafter left Alaska. A few weeks later he died of pneumonia, thought to have developed from a cold he caught while visiting Alaska. The Alaska Railroad remained a federally owned and operated rail line for the next 62 years. Only in 1985 did the state purchase the railroad from the federal government and set it up on a profit-making basis.

Though Anchorage was a comfortable and very livable city in the 1920s and 1930s, it wasn't until the 1940s ushered in World War II that Anchorage's real boom began. A huge influx of soldiers, construction workers and later their families quickly pushed Anchorage to the status of Alaska's largest city. At the same time the Alaska Highway, then known as the Alcan, was completed, enabling people to drive to and from Alaska.

As part of this growth, Anchorage became the air crossroads of the world, as had been predicted for Alaska by maverick U.S. Army General Billy Mitchell back in the 1920s. Anchorage was and still is the obvious gas station for planes operating on the Great Circle Route over the North Pacific, as well as for planes operating over the North Pole to and from Europe.

Things were going quite well for Anchorage when tragedy struck on Good Friday 1964: The largest earthquake ever measured on the North American continent occurred in late afternoon, and Anchorage was literally shaken to pieces.

Part of the problem was the makeup of the land, particularly the soil underlying the core of the city. This cloying clay turned to the consistency of jelly as tremors raced through the earth. Fourth Avenue sank several feet straight down. Whole housing districts broke away from shelves of land high above the inlet and slid almost to sea level.

But Anchorage was quickly rebuilt, bigger and better than before. Countless loads of rock and gravel were trucked in to replace sunken lands in downtown areas. Businessman Walter Hickel (elected governor in 1966 and 1990) built the first tower of the Captain Cook Hotel on a downtown street to demonstrate his confidence in Anchorage; this was the city's first high-rise hotel. Two more towers have been added in the years since, and the Captain Cook is one of Anchorage's finest hotels and a major city landmark.

On the heels of Anchorage's recovery from the earthquake came oil, lots of it discovered nearly 700 miles away at Prudhoe Bay on Alaska's Arctic Coast. While oil had been flowing from the Kenai Peninsula and offshore from lower Cook Inlet, the volume there was nothing compared to this new find up north—nine billion or more barrels of it. Anchorage boomed again, this time as the center where major oil companies established their Alaskan offices and as a gathering spot for lawyers who were involved in every aspect of the Prudhoe Bay field from Native land claims to environmental concerns. Since the smoke has cleared from the oil "rush" at Prudhoe Bay, Alaska holds the dubious distinction of having more lawyers per capita than any state in the United States. In recent years their ranks have swollen even more as sharp-eyed legal types surged north to participate in litigation generated by the *Exxon Valdez* oil spill in Prince William Sound in 1989.

The plethora of lawyers in Alaska best illustrates the Anchorage of the 1990s. Anchorage is not a manufacturing city; it is a city of offices. Most federal government agencies at work in Alaska are headquartered in Anchorage. Though Juneau is officially the state capital, much of the state's day-to-day business is conducted in Anchorage. The capital serves mostly as the governor's base and the host city for the legislature for four months every year. Even Native corporations, whose land and people are often far from Anchorage, have major offices there. Anchorage illustrates better than any other Alaskan city except perhaps Juneau the fact that a disproportionate number of Alaskans work for some sort of federal, state or local government agency. And, where the government offices are located, so too are the private businesses that exist to support it, protect it and litigate against it.

This situation does show a few signs of change. Tourism, generally regarded as Alaska's most promising growth industry, is bringing more and more jobs to Anchorage every year. Also, as the flow of oil from Prudhoe Bay begins to decrease, the state has less money to employ workers. These are the first signs of a gradual shift away from utter dependence on government as an economic engine in Anchorage. This shift will not be without trauma, nor will it happen quickly as in a boom; but it will happen eventually. Through it all, Anchorage will remain Alaska's largest city, and the city that most visitors will see at least briefly during their trips to Alaska.

GETTING THERE

There are really just two ways to reach Anchorage—by road and by air. Visitors starting in Fairbanks can arrive by rail, though they will have had to reach Fairbanks either by road or air first.

Several domestic and international carriers serve Anchorage. Most predominant is Alaska Airlines with several nonstop flights daily from Seattle. Alaska Airlines offers service to almost all major cities in the West and a few tourist destinations in northwestern Mexico, though all Alaska-bound flights originate in Seattle.

Delta, United, Continental, Northwest and MarkAir also provide service to Anchorage. Nonstops on Delta can be arranged from either Salt Lake City or Seattle. United flies once a day from Chicago and a couple of times a day from Seattle. MarkAir, a local Alaskan airline, began service to and from Seattle in late 1991, and offers several flights a day. Continental schedules one plane daily to Anchorage from Seattle. Anchorage is approximately 3 hours and 40 minutes from Seattle on an airliner.

Those driving to Alaska can turn southwest in Tok, the first major road junction after entering Alaska, and drive 300 miles or so to Anchorage via the Glenn Highway. Once you are in Anchorage, there are only two roads out of town, the Glenn Highway to the north and the Seward Highway leading to the Kenai Peninsula south of Anchorage.

A handful of cruise ships have made brief stopovers in Anchorage in recent years and will probably continue to do so. These ships are more the exception than the rule for cruise ships, as the bulk of the cruise ship traffic operates along the Inside Passage in southeastern Alaska.

In Anchorage, a subsidized city bus service offers a cheap way to get around, taxi cabs are plentiful and all of the major car rental companies are represented. Most of the downtown hotels provide airport pickup if desired. With the exception of the core area downtown, Anchorage does not lend itself to walkers; things are just a little too spread out.

Anchorage is not served by Alaska Marine Highway System ferries. Toll-free reservation/information numbers:

Alaska Airlines	1-800-426-0333
(in Mexico)	95-800-426-0333
Continental Airlines	1-800-525-0280
Delta Airlines	
(in Alaska)	1-800-221-1212
Hearing/Speech impaired	1-800-831-4488
MarkAir	
(inside Alaska)	1-800-478-0800
(outside Alaska)	1-800-426-6784
Northwest Airlines	1-800-225-2525
United Airlines	
(in Alaska)	1-800-241-6522

Anchorage and
the Surrounding Area

In one sense, writing about Anchorage is like writing about a city without definable borders. This section will include Anchorage's bedroom communities of Eagle River, Chugiak, Birchwood and Girdwood. It will, as well, include information on attractions as far away as Portage Glacier, about 35 miles to the south, and Eklutna, about 25 miles to the north.

Each of these smaller communities or attractions is interesting in its own right, but none are sufficient to command their own sections in this book, tied as they are physically and economically to Anchorage.

FESTIVALS AND EVENTS

Anchorage's two largest festivals occur almost back to back in late winter. First, for nine days in mid-February, is the annual **Fur Rendezvous Festival,** commonly called Fur Rondy. Anchorage's oldest scheduled celebration, it attracts attention all over the state.

Key Rondy events include the Grand National Championship sled dog races, the Miners and Trappers Ball and a parade. The sled dog races are a series of three heats on the final Friday, Saturday and Sunday of Rondy. Each day's heat takes from 90 minutes to 2 hours, and the start-finish line is downtown on 4th Avenue.

Tickets to the **Miners and Trappers Ball,** Alaska's largest costume party, are almost impossible to obtain if you're from out of state. These normally go on sale at 8 A.M. on a mid-January morning and are usually sold out within a couple of hours. People line up a day or more in advance to get first crack at these tickets, sleeping outside in the cold and the snow just for a chance to get into the ball.

The parade is held along 6th Avenue on the last Saturday of Rondy. Fur Rondy is normally held from the second Friday in February through the third Sunday of the month.

Less than two weeks after Rondy, Anchorage's other big gig rolls around, the start of the **Iditarod Trail Sled Dog Race,** a 1,049-mile endurance classic from Anchorage to Nome. A lot of the town is involved with Iditarod, and the major events are health checks for dogs during the first three or four days of the week, the **mushers banquet** at the Egan Center on Thursday night (either the last Thursday of February or the first Thursday of March) and the race start on 4th Avenue at 9 A.M. Saturday. The highlight of the banquet is the mushers drawing for their starting positions in the race, an affair that usually takes three or more hours as each musher pauses to address the crowd and to thank lengthy lists of sponsors and friends. There are normally 75 or more mushers entered in the Iditarod.

Various events are scheduled in Anchorage and its surrounding communities over the summer; some are annual events, others are not. Contact the **Anchorage Convention and Visitors Bureau, (907) 276-4118,** for the latest information on scheduled events.

OUTDOOR ACTIVITIES

THE ALASKA ZOO

This is a favorite spot for many visitors, especially visitors with children. Most of Alaska's larger mammals are on display, including some marine mammals, and some other-than-Alaska animals as well. Favorites include Binky the polar bear and Anabel the elephant. In recent years Anabel has been creating paintings with a brush she holds in her truck. These canvases are later sold at auction to help defray operating expenses.

Lucky visitors may also get to see orphaned polar bear or grizzly bear cubs kept by the zoo while homes are found for them in other zoos around the world. The keeping of orphaned animals while searching for homes for them is nothing new for the Alaska Zoo. All of the animals on permanent exhibit at the zoo were originally orphaned or injured and cannot safely be restored to the wild. This is the driving philosophy behind all exhibits at the Alaska Zoo.

To reach the zoo, drive south from downtown on the Seward Highway to O'Malley Road. Turn east (uphill) on O'Malley and drive until you reach the zoo, which is well marked. Call **(907) 346-3242** for information and scheduled hours.

CHUGACH STATE PARK

This huge state park all but surrounds Anchorage on its landward side. Great hiking trails, wildlife viewing, wildflowers, rock climbing and (in winter) ice climbing are a few of the options for those looking for fresh air and a close look at the Chugach Mountains.

Several roads offer access to the park, including O'Malley and DeArmond roads in south Anchorage (just drive uphill until the road ends at a trailhead), Eagle River Road in Eagle River, Eklutna Road north of Anchorage, and through Girdwood near the Alyeska Ski Resort south of Anchorage. Most of the land along the Seward highway for its first 25 miles south from Anchorage is within the park.

Be careful leaving your car at trailheads off the roads leading from south Anchorage. In recent years there has been a lot of vandalism; cars in the parking lots are regularly broken into. Do not leave anything in your car that would tempt a thief. Call **(907) 345-5014** for more information on Chugach State Park.

CITY WALKING TOUR

A splendidly laid out walking tour of downtown Anchorage begins and ends at the **Anchorage Log Cabin Information Center** on 4th Avenue. Allow about two hours—more if you like to linger—for this trek through the core of Alaska's largest city. Maps are available at the information center. Call **(907) 274-3531** for additional details. Morning seems to be the favorite time for most walkers.

EARTHQUAKE PARK

Overlooking Cook Inlet, this park's walkways wind through areas twisted and reshaped by the 1964 earthquake. Most of this land was condemned for future building because of the unstable nature of the soil, thus it is available as a kind of laboratory for looking at the massive amount of destruction a major earthquake can do to the landscape. Maps and information are available at the **Anchorage Log Cabin Information Center** on 4th Avenue, **(907) 274-3531.**

EKLUTNA VILLAGE HISTORICAL PARK

This is the oldest inhabited site in the immediate Anchorage area. The original Russian Orthodox church dates back to 1830 (it was reconstructed in the 1970s), though religious services are now held in the church next door built by Eklutna residents in the 1950s. Centuries-old icons fill the church and are still used as part of the religious services.

Entering the park you will pass through the Heritage House, kind of a museum featuring historical displays portraying Native lifestyles and you'll see examples of Native art from south-central Alaska. Occasionally there are demonstrations by various artists.

The nearby cemetery holds colorfully decorated Spirit Houses, small structures erected over graves of deceased relatives. This practice came from a melding of Athabaskan and Russian Orthodox beliefs and practices.

Summer hours are 9 A.M. to 9 P.M. Drive north from Anchorage about 30 minutes on the Glenn Highway and take the Eklutna exit. Turn left as you exit the highway and drive a short distance to the park. For information, contact **Eklutna Village Historical Park, 510 L Street, Suite 200, Anchorage, AK 99501,** or call either **(907) 276-5701** or **(907) 688-6026.**

FISHING

You can catch a 50-pound king salmon or a tiny trout stocked in a lake within the city limits of Anchorage. Though this is far from the wilderness fishing for which Alaska is famed, it still can be quite an experience, particularly in the case of the king salmon.

The city's king fishery is **Ship Creek** near the railroad yards. Rules are extremely specific as to when and where you can fish, so check the state fishing regulations carefully before heading out to cast your line in the shadow of Anchorage's high-rise buildings.

Stocked rainbow trout are available in a number of ponds and small lakes in and around the city. Best bait is usually salmon eggs, either the commercial variety that come in a jar or fresh roe taken from a recently caught salmon. Best trout fishing is usually early (May and June) or late (September) in the season. Ice fishing is especially good in February and March.

Anchorage's real fishing thrills, however, are the wide variety of fly-in opportunities offered by several floatplane operators at Lake Hood near the international airport. Pilots can drop you off for a day, a week or a month of superb stream-side fishing in wilderness areas just a few minutes' flying time from Anchorage. Costs vary, but trips can be had for as little as $100 a day per person during special promotions, which includes tackle and, occasionally, the necessary fishing license. Normal prices range from about $150 to $200 a day per person depending on how long you are staying and whether your air service provides such amenities as a cabin, camping gear and a boat at the fishing site.

As a general rule for fly-in fishing, figure king salmon in late May and June, red salmon in July, silver salmon in August and rainbow trout in September when planning fly-in wilderness fishing out of Anchorage. These seasons do overlap, and are subject to slight variation from year to year, but they should get you started in the right direction.

Most air services encourage catch-and-release fishing for rainbows, particularly the larger fish that take decades to reach 20 or more pounds in Alaska's clear waters. As for salmon, there is generally no harm to the resource if you catch and keep fish according to the limits established by the Alaska Department of Fish and Game.

Though there are several air services at Lake Hood that can provide excellent fly-in fishing opportunities, two that have been in business a long time and are well respected are **Ketchum's Air Service, (907) 243-5525** or **1-800-433-9114,** and **Rust's Flying Service, (907) 243-1595** or **1-800-544-2299.** Both are long-time family businesses in the Anchorage area, and both will go the extra mile to see that you have a good time and every opportunity to catch a few braggin'-size fish. For best results, book early for peak fishing periods.

Besides the fish species listed above, there are also opportunities for pink salmon and chum salmon in the Anchorage area. These fish tend to overlap with silver salmon in August. They are not generally sought after, only taken as incidental fish on trips for reds and silvers.

The lack of interest in pink salmon is a bit of a shame. Pinks, though the smallest of the five species of Pacific salmon, are great fighters on light tackle and good table fare when taken from salt water or right at the mouths of spawning streams. And pinks are the most abundant salmon; fishing for pinks is quite literally a fish-every-cast proposition when you find them schooled up for spawning.

For the latest information on Anchorage-area fishing, call **(907) 349-4687**. The **Alaska Department of Fish and Game** continually updates a recording at that number telling what species of fish are biting where in the Anchorage area. To talk to a fisheries biologist or to request a copy of current fishing regulations, call **(907) 267-2218**.

FLIGHTSEEING

Virtually all of the air services that offer fly-in fishing also offer attractive packages for those who wish just to take in Alaska's magnificent scenery from the air. A wide variety of offerings are available including close-up views of mountains and glaciers, drop-offs for wilderness treks or just an aerial view of the Anchorage area. Some fly-in trips may include a short stop on a glacier. If the weather is good, these are hard to beat; it is extremely difficult to see more than just a little of Alaska from the ground.

Costs depend primarily on how long your flight will be in the air. Shorter flights may be as low as $75 per person with longer flights running to $150 or $200. Costs may also vary according to the number of people going together at the same time. The **Anchorage Log Cabin Information Center, (907) 274-3531**, can provide information on various carriers offering flightseeing packages.

GOLFING

Anchorage offers only one golf course at **Russian Jack Park.** Call **(907) 333-8338** for hours and green fees. Active duty and retired military personnel and their guests can use the course available at **Elmendorf Air Force Base** on the edge of town. Call **(907) 552-1110** (base information) for details.

Though gradually increasing in popularity, golf is not a big activity in Anchorage, or anywhere in Alaska for that matter, because of the extremely short summer season.

MOTOR-HOME RENTALS

A favorite way to explore Alaska is from a motor home or other recreational vehicle. However, not all people have the time to drive their own rigs up the Alaska Highway and then spend time poking around in Alaska. As such, it's become increasingly popular for visitors to fly into Alaska and then rent a rig for one or two weeks.

Costs range from of about $110 a day plus 20 cents a mile for a camper van to $250 a day plus mileage for a large class-A motor home. Rigs are generally equipped with cooking gear, eating utensils and bed linens. You buy your own food and cook your own meals with these programs. If you provide your own insurance, there's generally a $500 cash deposit required in advance. Depending on which dealer you rent from, there may be an additional charge for the housekeeping kits that include the dishes, pots and pans, flatware and linens—about $30 per person.

Three good motor-home rental firms are

#1 Motorhome Rentals of Alaska—322 Concrete Street, Anchorage, AK 99501, (907) 277-7575.

Murphy's RV—P.O. Box 202063, Anchorage, AK 99520-2063, (907) 276-0688.

Sourdough Camper Rentals—P.O. Box 9-2440, Anchorage, AK 99509, (907) 563-3268.

PORTAGE GLACIER

Little more than a half-hour's drive from Anchorage, Portage Glacier, part of the Chugach National Forest, is the most-visited attraction in Alaska. A spectacular new visitors center was completed by the USDA Forest Service during the 1980s and overlooks the iceberg-filled lake at the foot of the glacier. In 1990, a commercial operator began offering boat trips on the lake aboard the M/V *Ptarmigan;* these board near the visitors center. This is an awesome experience, one that may permit you close-up encounters with the glacier calving icebergs into the lake. The cruise costs about $20 per person, or $50 per person with bus transportation from Anchorage.

Drive south from Anchorage on the Seward Highway to the head of Turnagain Arm, about 35 miles. Turn left at the well-marked junction and proceed the additional few miles to the visitors center. Moose are often seen after turning off the Seward Highway. There's a small campground available for RVers and tent campers about halfway from the Seward Highway to the visitors center.

The **Begich-Boggs Visitors Center** at the lake was named in honor of Alaska Congressman Nick Begich and Louisiana Congressman Hale Boggs, who disappeared on a flight from Anchorage to Juneau in October 1972. Despite a massive military and civilian search lasting several weeks, no trace of their plane was ever found. The Begich-Boggs disappearance remains one of many unsolved aviation mysteries in Alaska.

Contact the visitors center at **(907) 783-2326** for additional information about visiting Portage Glacier.

SHOOTING

Two splendid outdoor ranges offer hunters the chance to sharpen their skills before setting forth on a once-in-a-lifetime Alaska hunt or recreational shooters to compete with locals in various competitions.

The **Rabbit Creek Range** run by the Alaska Department of Fish and Game is just a few miles south of downtown Anchorage on the Seward Highway. As you drive out of the forested residential areas in south Anchorage, the range is on the first open, flat stretch of ground you come to; it's hard to miss and well marked. Ranges are available for rifle and handgun as well as trap shooting for shotgunners. Hours

vary. Call **(907) 345-2502** for a recording of times the range is open. The most crowded period is usually in August, just before and during the opening of many of Alaska's big game and waterfowl seasons.

The **Izaac Walton League Recreational Park** in Birchwood may be Alaska's finest private shooting facility. Ranges are available for all calibers of rifles and handguns. Trap and skeet ranges are available, and an archery range challenges bowmen. There are frequent competitions, particularly trap and skeet. To reach the Izaac Walton League range, drive north from Anchorage about 20 miles on the Glenn Highway. Take the North Birchwood exit and drive west toward the airport. Drive past and around the airport to the well-marked range. Call **(907) 688-2809** or **(907) 688-3967** for additional details and shooting times.

SKIING

Whether your tastes in skiing run from sliding cross-country or booming down a mountain, the Anchorage area has something for you.

Cross-country skiers will find well-laid-out and groomed trails in **Russian Jack Springs Park** and **Kincaid Park.** Both have trails of varying levels of difficulty. Call **(907) 333-8338** for directions, information on trail conditions and hours at Russian Jack, or **(907) 248-4346** for similar details on Kincaid. Various competitions take place at these facilities, usually in March.

Downhillers will find Alaska's finest facilities in the immediate Anchorage area. **Alyeska Ski Resort,** Alaska largest, is located at Girdwood, about a half-hour's drive south of Anchorage on the Seward Highway. Vertical rise for this ski resort is 3,125 feet. Four double lifts and a quad lift can carry up to 5,000 skiers per hour. Trails covering everything from easy to expert are available. Skiing starts as early as October and lasts through April. For additional information, write **Alyeska Resort, P.O. Box 249, Girdwood, AK 99587,** or call **(907) 783-2222.** A 24-hour ski hot line for Alyeska (updated at least three times daily) can be reached at **(907) 783-2121.**

Alaska Sightseeing Tours in Anchorage provides daily bus service to and from Alyeska for those who don't wish to drive. Roundtrip fare is about $40.

Discounts are available at Alyeska for early-season skiing in November and December, and all season long for students and seniors. Various events are scheduled throughout the skiing season culminating with Alyeska's annual spring carnival in mid-April. The carnival is an absolute riot and draws lots of skiers and nonskiing spectators.

Within the actual city of Anchorage are two more downhill ski areas, Arctic Valley and Hilltop. Neither is as elaborate as Alyeska, but both are more convenient for local residents. Contact Hilltop Lodge, (907) 346-2165, or Alpenglow at Arctic Valley, (907) 694-7669, for additional details.

TONY KNOWLES COASTAL TRAIL

This combination bike path, jogging, walking and cross-country ski trail runs more than 20 miles around the western (Cook Inlet) side of Anchorage. No motorized vehicles are allowed. Whether you want just a short walk after dinner or an all-day hike around the outskirts of town, you can't miss with this trail.

The coastal trail was named for Tony Knowles, a two-term mayor of Anchorage during the 1980s, who is generally credited with being the driving force in getting it built. Contact the Anchorage Department of Parks and Recreation, (907) 343-4355, for detailed information.

WHALE WATCHING

From about mid-July through most of August, white beluga whales follow migrating salmon into Turnagain Arm of Cook Inlet. A 10- to 15-minute drive south on the Seward Highway will bring you to Beluga Point with a large parking area and a good view of the arm. Most belugas can be seen with the naked eye, though binoculars will help. Whales will be closer to shore during high tide.

Besides the whales, on the inland side of the road in the same general location are Dall sheep. Mostly ewes and lambs, these animals frequently come down almost to the roadside. Several trails are available near some of the roadside turnouts so you can walk uphill to get closer to the small bands of sheep.

INDOOR ATTRACTIONS

ALASKA CENTER FOR THE PERFORMING ARTS

This huge edifice occupying an entire block in downtown Anchorage boasts three theaters and all manner of live performances throughout the year. Everything from local productions to top-rated entertainers and performers are included on its bill of fare. Call (907) 263-ARTS for the latest information on scheduled performances and ticket prices.

This recent addition to Anchorage's cultural scene has been embroiled in controversy almost since its inception. Massive overruns forced its cost to $70 million or more before it opened, and costs are still escalating as the building is modified after the fact to provide for handicapped access and to fix such construction flaws as a leaky roof. As government revenues continue to decline in Alaska as a whole and Anchorage in particular, the Anchorage Center for the Performing Arts is high on the list of city activities that some politicians would like to eliminate from funding requests. Every year at budget time there is considerable concern as to whether the center will be able to continue to operate. It requires considerable subsidies from the city to avoid setting ticket prices out of reach for most people.

ANCHORAGE MUSEUM OF HISTORY AND ART

This is Alaska's largest and most comprehensive museum at **121 W. 7th Avenue.** Features include Alaska Native cultures and art by local—some well-known—artists. It requires several hours to do justice to the exhibits on display. Call **(907) 343-6173** for a recording about current exhibits and hours. For questions, call **(907) 343-4326.**

BASEBALL

Two semipro baseball teams call Anchorage home, the Anchorage Glacier Pilots and the Anchorage Bucs. There are games most evenings in June and July, and the admission is fairly cheap. They have lots of great action and are never very crowded. Call the **Glacier Pilots** at **(907) 274-3627** or the **Bucs** at **(907) 272-2827** for game times and locations.

THE IMAGINARIUM

This is hands-on, fun science—biology, physics, chemistry, astronomy, etc.—for children of all ages. Every adult who visits has a great time as well, so it's well worth a half day or even a day of your time in Anchorage. Major exhibits in recent years have included whales and dinosaurs. The Imaginarium is right downtown at **725 W. 5th Avenue.** There is usually a cover charge that varies depending on the cost of the particular display being highlighted. Call **(907) 276-3179** for information on current exhibits and hours.

THE PINES CLUB

Anchorage's biggest country-western bar is crowded almost every night. Live music and a huge dance floor make this a popular nightspot for those who want to let their hair hang down a little. Call **(907) 563-0001** for information.

SHOPPING

Three major malls and a host of smaller malls supplement the extensive downtown business district of Anchorage. Alaska's largest mall, **Dimond Center,** is in south Anchorage just off the Seward Highway at the Dimond exit. An ice rink, professional offices and more than 200 stores and restaurants combine to make Dimond one of the finest malls in North America.

Northway Mall, just as you enter Anchorage from the Glenn Highway on the north side of town, is the next largest mall with 150 or so stores and restaurants.

Downtown is the **5th Avenue Mall** between 5th and 6th avenues in the vicinity of C, D, and E streets. This is a city-center-style mall five stories high with a variety of shopping opportunities, though not nearly as many stores as either Dimond or Northway malls.

THE WHALE FAT FOLLIES

Owner of the Fly By Night Club and creator of the follies, Mr. Whitekeys bills his extravaganza as "the show the division of tourism doesn't want you to see." He and his talented crew spend about two hours every night poking fun at Alaska and Alaskans with skits and sketches like "Every Time Someone Does Something Dumb, an Alaskan Does Something Dumber," or "Spawn, Spawn, Spawn 'Til You Die." The performance is live, the house is packed almost every night and the humor is slightly risqué, though not obnoxiously so. A sample: Mr. Whitekeys picked up on the controversy over the Alaska Center for the Performing Arts by noting that the phone number for information, **263-ARTS,** can also be written 26-FARTS.

No one in Alaska is safe from Whitekeys' barbs, and as a result it's sometimes hard for visitors to get seats because local people have bought all the tickets. For an evening of hold-your-sides laughter, this is one you won't want to miss. Mr. Whitekeys has a real name, or so he claims, but so far no one except perhaps his family and his accountant know what it is. Call the **Fly By Night Club** at **(907) 279-7726** for tickets and reservations.

During the winter months, Whitekeys and his staff present a variation of the follies called "Christmas in Spenard," Spenard being the Anchorage suburb where the Fly By Night Club is located. It, too, is a laugh a minute, though the barbs tend to require a bit more local knowledge for complete understanding.

WHERE TO STAY

ACCOMMODATIONS

Anchorage has dozens of hotels and motels ranging from first class to extremely modest. It would be impossible to list all of them here. What follows is a sampling of varying levels of hotels/motels in the Anchorage area.

Reservations are almost always necessary during the summer months; Anchorage fills up quickly during the tourist season. If you have difficulty finding a hotel room, contact the **Anchorage Convention and Visitors Bureau, (907) 276-4118,** for assistance.

$$$–$$$$
The Anchorage Hilton

Rooms, suites, banquet and meeting rooms, good restaurants and comfortable lounges. Less than three blocks from the Anchorage Log Cabin Information Center. **500 W. 3rd, Anchorage, AK 99501, (907) 272-7411 or 1-800-245-2527** for Hilton's worldwide reservation service.

The Hotel Captain Cook

The original tower to this hotel was the first major construction begun in Anchorage after the 1964 earthquake. It is considered both an Anchorage landmark and possibly Anchorage's finest hotel. All facilities including an athletic club. Lower-priced rooms tend to be fairly small. **5th and K streets, Anchorage, AK 99501, (907) 276-6000.**

The Sheraton Anchorage

This is Anchorage's newest first-class hotel. The service is excellent and the lounge and restaurants are all that could be desired. **401 E. 6th Avenue, Anchorage, AK 99501, (907) 276-8700 or 1-800-325-3535** for Sheraton's worldwide reservation service.

$$–$$$
Anchorage International Airport Inn

Closest to the Anchorage airport. Large log structure with clean, comfortable rooms. Restaurant and lounge. Also close to Lake Hood floatplane base for those expecting fly-in fishing or flightseeing to be part of their vacations. Several miles from downtown. **3333 W. International Airport Road, Anchorage, AK 99502, (907) 243-2233 or 1-800-478-2233.**

Executive Suite Hotel

Every room is a small suite. Midway between the airport and downtown Anchorage. **4360 Spenard Road, Anchorage, AK 99517, (907) 243-6366.**

Holiday Inn

Pretty much the standard Holiday Inn. Indoor pool, restaurant and lounge. Upper-floor rooms overlooking 4th Avenue are great for watching the start of Iditarod Trail Sled Dog Race or Grand National Championships. **239 W. 4th Avenue, Anchorage, AK 99501, (907) 279-8671.**

Mush Inn Motel

Specialty rooms (jacuzzis, mirrors, etc.) available. Limited parking near motel. Not really close to anything. **333 Concrete, Anchorage, AK 99501, (907) 277-4554.**

Northern Lights Inn

Good restaurant and lounge, live entertainment. **598 W. Northern Lights Blvd., Anchorage, AK 99503, (907) 561-5200 or 1-800-447-9559.**

Regal Alaska Hotel

Right on Lake Hood, the largest floatplane base in the world, this hotel offers patrons the opportunity to be picked up by their chartered floatplanes right outside the door. An excellent choice for those planning fly-in fishing or flightseeing trips. Good restaurant and a great lounge. Almost a wildlife museum with all the stuffed critters hanging on the walls. **4800 Spenard Road, Anchorage, AK 99517, (907) 243-2300 or 1-800-252-7466.**

Voyager Hotel

Primarily because of its location, across 5th Avenue from the Hotel Captain Cook, this small hotel is so popular that it doesn't have to advertise. Most rooms are small suites with kitchenettes, and rates are extremely reasonable. Essentially, this hotel offers guests access to all the shops, meeting rooms, restaurants and lounges available at the Cook for less than half the cost. This small hotel is one of Anchorage's better-kept secrets. **501 K Street, Anchorage, AK 99501, (907) 277-9501.**

Westmark Anchorage

Nice rooms, good restaurant and lounge. Very limited parking available. In the heart of downtown Anchorage. **720 W. 5th Avenue, Anchorage, AK 99501, (907) 274-6631 or 1-800-544-0970.**

$–$$

Hillside Motel

Near Chester Creek Park with bike, jogging and ski trails. **2150 Gambell, Anchorage, AK 99503, (907) 258-6006.**

John's Motel

Close to Elmendorf Air Force Base gate. **3543 Mountain View Drive, Anchorage, AK 99508, (907) 277-4332.**

BED AND BREAKFASTS

The 1980s and the early 1990s saw a virtual explosion of bed and breakfast accommodations in the Anchorage area. The following list, though lengthy, is by no means complete but gives an idea of the wide range available. Bed and breakfasts average $50 to $75 per night per person.

Because B&Bs are opening and closing almost daily in Alaska, there may be facilities on this list that have closed for one reason or another before you arrive. The best that can be said is that all these were active when this book was written.

For assistance in sorting through the maze of these accommodations in Anchorage, three B&B referral services have been created. All are skilled at matching customers with B&B hosts. **The Anchorage Convention and Visitors Bureau Log Cabin Information Center, (907) 274-3531,** can provide information about these referral services.

6 Bar E Ranch B&B—c/o Margaret Ekvall, Earth Tours Inc., 705 W. 6th Avenue, Suite 205-7, Anchorage, AK 99501, (907) 279-9907 or (907) 346-2665.

Alaskan Comfort B&B—2182 Stanford Drive, Anchorage, AK 99508, (907) 258-7500.

Alaskan Friends B&B—3107 Willow Street, Anchorage, AK 99517, (907) 276-1210.

Alaskan Frontier Gardens B&B—c/o Rita Gittins, 1011 E. Tudor Road, Anchorage, AK 99503, (907) 561-1514 or (907) 345-6562.

Alaska Private Lodgings—4831 Caravelle Drive, Anchorage, AK 99502, (907) 248-2292.

All the Comforts of Home B&B—12531 Turk's Turn, Anchorage, AK 99516-3309, (907) 345-4279.

Anchorage Downtown B&B—1401 W. 13th Avenue, Anchorage, AK 99501, (907) 278-9275.

Arctic Loon B&B—P.O. Box 110333, Anchorage, AK 99511, (907) 345-4935.

Arctic Poppy B&B—307 E. 15th Terrace, Anchorage, AK 99501, (907) 258-7795.

Bed & Breakfast Colonial Inn—1713 Northwestern Avenue, Anchorage, AK 99508, (907) 277-6978.

Big Bear B&B—3401 Richmond Avenue, Anchorage, AK 99508, (907) 277-8189.

Birch Haven B&B—4602 Garfield Street, Anchorage, AK 99503, (907) 561-1307.

Bonnie's B&B—8501 Upper Huffman, Anchorage, AK 99516, (907) 345-4671.

Caribou Manor House—501 L Street, Anchorage, AK 99501, (907) 278-5776.

Country Garden B&B—8210 Frank Street, Anchorage, AK 99518, (907) 344-0636.

Cranberry Cliffs B&B—18735 Monastery Drive, Eagle River, AK 99577, (907) 696-3326.

Crossroads Inn B&B—1406 W. 13th Avenue, Anchorage, AK 99501, (907) 258-7378.

Far North B&B—4001 Galactica Drive, Anchorage, AK 99517, (907) 248-3393.

Fireweed B&B—10980 Corrie Way, Eagle River, AK 99577, (907) 696-7212.

Gallery B&B—1229 G Street, Anchorage, AK 99501, (907) 274-2567.

Hansmeyer's Homestead B&B—2535 Glenkerry Drive, Anchorage, AK 99504, (907) 333-0015.

Hillcrest Haven—1449 Hillcrest Drive, Anchorage, AK 99503, (907) 274-3086.

Hog Heaven B&B—4334 Spenard Road, Anchorage, AK 99517, (907) 248-5300.

Lynn's Pine Point B&B—3333 Creekside Drive, Anchorage, AK 99504, (907) 333-2244.

Maison Nanette B&B—2100 North Star, Anchorage, AK 99503, (907) 279-2063.

Polarwise B&B—4829 Kent Street, Anchorage, AK 99503, (907) 562-COLD.

Randy's Valley View B&B—P.O. Box 770515, Eagle River, AK 99577-0515, (907) 694-8266.

Mountain Air B&B—HC 83 Box 1652, Eagle River, AK 99577, (907) 696-3116.

Sixth & B Bed and Breakfast—145 W. 6th Avenue, Anchorage, AK 99501, (907) 279-5293.

The Smith's Sack 'n Snack B&B—516 North Park, Anchorage, AK 99508, (907) 274-8946.

Spring Hill Manor B&B—9451 Spring Hill Drive, Anchorage, AK 99507, (907) 346-2112.

A View With a Room B&B—8601 Sultana Drive, Anchorage, AK 99516, (907) 345-2781.

Wright's B&B—1411 Oxford Drive, Anchorage, AK 99503, (907) 561-1990.

CAMPGROUNDS

Unfortunately, Anchorage does not offer a large amount of camping space or RV parking. The city has one area, **Centennial Park,** off the Glenn Highway, **(907) 333-9711.** This is a pretty nice park with a large number of spaces, but it fills up fast during the summer months, so don't pull in unannounced late in the evening and expect to find space.

Private RV parks in the Anchorage area include

Golden Nugget Camper Park—(86 spaces), 4100 DeBarr Road, Anchorage, AK 99504, (907) 333-5311.

Hillside Motel and RV Park—(59 full hookup spaces), 7150 Gambell, Anchorage, AK 99503, (907) 258-6006.

John's Motel and RV Park—(50 full hookup spaces), 3543 Mountain View Drive, Anchorage, AK 99508, (907) 277-4332. (Good Sam member)

This is by no means a complete list, but it does cover some of the larger privately owned parks. If Anchorage-area parks are full—extremely likely during the summer season—there are a number of fine parks in the Palmer-Wasilla area about 45 miles northeast on the Glenn Highway.

—— WHERE TO EAT ——

Listing all the available restaurants in Anchorage would be impossible. There's eight or more yellow-page listings for pizza parlors alone. However, we can vouch for anything listed here because we've tried them all at one time or another.

$$$–$$$$

The Corsair
Try the rack of lamb. Very good wine cellar. **944 W. 5th Avenue** (across from the Hotel Captain Cook).

The Crow's Nest
Superb, with splendid views overlooking the city and Cook Inlet. Usually pretty dressy, though there is no actual dress code. Top floor of the west tower of the Hotel Captain Cook, **5th and K streets.**

Elevation 92
Excellent Alaskan seafood and beef. Not much of a view but the food is very good. Not quite so dressy as the Crow's Nest or Josephine's. **1007 W. 3rd Avenue.**

Josephine's
Middle floor of the Sheraton Anchorage. Tends to have a European flair to the cooking. Probably the most romantic spot to take that special someone. No dress code, though gentlemen will feel out of place without a jacket and tie. Most women wear dresses. **401 E. 6th Avenue**

$$–$$$

Akai Hana
An excellent sushi-bar type of Japanese restaurant across 5th Avenue from the Hotel Captain Cook. The restaurant is tucked back in an alley, so you have to look a little for it. There is a lighted sign on 5th Avenue at the entrance to the alley. Generally not very crowded; reservations probably not necessary. Quiet; nice for lingering over dinner. **950 W. 5th Avenue.**

Double Musky Inn
About 30 miles south of Anchorage on the Seward Highway turn left toward Girdwood (Alyeska Ski Resort). As you enter town, the restaurant is easily spotted on the left. Excellent Cajun food in generous quantities, as well as steaks and seafood. Always crowded and reservations are not accepted. Expect a long wait in the lounge, but remember, you still have to drive home. Well worth visiting; this has been a favorite Anchorage-area restaurant for years.

La Mex
Full range of south-of-the-border dishes, excellent lounge. Lounge is usually noisy, particularly during the cocktail hour. Dining area is more subdued and tables are arranged to maximize privacy. Reservations are handy but not necessary if you don't mind a short wait for a table. Two locations: **2552 Spenard Road** and **900 W. 6th Avenue.**

Romano's
An excellent Italian restaurant with a wide variety of pastas and sauces. Tables are reasonably private and the service is good. Reservations usually not necessary. **2415 C Street.**

Sack's Cafe
This is one of Anchorage's trendier lunch spots with a somewhat sophisticated clientele. Great pastas and seafoods. **625 W. 5th Avenue.**

Simon & Seafort's Saloon & Grill
In the vernacular of the 1980s, this was and is Anchorage's favorite yuppie hangout. The lounge can be lively during the cocktail hour, especially on Thursdays and Fridays. Superb seafoods, including a variety of fresh fish and shellfish as daily specials. Good views of Cook Inlet if you can get a window seat. Reservations necessary

unless you want to wait in the bar. If you tarry on summer evenings, you'll have a good view of the late sunsets. Fairly noisy; not a good place for quiet conversations. **420 L Street.**

$–$$

Like most other American cities, Anchorage offers the full range of fast-food franchises that have sprung up in the last couple of decades—hamburgers, chicken, pizza, whatever. Children find these a reminder of home, adults use them for quick, cheap meals. Because most are familiar with these places, and the ones in Anchorage hardly differ from the ones in Chicago, they are ignored in this guide. You'll find the same food at roughly the same prices as in the Lower 48.

Club Paris

A favorite of the Alaska press corps, this is a fine spot for burgers and beer at lunch time, or even something stouter from the bar. Pretty dark inside and usually noisy at lunch time. **417 W. 5th Avenue.**

North Slope Restaurant & Sophie's Saloon

Hearty burgers and other American fare. Excellent breakfasts. **11501 Old Glenn Highway** (Eagle River).

Peggy's Restaurant

Across from Merrill Field as you drive into Anchorage from the north, Peggy's has been an Anchorage fixture forever, or so it seems. Mostly down-home cooking—meatloaf, roast beef, chicken, hamburgers and so on. For dessert, try a slice of homemade pie—with ice cream, of course. Hearty breakfasts; opens early. **1675 E. 5th Avenue.**

Red Robin Burger & Spirits Emporium

Though this is one of a chain of restaurants, its popularity in Anchorage makes it worth listing here. Mostly American food—wide variety of hamburgers, ribs, chicken, etc. An excellent place to take a family. Always crowded and noisy; expect to wait for a table. A full-service bar and lounge, unusual in this price range for a family restaurant. **3401 Penland Parkway** (behind the Northway Mall where the Glenn Highway enters Anchorage).

Royal Fork Buffet

An excellent all-you-can-eat buffet—soups, salads, entrees, side dishes and desserts. Go back as many times as you want. **800 Northway Drive.**

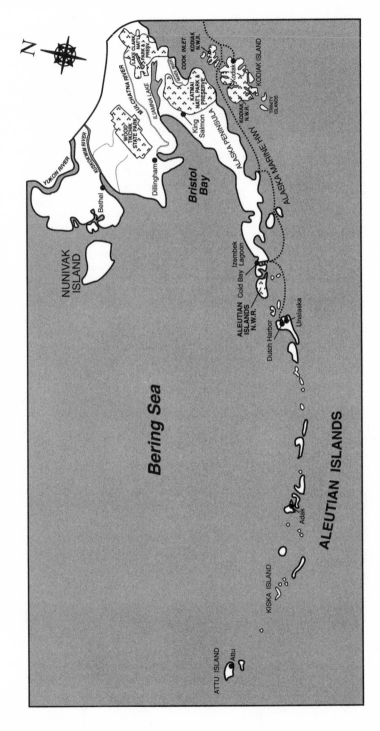

Southwestern Alaska

⸏SOUTHWESTERN ALASKA⸏

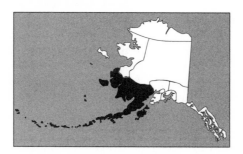

OVERVIEW

It was here that the Russians first came to Alaska in force, and solely because of greed. The wind-swept and wave-battered Aleutian Islands were home to the sea otter, a lushly furred mammal whose pelts were eagerly sought by the wealthiest and most powerful Russians.

These first Russians in Alaska were greedy, uncultured and little concerned with the fate of the peaceful Aleuts who greeted them in the mid-1700s. In a few decades these *Promelshki*, as they were called, would hunt the sea otter to near extinction and show little more regard for the fate of the Aleuts. What few written accounts survive of the era tell of Russians lining up a number of Aleut boys one behind the other, then shooting a musket into the chest of the first to see how many could be killed in a single shot.

By the time Aleksandr Baranov arrived with a charter from the czar granting him charge of the Russian American Company, most of the otters were gone from the Aleutians. He established the first Russian capital in Alaska on the north side of Kodiak Island, where the city of Kodiak is today. Even it was short-lived: Within a few years the fur traders were ranging ever further eastward in search of more pelts, and the capital was subsequently moved to Sitka, where it would remain until the United States purchased Alaska in 1867.

The establishment of Kodiak, however, brought some measure of peace for the desperate Aleuts. Baranov brought priests from the Russian Orthodox church with his entourage, and these men began to establish at least a minimal degree of order. Thus the Russian church became the first of the

95

organized European religions to establish itself in Alaska. Throughout the nation today, the strongest influence of the Russian Orthodox is still in Alaska.

Virtually all of the long-established communities in southwestern Alaska, particularly those with large Native populations, have the distinctive onion-domed sanctuary of the Russian Orthodox church as a prominent feature of the town. Traditionally, no chairs or pews are provided the worshipers, save for the ill or infirm. Treasured, gilt-edged icons decorate the walls and the alters. Christmas is celebrated in January, weeks after other institutions have turned to other matters.

Yet amidst these churches that many consider relics from a distant age are modern if modestly sized cities. As in the time of the Russians, these cities, towns and villages are still relatively isolated. No roads lead to southwestern Alaska, major airports with scheduled passenger service are relatively few, and other than fishing boats, supply barges, and here and there a ferry, no major ships call with any regularity. If one thinks of Alaska itself as remote, then this would qualify as the remotest part of Alaska.

Many, if not most Alaskans have never been to the southwestern part of the state. Relatively few would even recognize the names of the communities therein, except perhaps for Kodiak, Dillingham, King Salmon or Dutch Harbor. With the exception of Kodiak, most Alaskans could hardly find these places on a map without a moment or two to study it first. These Alaskans, and most of the rest of the world, don't know what they are missing.

Wildlife abounds throughout the region—hundreds of bird species, giant brown bears, caribou, sea otters, killer whales, and seals to name a few. Waterfowl by the score gather in Izembek Lagoon near Cold Bay each fall waiting for just the right storm to push them south in their annual migrations.

The landscape is rugged, stunning, all but untouched by man. The weather is worse than most people can imagine. Williwaws, with gusts exceeding 100 miles per hour, can abruptly shatter the calmest of days. Summer temperatures in the Aleutians rarely rise much above 60 degrees; winter temperatures rarely fall much below freezing at sea level— if you discount the wind-chill factor.

And, to add insult to injury, the Aleutians and the Alaska Peninsula are the northern arc of the Pacific's Ring of Fire. Volcanoes are frequent, felt but rarely seen because of the weather. Most eruptions are reported by passing pilots who might happen to get a glimpse through a hole in the clouds. Every year, too, earthquakes that would devastate California hardly merit a comment. A keen observer might note that there are very few multistory buildings in the region.

If you're looking for wilderness, the wilds for which Alaska is so justly famed, this is the ultimate region to visit. Nothing else even comes close.

The Aleutian Islands

On a map, the 1,000-mile arc of these islands, stretching westward toward Asia from the Alaska Peninsula, usually appears as a string of emerald green, irregularly shaped dots set in an azure sea. Looking more closely at the map, you will see very few communities. Those that are listed probably have Russian or Aleut names, names like Akutan, Nikolski, Attu and Adak.

Almost all the land on these islands is part of the Aleutian Islands National Wildlife Refuge, perhaps the most remote of all the lands managed by the U.S. Department of the Interior. The only grounds not part of the refuge are isolated holdings near the towns and villages and certain lands deeded to Aleuts as part of the Alaska Native Claims Settlement Act of 1971.

Scheduled airline service is only available to a few selected sites—Dutch Harbor and Adak being the most prominent.

Two military bases sit on these lonely rocks: **Adak Naval Station** and **Shemya Air Force Base.** Both are classified facilities, though it is possible to get to Adak as there is a small civilian town there as well. Don't even try to visit Shemya at the far western end of the chain. The Air Force folks out there don't like visitors in any form.

Fishing and crabbing are the major industries in Dutch Harbor. (Photo by Ron Dalby)

Dutch Harbor/Unalaska

Daily air service—weather permitting—is available to this, the largest community in the Aleutian Islands. Few hotel rooms can be found during the summer season without reservations far in advance.

Fishing and crabbing are the major industries in Dutch Harbor. Every year the town is listed in the top five U.S. fishing ports in terms of volume and value of catch; usually it's number one or number two. What hotel rooms are available are quickly rented by seasonal workers in the employ of some segment of the fishing industry.

However, visitors do come to Dutch Harbor. During World War II, Dutch was bombed by planes from Japanese carriers covering the landings of Japanese soldiers on Attu and Kiska islands near the western end of the chain. Attu, Kiska and Dutch Harbor thus became the only parts of North America to suffer damage or invasion as a result of the war. Many who visit Dutch Harbor are former soldiers coming to see where they spent part of their youth.

Birders also visit Dutch Harbor. Bald eagles and sea birds are the prime attractions, but there are others as well. If you've got some gaps in your life list, this is a good place to start an expedition to fill in some of the holes.

Visitor services in Dutch Harbor are not extensive. There is the **Grand Aleutian Hotel** ($$$), which has two restaurants and a lounge, **Pouch 503, Dutch Harbor, AK 99692, (907) 581-3844.** There's also a light aircraft for charter and a weekly Alaska Marine Highway ferry. Scheduled air service to and from Anchorage is available from Reeve Aleutian Airlines, and it's pretty expensive. Expect to pay the highest seat-mile rates in the airline industry for a trip to Dutch or further out on the chain.

Few planned tours are available on a regular basis to Dutch Harbor or the Aleutian Islands. Birding clubs and other groups with a specific interest in the islands occasionally put programs together, but these are sporadic at best. Your best bet if you want to visit here is spend some time with a travel agent seeing what can be put together. Or, if you're a birder, watch publications dedicated to your hobby for announcements of group tours.

Smaller communities served by scheduled commuter air services out of Dutch Harbor include Akutan and Atka, with occasional flights to lesser known places.

The Alaska Peninsula

COLD BAY/IZEMBEK LAGOON

No more compelling wildlife spectacle exists in North America than the fall gathering of geese in Izembek Lagoon near the southwestern end of the peninsula. Starting in late September, Canada geese, cacklers, brandt and emperor geese straggle into the lagoon to feed on eel grass and await just the right moment for the major leg of their southern migration to commence.

The timing of their departure takes advantage of a fast-moving storm in early November. The birds, sensing the right moment, arise almost en masse, climb into the clouds and are pushed in a southeasterly direction by the wind patterns of the storm. Almost overnight, a huge bay populated by millions of birds the day before empties.

Waterfowl aren't the only treat in Izembek National Wildlife Refuge. On land there are brown bears and caribou, the latter generally migrating into the area in late October or November.

Most journeying to Cold Bay come by air, again on Reeve Aleutian Airways. There is a weekly ferry in the summer months, but it's used more for freight than passengers. A small hotel, more like a bunkhouse (two sets of bunk beds in a 10-by-10 room, bathrooms down the hall), a small restaurant and a bar sum up the available facilities. A limited number of rental vehicles are available at the airport, and the limited road system of the area does allow you to drive the few miles to the edge of Izembek Lagoon.

These rental vehicles are not what most people expect. The "deluxe van" available in 1989, was a Dodge of uncertain vintage (at least 20 years old), battered almost but not quite beyond repair. Carbon monoxide from the engine was a problem inside, but one that was easily resolved by a sprung door that wouldn't stay latched and thus provided plenty of ventilation. The windshield wipers only worked when the headlights were turned off, and the dashboard only lit up on an irregular basis. This vehicle rented for $55 a day. It did, however, start every time the key was turned.

Probably the opportunity to hunt geese at Izembek brings Cold Bay most of its recreational visitors. A couple of big game guides also operate from the town, taking hunters for brown bear and caribou. There is limited fishing for salmon in the area, usually in the fall for silvers.

Sitting down with a knowledgeable travel agent coupled with a bit of patience is about the only way to arrange a vacation in Cold Bay. Or, if you really thirst for a bit of RV adventure, put your rig on the Alaska Marine Highway in Homer and use it as a base to explore the region. Contact the **ferry system** at **1-800-642-0066** for details on sailing times and prices. This trip is not recommended for the really large, lushly appointed class-A motor homes. What roads there are in the region are suited more to pickup campers and smaller rigs like class-C motor homes or smaller travel trailers.

99

McNEIL RIVER

Countless wildlife documentaries and magazine articles have depicted the bears of McNeil River feasting on salmon in the summer months. The state of Alaska maintains a small facility there to serve visitors. Usually visitors arrive for a three-day stay (bring your own tent and sleeping bag, charter your own airplane to get there).

Resident Alaska Fish and Game biologist Larry Aumiller guides visitors daily to an overlook to watch and photograph the bears and ensures that no contact detrimental to either the bears or the people takes place. Those who visit McNeil actually live with the bears throughout their stay. A cook shack is used to keep food items away from the tents.

Because of the high demand to visit McNeil during the salmon runs, Alaska runs a lottery to determine who gets to visit and who doesn't, which is held in April for the upcoming summer. If you are interested in entering the lottery, write to the **Alaska Department of Fish and Game, Attn: McNeil River, 333 Raspberry Road, Anchorage, AK 99518,** or call **(907) 267-2180**. ADF&G personnel will explain the lottery system to you and send an application so you can participate in the drawing. If selected to visit McNeil River, the visitor must bear all expenses relating to travel and equipment.

KATMAI NATIONAL PARK

North America's largest volcanic explosion in the twentieth century blasted southwestern Alaska when Novarupta blew in 1912. Big even by Alaska standards, this event blanketed more than 40 square miles of formerly green valley with up to 700 feet of ash and pumice, and created an almost moonlike landscape only now showing signs of recovery. For decades, the Valley of 10,000 Smokes delighted hikers bold enough to venture into the region. In recent years, however, the steaming vents have gradually been disappearing or weakening.

The opportunity to observe brown bears and the tremendous sport fishing for salmon and rainbow trout bring most visitors to Katmai these days.

Katmai is considered a haven for native populations of rainbow trout, and fishermen are asked to practice a careful program of catch-and-release for these spectacular game fish. If you want fish for dinner or for the larder, stick with the salmon.

Brooks Lodge

In the heart of Katmai National Park, Brooks Lodge has long been famed for its bear-watching and fishing opportunities.

Day trips to the Valley of 10,000 Smokes and Park Service guided nature walks are also available. During the salmon runs, bears feeding on fish are generally visible from the lodge. Park Service campgrounds for tenting are also available near the lodge. Write **Katmailand, 4700 Aircraft Drive, Anchorage, AK 99502,** or call **1-800-544-0551** for information and reservations.

Brooks Lodge is normally accessed from King Salmon, a 280-mile flight from Anchorage via scheduled air service. Three-day, two-night trips, double occupancy, are slightly more than $700 per person, which includes air transportation from Anchorage. Prices are higher in July, the prime bear-viewing month. Flightseeing tours, the Valley of 10,000 Smokes tour, guided fishing and other services cost extra.

Those strictly interested in fishing should consider Katmailand's other lodges, Kulik and Grosvenor. Combination trips to Brooks Lodge and one of the fishing lodges are available. Three-day, three-night packages at these lodges start at around $1,500 at Grosvenor and can exceed $4,000 for a one-week package at Kulik.

KING SALMON

As is obvious from the name of the town, there are fish here, lots of them. Fishing, both commercial and sport, is the key industry, along with the services necessary to help people reach backcountry areas.

Commercial air service is available from Anchorage with a couple of flights daily.

Since so few facilities are available, pricing guides are not listed. There is very little competition to make such a guide relative to anything. Plan for moderately high prices in town.

Quinnat Landing Hotel

On the Naknek River, floatplane dock, cable TV, restaurant and lounge. Spacious, modern rooms by Alaska bush standards.

Winter: **(907) 561-2310.** May 15–October 15: **(907) 246-3000.** Can also book guided fishing with Freebird Charters through the same phone numbers. Combination fishing and sightseeing packages available.

Katmai Lodge

Despite the name, this lodge is not located in the national park; it's on the Alagnak River a short distance west of King Salmon. The Alagnak is the easternmost of the famed Bristol Bay watersheds, and the fishing in all these streams is nothing short of fantastic: salmon and big rainbows primarily—also grayling and northern pike. One-week packages, including airfare from Anchorage, start at about $3,000. Call Tony Sarp, **(206) 337-0326,** for details and reservations.

A Grizzly bear misses a salmon at Brooks Falls in Katmai National Park. (© 1993 Alissa Crandall)

Dillingham

The Bristol Bay region's largest city primarily serves commercial fishermen and government agencies at work in the area.

In a sense, Dillingham is a model of too much government. Two separate school districts are headquartered in the city, complete with support staffs and administrators. First there's the Dillingham city district, then there's the regional district serving the outlying villages. Either the city didn't want to be part of the rural school district or the rural areas didn't want to be connected with the city. Whichever the case, state dollars completely support both school districts in a spectacular example of duplication of effort.

Most visitors to Dillingham are fishers or hunters; very few others make it this far. Those who do come spend little time in town. The fishers are either en route to a remote lodge or float trip, the hunters are meeting a guide or being flown into remote areas to hunt on their own.

Most of the fishers are on their way to lodges in Wood-Tikchik State Park, the largest state park in the nation. For decades these lodges have been thought of as the ultimate North American adventure for the dedicated fishing fraternity. Prices start at about $4,000 a week per person and include considerable fly-out activity as well as boat travel along the streams and interconnected lake systems of this park. Five lodges serve the area and each caters to a very limited number of guests (only four of the lodges were open in 1992).

For a list of these lodges, contact the **Alaska Public Lands Information Center, 605 W. 4th Avenue, Anchorage, AK 99501, (907) 271-2737,** and inquire about Wood-Tikchik State Park.

Nushagak Tidal Area, Dillingham, Alaska. (Photo by Rex Melton, Alaska Division of Tourism)

Kodiak Island/Kodiak City

Of all the possible destinations in southwestern Alaska, Kodiak is the best known, and, even so, relatively few visitors make it this far.

Like the other major towns in southwestern Alaska, Kodiak is primarily a fishing port, and like Dutch Harbor it is regularly reported in the top five ports nationwide for value and volume of its catch. There is also some logging activity on neighboring Afognak Island and a modestly sized but gradually growing tourism industry.

Guided hunting for the giant Kodiak brown bears has long been Kodiak's most famous offering in sporting circles. Though the hunting activity is still important, it is carefully regulated these days as to numbers of resident and nonresident hunters. Expect to pay about $10,000 for a guided hunt for Kodiak bear; demand far exceeds supply.

Sportfishing has been growing on Kodiak Island in recent years. A number of saltwater day charters for halibut and salmon are now available in Kodiak harbor, and several lodges cater to fishermen.

Lions Den Wilderness Lodge

Kevin and Katy Adkins run this lodge in Port Lions, a short distance across a small bay from Kodiak. One-week fishing packages are about $1,500 per person and include transfer from Kodiak and all the fishing. Deer and waterfowl options are available in the fall, with combination trips possible. Week-long deer-hunting packages start at around $800, unguided, and bring your own sleeping bag. Call Kevin or Katy at **(907) 454-2301** or **(907) 454-2418** for details and reservations.

Saltery Lake Lodge

Doyle Hatfield, a retired Kodiak teacher, manages this lodge a 20-minute flight south of Kodiak (city). Offers great freshwater opportunities for salmon and rainbows (including Karluk River float trips), and saltwater fishing for halibut and salmon. Deer-hunting combinations with the fishing are available from August 1. Cost is $1,770 per person per week, with extra charges for fly-outs and the Karluk float trip. Call Doyle at **1-800-770-5037** for details and reservations.

$$$
Buskin River Inn

Kodiak's newest hotel overlooks the Buskin River at the edge of town and is used as a base by many visitors. Lounge and dining room. Staff can assist in reservations for ocean charters, hunting charters, flight services and tours. Call **1-800-544-2202** (from outside Alaska) or **1-800-478-2701** (from within Alaska) for information and reservations.

TOURS

MarkTours, a division of MarkAir, offers one- and two-day package tours to Kodiak, which include airfare from Anchorage, museums, entertainment and other activities. Call **(907) 243-6275** for information and reservations.

═ Lake Clark National Park ═

This wilderness park protects a beautiful area centered on Lake Clark on the northern edge of the Aleutian Mountains across Cook Inlet from Anchorage. There are very few facilities, a few private inholdings within the park and a couple of small communities on the lake: Port Alsworth and Nondalton. Access is by charter air from Anchorage, or infrequently scheduled commuter service to Port Alsworth.

Contact the **Alaska Public Lands Information Center, 605 W. 4th Avenue, Anchorage, AK 99501, (907) 271-2737,** for information on Lake Clark National Park. Primary attributes of this park are the little-touched wilderness and rarely disturbed wildlife. Some fishing is available in Lake Clark.

A cloud hovers over beautiful Lake Clark. (Photo by Rex Melton, Alaska Division of Tourism)

Bethel

Primarily a shipping and communications center for the numerous small villages in the Kuskokwim River delta, Bethel has limited facilities and limited offerings for visitors. Most visitors passing through Bethel are either coming from or going to a fishing or hunting trip.

There are a couple of small restaurants available. Charter air services serving the surrounding bush villages have airplanes available for charter into the backcountry.

Scheduled air service is available from Anchorage, and there is scheduled commuter service to most villages in the region.

Distances are vast in Alaska as is the tundra on the North Slope. (Photo courtesy of the Alaska Division of Tourism)

Western Alaska

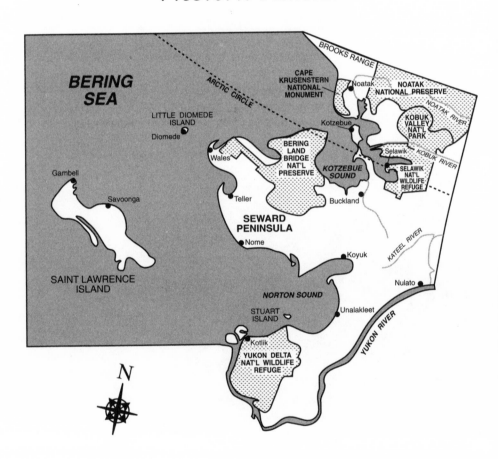

BROOKS RANGE

BERING
SEA

ARCTIC CIRCLE

LITTLE DIOMEDE
ISLAND
Diomede

CAPE
KRUSENSTERN
NATIONAL
MONUMENT

Noatak

NOATAK
NATIONAL PRESERVE

NOATAK RIVER

Kotzebue

KOBUK
VALLEY
NAT'L
PARK

Wales

BERING
LAND
BRIDGE
NAT'L
PRESERVE

KOTZEBUE
SOUND

Selawik

KOBUK RIVER

SELAWIK
NAT'L
WILDLIFE
REFUGE

Gambell

Savoonga

Teller

Buckland

SEWARD
PENINSULA

Nome

Koyuk

KATEEL RIVER

SAINT LAWRENCE
ISLAND

Nulato

NORTON SOUND

STUART
ISLAND

Unalakleet

YUKON RIVER

Kotlik

YUKON DELTA
NAT'L WILDLIFE
REFUGE

N

WESTERN ALASKA

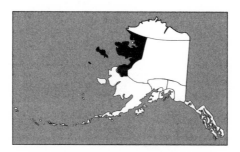

OVERVIEW

The second of Alaska's three most remote regions, western Alaska, as described here, extends from the Yukon River delta in the south to the western Brooks Range in the north, and includes the Seward Peninsula, Little Diomede Island and St. Lawrence Island. The eastern boundary is approximately that latitude where the Yukon River shifts from flowing west to flowing south near the village of Nulato. While these boundaries may seem a bit nebulous, they do give us some firm geographic reference, something fairly important in a land that has few other references.

Nobody can drive to western Alaska; nobody can get there as a paying passenger on a boat. Only airplanes, mostly from either Anchorage or Fairbanks, can take you to western Alaska. (There is, however, a record of a man who rode a bicycle to Nome from Dawson City, Yukon, at the turn of the last century, but that's a little much to consider these days since no major gold rush is around to prompt such feats.) Alaska Airlines and MarkAir both serve Nome, Kotzebue and other smaller communities in the region from Anchorage and Fairbanks.

Though much of the scenery in the region is gorgeous, it does fall a little short of the stupendous. To that extent, it's hard to talk in the same kind of effusive terms used when describing other parts of the state. At the same time, if it's wilderness and solitude you're seeking, this is another good place to find it. Huge tracts of land in this region are rarely visited except for perhaps a wandering trapper seeking new sources of fur in the deepest part of winter.

By way of example, a few years back the Bering Land Bridge National Preserve between Kotzebue and Nome showed only seven visitors signing the guest register for an entire summer season. Though more than just those seven probably found their way into the preserve for short periods, it probably wasn't very many more. For a National Park Service facility to have that low a number, this must be a remote area.

Even the fishing crowd tends to stay away from this part of Alaska. Though there are spots offering northern pike, sheefish and grayling, the major salmon runs so attractive farther south, and the big tackle-busting rainbows are notably absent from western Alaska. The only exception is a king salmon run in the Unalakleet River south of Nome—and it's fairly short-lived.

There are, however, things worth making time for; much of Alaska's contemporary history starts in this part of the state.

An aerial view of Nome, Alaska. (Photo by Ron Dalby)

Nome

It's pretty hard to go to Nome and not have a good time. Nome is probably the last reminder in the United States of what our frontier used to be, and most local residents hope to keep things just that way.

About a dozen years ago, a Coast Guard icebreaker anchored offshore after several months in the arctic ice pack. The skipper made plans to grant the crew a well-deserved liberty in town, but before doing so he came ashore to visit with the local police department and state troopers. At the police department, he explained the situation to the city's chief of police and a sergeant known locally as "Huggy Bear" because of his huge size and big red beard. A couple of state troopers (wildlife protection division), assigned to help keep the peace during the next couple of evenings, were there as well.

The skipper patiently explained about how long his men had been penned up and that while he was expecting a rowdy liberty he didn't think anything malicious would happen. He ended his little talk by noting that his officers and petty officers would be visible in town during the liberty period and asked the police to please use them if they needed help with any of his men.

As the skipper disappeared, Huggy Bear ducked into a back room, returning a few minutes later with a couple of spiked dog collars and a leash for each.

About an hour later, when the first bargeload of "Coasties" reached the beach for liberty, they were greeted by two huge policemen (in uniform) wearing spiked dog collars and leashed to state wildlife officers. Huggy Bear in particular was hopping up and down, grunting and making threatening gestures. The wildlife officer jerked his leash and admonished him, "Not yet, Huggy Bear. They haven't done anything yet."

Nome was ready to party that night and so were the Coasties. Within an hour, all of Front Street was really rocking. And the police, quite visible, soon started escorting drunks to the local jail. Tourists, in town on their vacation, joined in the fun. Even by Nome standards it was a heavy-duty evening.

The next morning, inventory was taken in the slammer. Every person jailed the night before was a local resident—there wasn't a Coast Guardsman or tourist in sight. And all of the jailed celebrants were sporting massive hangovers. Rather than try to process all the paperwork, the doors were opened a little after 8 A.M., and all were allowed to return home. No damage was done, no one was injured or threatened with injury, and Nome added another notch to its reputation.

Lest you think this kind of thing only happens in the summer months, Nome in winter can be an absolute riot, particularly in mid-March when the **Iditarod** mushers wind up their 1,049-mile race from Anchorage under the arch on Front Street.

Nome devotes a whole week or more to celebrating the Iditarod—everything from a wet T-shirt contest to a golf tournament to a banquet. A golf tournament?

Yes, indeed. The **Bering Sea Golf Classic** is played out every March on the frozen ocean just behind the sea wall. Each hole on the six-hole, par-75 (or so) course is a tuna can sunk in the ice and surrounded by green astroturf-type material. Each entrant pays a fee, chooses a club, a brightly colored golf ball (white ones would be too hard to find on the ice pack) and a pint bottle of his favorite antifreeze. Crying towels are also provided. The first, third and fifth tees are on the seawall behind local saloons, just in case the pint provided with the entry fee was insufficient for warding off frostbite. Though none have been seen in recent years, snow snakes are thought to be a menace as well, and the antifreeze often doubles as preventative snakebite medicine—just in case.

Most of the day is spent looking in crevasses for golf balls, chiding each other on the greens (no hushed silence while awaiting the putt here) and in general seeing who can have the most fun at the expense of others. There is absolutely no finesse or strategy involved.

And of course there's local government, a constant source of irritation in Nome just as it is in much of the rest of the country. A few years back, the city council outlawed the sale of fireworks in the city limits. Nome, after all, has burned down a couple of times over the years. Significantly, they didn't ban the use of such items, just the sale of them in town.

This, naturally, angered the larger distributors of such devices, the largest also being the mayor of Nome, who was also an upstanding local businessman. The mayor had a surveyor establish the exact boundary of town, built a fireworks stand just inches outside that boundary and did a brisk business with anyone willing to step outside the municipal boundaries for just a moment. Nome will be Nome.

Most who visit Nome do so as part of a package tour, usually run out of Anchorage. These generally include airfare, a couple of tours and lodging. If you are looking for a place to stay on your own, try one of these ($$): **Nugget Inn, (907) 443-2323; Oceanview Manor, (907) 443-2135; Polaris Hotel, (907) 443-2000;** and **Ponderosa, (907) 443-5737** or **443-2368.** All are located close to restaurants, gift shops, etc.

MarkTours

The standard package is a two-day, one-night trip, part spent in Nome and part in Kotzebue. Participants can select lodging in either Kotzebue or Nome according to their preferences. Outside Alaska, call **1-800-426-6784** for details and reservations. From within Alaska, call **1-800-478-0800.**

Grayline of Alaska

Tours are offered similar to the MarkTours described above using either Alaska Airlines or MarkAir as the local carrier. Call **1-800-544-2206** for details and reservations.

General Visitors Information

Contact Lois Wirtz, **Nome Convention and Visitors Bureau, P.O. Box 251, Nome, AK 99762, (907) 443-5535.**

Plan early for your trip to Nome if you want to be there for the Iditarod celebration in March or for the Midnight Sun Festival at the end of June. Remember: "There's no place like Nome."

Kotzebue

While Nome is primarily a non-Native town, Kotzebue, less than 200 miles to the north and just across the Arctic Circle, is essentially a large Native village. Demonstrations of traditional Native lifestyles and entertainment are the most notable attractions, as are local delicacies like reindeer stew and freshly caught fish.

The modern, recently refurbished Nullagvik Hotel overlooking Kotzebue Sound serves visitors to Kotzebue, and ground tours of the local area are available. Contact **Tour Arctic, Box 49, Kotzebue, AK 99752, (907) 442-3301** for details and reservations on a visit to Kotzebue.

Kotzebue is also National Park Service Headquarters for **Kobuk Valley National Park, Noatak National Preserve and the Bering Land Bridge National Preserve.**

Kotzebue, pictured here from the air, is located north of the Arctic Circle. (Photo courtesy of the Alaska Division of Tourism)

Kobuk Valley National Park/
Noatak National Preserve

This park and preserve adjoin each other and are best described as a single entity. The park is centered around the Kobuk River between Ambler and Kiana; the preserve surrounds much of the Noatak River north of the park.

These are wilderness parks with no visitor facilities. To reach them, you will have to charter an air service from Kotzebue. Also, you must be aware that there are numerous parcels of private land within the park and preserve, withdrawals made under the auspices of the Alaska Native Claims Settlement Act of 1971. If at all in doubt about the land you plan to visit,

inquire at Park Service headquarters in Kotzebue before departing for the wilds.

The western reaches of the Brooks Range lies between the two river valleys. Dall sheep, caribou, moose, grizzly bears and wolves are quite common, as are numerous species of birds and smaller mammals. A great way to see either the park or the preserve is a float trip down either of the rivers running through them.

For additional information about visiting either of these areas, contact the **Alaska Public Lands Information Office, 250 Cushman Street, Fairbanks, AK 99701, (907) 451-7352.**

A large field of wildflowers is edged by the buildings of Kotzebue. (Photo by Ernst Schneider, Alaska Division of Tourism)

Bering Land Bridge
National Preserve

This, as noted earlier, is probably the least-visited National Park Service facility in Alaska. Essentially it covers beach areas on the north side of the Seward Peninsula and an inland area that may have been an important overland access route to Alaska's Interior when people first migrated to North America during the last ice ages. Generally, 12,000 years ago is accepted as the time the first people crossed from Asia to what is now Alaska, though more and more evidence is beginning to hint at dates as early as 40,000 years ago.

It is generally accepted that during the ice ages the level of the oceans dropped sufficiently to create an overland connection between Asia and North America over what is now the Bering Strait. Wandering bands of hunters and others crossed over at these times and began the slow process of populating the Americas. The migration was not, as once believed, a single mass movement, but more a series of fits and starts over thousands of years.

Descendants of at least several distinct Asian cultures are believed to have crossed at one time or another, and many of these cultures had more than one distinct crossing period centuries apart. For example, the language patterns of Athabaskan Indians in Alaska and Canada closely resemble those of the Navajos of the American Southwest. In between them are a variety of other Indian tribes whose language roots have seemingly no connection to the origins of the Navajo and Athabaskan tongues.

The Bering Land Bridge National Preserve is dedicated to preserving artifacts of the Alaskan migration that have yet to be found. It is a wild and rugged region, but it is here at least 100 centuries ago—and maybe as many as 400 centuries ago—that humans first came to North America.

For more information on visiting the preserve, contact the **Alaska Public Lands Information Office, 250 Cushman Street, Fairbanks, AK 99701, (907) 451-7352.** If you do visit, please remember that all artifacts must be left as found. It is against the law to remove any archaeological evidence from a national park or preserve.

The Kenai Peninsula

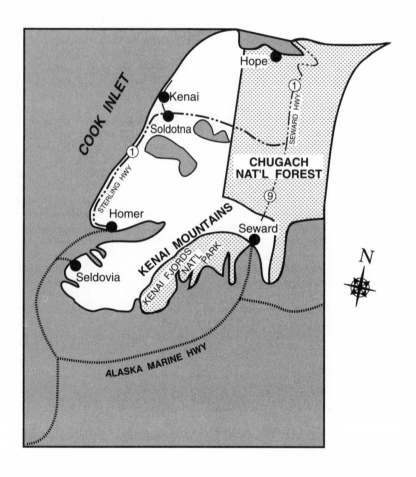

⹀ THE KENAI PENINSULA ⹀

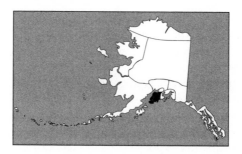

───────── **OVERVIEW** ─────────

Relative to the overall size of Alaska, the Kenai Peninsula south of Anchorage isn't much. But in terms of user days by visitors (tourists and Alaskans combined), it looms larger than any other region of the state.

The reasons for this are varied. Most significant is its proximity to Anchorage, Alaska's most densely populated region. On a Friday afternoon in June or July the road south from Anchorage can be and often is a 100-mile line of almost bumper-to-bumper cars, pickups and recreational vehicles. The Kenai is Anchorage's summer playground.

Why does seemingly all of Anchorage head for the Kenai on a summer weekend? Fish, primarily, but also hiking trails, USDA Forest Service cabins and some special scenery, particularly in Kenai Fjords National Park. As far as the fishing goes, there are rainbow trout, grayling, "barndoor" halibut and all five species of Pacific salmon at intervals during the summer months.

All these different fishing opportunities and the relative ease of access for locals and tourists alike have, in the last 20 years, led to another reason for the Kenai's popularity—hype. In the past 20 years or more, probably no segment of Alaska fishing has gotten more ink in newspapers and magazines or more air time on television and radio than the Kenai Peninsula. In particular, the huge king salmon occasionally caught in July generate most of the press coverage.

Indeed, there are a lot of fish caught on the Kenai, and every so often an unusually large king comes to the net. The rod-and-reel record for kings is a 97-pound, 4-ounce behemoth caught by Les Anderson of Soldotna on the Kenai River in 1987. Every year a couple of 80-pounders are brought in and, more rarely, a fish over 90 pounds shows up. That the Kenai has a genetic trait producing an occasional whopper is not in dispute. However, in terms of numbers of kings available to anglers in the river, the Kenai comes in way behind a large number of streams in Alaska.

Besides the kings, there is a huge run of red salmon (sockeye) in July on the Russian River, a Kenai River tributary. This particular fishery has become Anchorage's "meat" fishery, and the angling conditions are locally known as "combat fishing."

The only allowable bait for reds on the Russian is a fly. However this river provides little opportunity to practice traditional fly-fishing. Anglers line up shoulder to shoulder along the accessible portions of the stream, and when somebody does hook a fish, he or she needs to drag it out of the water as quickly as possible to avoid tangling the lines of others. Thus a typical rig for Russian River reds (average fish about 10 pounds) is a stout spinning rod with 15- or 20-pound-test line, a spark-plug-sized weight and a streamer fly. No finesse at all involved here—hook 'em and get 'em on the bank. And while you are unhooking your fish and storing it in the cooler, it's likely that someone else will come along and take the spot on the bank where you were standing to fish. More than one commentator has noted that "you gotta bring your own rock to stand on" when fishing the Russian River for reds.

The Kenai Peninsula's other major draw for anglers is halibut fishing in Homer. Here again, there's a lot of competition, but since halibut fishing is done from oceangoing charter boats, there's more space in which to spread out.

Other opportunities for exercising a fishing license on the Kenai include clam digging on the lower west-side beaches, rainbows in several rivers (best very late in the fall after the salmon runs are finished), pink salmon in even-numbered years and grayling.

For the most part, a visit to the Kenai for the fishing will not result in the wilderness experience so many people associate with the idea of fishing in Alaska. Road-accessible streams on the Kenai are as crowded, if not more, as popular streams elsewhere in the country. And, because of the fishing pressure and the limitations on the number of available fish, bag limits can be fairly restrictive. For the previous couple of years leading up to 1993, the Kenai River itself experienced several major closures during the king salmon season, and severe restrictions mandating catch-and-release when anglers were allowed to fish. Russian River red salmon bag limits were cut to two fish per day in 1993, a change from the three-fish-per-day limits that have been in effect for years.

If visiting the Kenai is part of your Alaska vacation plan, there are a few things you can do to avoid the crowds or at least the worst ones. The Kasilof River, Deep Creek and the Anchor River, all south of the Kenai River and on the road system, offer many opportunities for salmon and other fish. Although crowded at times, these streams are not hit nearly as hard as the Kenai and Russian rivers. Opportunities both for halibut and saltwater fishing for salmon are also available near the mouth of Deep Creek, and so far the king salmon closures haven't been applied this far south. Also, if you are on vacation and can adjust your time accordingly, avoid going to the Kenai Peninsula on weekends when you're competing with what seems to be the whole city of Anchorage as well as other tourists. Head south from Anchorage on Sunday afternoon or Monday morning when all the local folks are headed home. Then head north again on Friday morning.

If you've got a yen to really get away from the crowds on the Kenai and still catch some fish, hike in 10 miles or so on the Johnson Pass trail north out of Moose Pass. Johnson Lake and its outlet stream on the south side of the pass offer excellent fishing for rainbows, and Bench Lake, a mile or so to the north on the other side of the pass, is full of feisty grayling. Another option is to canoe either the Swanson River or Swan Lake canoe trails in the Kenai moose range north of Soldotna. Rainbow fishing along these routes can be excellent, and there's plenty of space for spreading out and avoiding the few others you might meet.

Finally, on a visit to the Kenai Peninsula, look beyond the fishing. It offers superb opportunities for sightseeing and exploring.

Hope

Driving south from Portage on the Seward Highway, you'll cross Turnagain Pass, then start down a section of winding road. A few miles south of the pass is the northern trailhead for the Johnson Lake trail mentioned earlier. A few miles beyond that is a side road on the right leading to Hope.

Hope was and still is, more or less, a gold-mining town. In its heyday, hydraulic mining—blasting cliffs with streams of high-pressure water—was used extensively. These days, what mining exists is on a much smaller scale. There are opportunities for gold panning in and around Hope, though make certain you are not trespassing on someone's claim before dipping a pan to try your luck.

Much of modern-day Alaska has pretty much passed Hope by. There is a **Chamber of Commerce,** but as chambers go, this one is pretty loosely defined. **(907) 782-3141.** There's a small cafe, limited RV parking, a motel and a grocery store. A USDA Forest Service campground is at the end of the road.

The 38-mile Resurrection Pass trail's northern trailhead is on a side road 4 miles off the Hope Highway, about 16 miles after turning off the Seward Highway. This is an extremely popular hiking trail on the Kenai Peninsula, with most parties taking about three days for the trip to the southern trailhead on the Sterling Highway west of Soldotna. Forest Service cabins are available for shelter along the trail and can be reserved in advance through the **USDA Forest Service, Chugach National Forest, 201 E. 9th Avenue, Suite 206, Anchorage, AK 99501.** Cost is $20 a night per cabin; bring your own sleeping bag and food. Three nights' stay maximum per cabin, and reservations should be made as far in advance as possible as the Resurrection Pass trail is an extremely popular hike. Cabin permits are awarded by drawing when there are two or more reservation requests for the same date. Reservations can be made a maximum of six months in advance.

Seward

Seward, 127 miles south of Anchorage on the Seward Highway, sits at the head of Resurrection Bay. Although accessible by road, Seward is also the southern terminus of the Alaska Railroad, so it is possible to purchase a train ticket to the town from Anchorage. Call the **Alaska Railroad** at **1-800-544-0552** for details and information.

Though they had no permanent settlement here, the Russians established a small shipyard in Resurrection Bay in the late 1700s to build a single sailing ship. The actual site of the former shipyard is be-lieved to be on the west side of the bay some miles south of Seward. Several tantalizing clues have surfaced over the years, but no one has officially pinpointed the site where the Russians built a small fort to house their people while building the boat.

Seward's major reason for growth in recent times was the decision in 1902 to make it the southern terminus of the Alaska Railroad. The primary consideration for this decision was the year-round ice-free harbor offered in Resurrection Bay.

FESTIVALS AND EVENTS

Contact the **Seward Chamber of Commerce, P.O. Box 749, Seward, AK 99664,** (907) 224-3094 for information on the following and other attractions in Seward.

MT. MARATHON RACE

Part foot race, part mountain climbing and part slip-sliding down 3,022-foot Mt. Marathon, this test of skill and endurance has been part of the Seward scene since 1915. Held each year as part of an overall July 4 celebration, this is a great race for either spectators or participants. The winner usually completes the course from downtown to the top of the mountain and back in under an hour. Stitches are usually required for some of the racers who fall coming back down the mountain behind the town.

ANNUAL SEWARD SILVER SALMON DERBY

It begins on the second Saturday in August and runs nine days to Sunday of the next weekend. Probably Alaska's best-attended salmon derby, it has $50,000 in prizes, with $10,000 going for the largest fish by weight. Seward fills up quickly for this event, particularly on the two weekends, so make your reservations early for both lodging and a fishing charter boat if you don't have your own boat. Weather permitting, even fairly small craft can troll for salmon in Resurrection Bay. Keep a weather eye out, though; winds can come up suddenly and quickly make the bay unsafe for smaller craft.

ACTIVITIES

FISHING

Charters are available for salmon and halibut. A boat launching facility and transient slips in the harbor are available for those with their own boats.

Arctic Wilderness Charters—(907) 344-2845.

Aurora Charters—(907) 224-3968.

Command Charters—(907) 694-2833.

Mackinaw Charters—(907) 224-3910.

Mariah Charters—(halibut), (907) 224-8625.

Quicksilver Charters—(907) 224-7225.

Sablefish Charters—(907) 224-3415.

Seward Fishing Adventures—(907) 224-8087.

FLIGHTSEEING

Several spectacular areas are close to Seward, including Kenai Fjords National Park, its glaciers and one of Alaska's major ice fields.

Harbor Air—(907) 224-3133.

TOURS

(See Kenai Fjords National Park write-up in next section.) **Town Shuttle & Historical Tour, Seward's Trolley, (907) 224-7373** or CB Channel 15.

———— WHERE TO STAY ————

ACCOMMODATIONS

All Seward-area accommodations fall in the $$–$$$ categories depending on size of room and type of accommodation selected.

Breeze Inn

Motel, restaurant and lounge. Close to the small boat harbor. **(907) 224-5237.**

Hotel Seward

Best Western in the center of town. Free movies and cablevision. **(907) 224-2378.**

New Seward Hotel and Saloon

Downtown with lounge. Modern rooms. **(907) 224-8001.**

Taroka Inn

Nine units, private baths, kitchenettes. Corner of 3rd and Adams. **(907) 224-8687.**

Van Gilder Hotel

National Historic Site, **308 Adams Street. (907) 224-3079.**

BED AND BREAKFASTS
Benson B&B—(907) 224-5290.

Creekside Cabins B&B—(907) 224-3834.

Mom Clock's B&B—(907) 224-3195.

Seward Waterfront Lodge B&B—(907) 224-5563.

Swiss Chalet B&B—(907) 224-3939.

Ursa Major B&B—(907) 224-3740.

The White House B&B—(907) 224-3614.

CAMPGROUNDS

Bear Creek RV Park—(6.6 miles north of town), **(907) 224-5725.**

Salmon Creek RV Park—(907) 224-3433.

In addition to these private parks, there are several USDA Forest Service campgrounds north of town, and a National Park Service campground near Exit Glacier. Also, during the salmon derby considerable self-contained RV parking is generally available near the small boat harbor.

WHERE TO EAT

As with lodging, the bulk of Seward's eating establishments fall within the $$–$$$ range.

Frontier Restaurant—5th and Washington, (907) 224-3141.

Harbor Dinner Club and Lounge—5th Avenue, downtown, (907) 224-3012.

Kountry Kitchen—3rd and Adams, (907) 224-8935.

Peking Chinese Cuisine—338 4th Avenue, (907) 224-5444.

Ray's Waterfront—Small Boat Harbor, (907) 224-5606.

Seward Salmon Bake and Barbeque—Small Boat Harbor, (907) 224-7051.

Digging for clams is muddy work. Clam Gultch, Kenai Peninsula. (Photo by Ron Dalby)

= Kenai Fjords National Park =

Other than Denali National Park between Anchorage and Fairbanks, this is Alaska's most accessible wilderness national park. Major attractions are a wide variety of sea mammals, sea bird rookeries, glaciers, fjords and Harding Icefield.

The Kenai Fjords visitors center is open seven days a week in the summer and is next to the harbormaster's office overlooking the small boat harbor. Call the **Park Service** at **(907) 224-3175** for additional information.

——— ACTIVITIES ———

DAY CRUISES

Probably the best way to get a feel for this park is to take a day cruise out of Seward on one of several available boats. The Kenai Fjords Tours offers a great package. The boat leaves the dock at 11:30 A.M. daily and is out for about six to seven hours, less time than some of the other operators because his boat is faster and can cover the less scenic stretches of the voyage more quickly. The crew serves a hot lunch on board as part of the ticket price, and during the tour you will see countless sea birds in their rookeries, sea lions, seals, sea otters, whales (humpbacks and orcas), glaciers, fjords and other things too numerous to list. Call **Kenai Coastal Tours** at **1-800-937-9119** for information and reservations. Also ask about packages that include transportation from Anchorage to Seward for the cruise, then back to Anchorage. In Seward, **Kenai Coastal Tours'** number is **(907) 224-8068**. Price for this tour in 1993 was $95 per person.

Other day-cruise operators for Kenai Fjords include:

Major Marine Tours—(907) 224-8030.

Mariah Charters & Tours—(907) 224-8625.

FLIGHTSEEING

See write-up under Seward in previous section.

HIKING

Exit Glacier in the park can be approached on foot after a short hike. The access road (Exit Glacier Road) to the trail is 3.7 miles north of Seward, and leads 9 miles to the parking area. Two trails are available, neither very long.

There are no accommodations or facilities within the park except for a 10-site, walk-in campground at the end of Exit Glacier Road.

Soldotna and Kenai

Here the king salmon is king. Soldotna sits astride the Kenai River and Kenai is near its mouth; in June and July this is the frantic center of activity for pursuit of the stream's most sought-after fish, famed as the largest kings in the world. During July, the month when king salmon fever peaks on the Kenai and the red salmon arrive as well, it can be all but impossible to find lodging anywhere in or around Soldotna or Kenai on short notice.

Area campgrounds, too, are beehives of activity. People are coming and going at all hours of the day and night, it's rarely quiet at any hour, and nobody seems to sleep. Besides the regular camping spaces, every bit of parking in overflow lots and picnic areas is filled with self-contained RVs. Camping and fishing in the Soldotna–Kenai area is not for the fainthearted in July.

Fishing is far and away the only activity that causes the hordes of people to descend on this small area. Though there are other attractions in the area, including rafting trips on the Kenai River and some historic sites in and near Kenai, until after the king salmon season on the river closes at the end of July nothing else seems to matter.

There is, however, at least one way to beat this madhouse if you make your reservations early enough. The Great Alaska Fish Camp sits on an old homestead site at the juncture of the Kenai and Moose rivers a few miles east of Soldotna on the edge of the small community of Sterling. The lodge property offers its guests the greatest expanse of private property frontage on the Kenai River. Lodge guides take guests out by boat to fish the river during the day, and are available along the riverbank in the evenings for those who want to fish an extra few hours. Additionally, the lodge maintains a halibut boat in Homer, pro-

vides options for fishing other area rivers and has access to charter aircraft for flyouts to more remote locations.

Once you fight through the crowds to the Great Alaska Fish Camp, you can kick back and relax and go after the big fish for which the region is known. Packages at the Great Alaska Fish Camp include all meals, lodging and guided fishing—even a free bar in the evening for reminiscing over the day's adventures. Contact either Laurence John or Kathy Haley at **1-800-544-2261** for information and reservations. Compared to many of the other full-service lodges in Alaska, prices at the Great Alaska Fish Camp are a bargain.

For those not staying at the Great Alaska Fish Camp, there are other lodges and countless day charters available on the Kenai River. The following list is by no means complete, but it does offer a few recommendations. For a more extensive list of hundreds of Kenai River charter operators and lodges, contact the **Kenai Peninsula Tourism Marketing Council** in Kenai at **(907) 283-3850.**

Alaska Rivers Co.—(907) 595-1226.

Alaska Wildland Adventures—1-800-478-4100 (within Alaska only), **(907) 595-1279.**

Angler's Lodge and Fish Camp—(907) 262-1747.

Denise Lake Lodge B&B—(907) 262-1789.

Jughead Salmon Charters—(907) 262-7433 (June–August); **(907) 277-1218** (September–May).

King's Inn—(907) 283-6060.

King of the River—(specializes in people with disabilities), **(907) 262-2139.**

Marlow's Kenai River Drifters—(907) 262-5218.

Osprey Alaska—1-800-533-KENI.

Run Wild Alaska River Adventures—(907) 276-3418, or (907) 595-1422.

RW's Guide Service—(907) 262-9600 or 1-800-666-3436.

Several of the operators listed above can also make arrangements for halibut charters in Homer or Deep Creek and for one-day rafting adventures on the Kenai River.

Those flying into the area for their fishing adventures should make their airline reservations to the Kenai airport; Soldotna itself has no regularly scheduled air service. A number of flights daily are available to Kenai from Anchorage, and it's just a short hop of about 20 minutes or so. Driving time from Anchorage to Soldotna is about three to four hours, except on Friday afternoons in June or July when it can often take twice as long.

One other activity that requires a fishing license but isn't exactly a hook-and-line event is clam digging on Kenai Peninsula beaches south of Soldotna. For a few days each month during full moon periods, low tides on the beaches expose dense beds of razor clams. An hour or so spent groveling in the mud with a shovel should easily yield a limit of 60 clams. Inquire locally for a copy of the tidetables (usually free) to determine when the best times are for clam digging. Beaches around Clam Gulch and Deep Creek are usually the most popular and the most productive. Clams are available as far north as the Kasilof River, though they seem to get progressively smaller as you move north of Clam Gulch.

Finally, the end of king salmon season on the Kenai River doesn't mean the end of the fishing season in the Soldotna–Kenai region. Just about the time the kings quit coming in, the silver salmon arrive. There are a lot more of these feisty fish and a whole lot fewer people chasing them in August and September. Most of the guides listed above for king salmon can take you out for silvers as well, and at a much lower price in most cases. Bag limits for silvers are more generous and there are many more of these fish ranging to about 20 pounds, so the action is usually much more intense.

Homer

Whereas the king salmon reigns in Soldotna and Kenai, in Homer the halibut rules. This is Alaska's most famed sport-fishery for these big bottom fish, and the big barndoor halibut can get up to 440 pounds.

This, obviously, is heavy-duty fishing requiring lines of 100-pound test or more and lead weights of six or seven pounds to keep your bait on the bottom of the ocean at depths of several hundred feet. Charter operators provide all the tackle for halibut, you just provide the brawn necessary to use it.

Day charters for halibut are usually 12 hours long, or less if everybody catches their limit of two fish early in the day. Prices range from $135 to $150 a day per person. The larger boats take 12 to 16 people fishing, the smaller ones take six or even as few as four.

There are hundreds of halibut charters available in Homer, and some are better than others. If you don't have an advance reservation or are uncertain about with whom you wish to fish, head down to the dock in the evening when the boats come in. Watch for two key indicators: which boats are unloading fish and which boats do the people disembark from looking as if they've had a good time, fish or no fish. Surly customers at the end of the day are a good indication that a less than a pleasant experience was had by those on board. Pick out a couple of boats that look good to you and either talk to the skipper about a reservation or stop in at the appropriate dockside office to sign up.

Most halibut trips are bring-your-own-lunch affairs. Very few of the skippers provide anything at all in the way of refreshments except perhaps coffee and soft drinks. Take along your raingear as well. You'll be outside fishing most of the day, and rain is frequent on Kachemak Bay outside of Homer and the nearby waters of lower Cook Inlet. Expect the temperatures to be fairly cool out on the water.

If you're confused about where to start looking for a halibut charter, contact the **Central Charter Booking Agency** in Homer, **(907) 235-7847.** These folks represent a whole fleet of boats and can help you pick the right one. And, because they have so many operators to choose from, they can probably find you an opening on short notice with little effort, no matter what the size of your party.

CHARTERS

Following is a list of some of Homer's halibut charter services if you want to do some calling on your own. It is far from complete and does not even begin to list every competent skipper in town.

Cie Jae Ocean Charters—1-800-677-5587.

Halibut King Charters—(907) 235-7303.

Homer Ocean Charters—(907) 235-6212.

Lucky Pierre Charters—(907) 235-8903.

North Country Halibut Charters—(907) 235-7620.

Silver Fox Charters—(907) 235-8792.

Thompson's Halibut Charters—(907) 235-7222.

Tutka Bay Charters—(907) 235-7272.

TOURS

Halibut fishing is not the only thing to do in Homer. Kachemak Bay at the town's doorstep offers a variety of opportunities for sightseeing and cruising.

One of the most pleasant ways to spend the day is take a trip across the bay to the small community of Seldovia. Take lunch at the Saltry while in Seldovia and explore this tiny beachfront community in Halibut Cove. En route to and from Seldovia you'll also have opportunities for bird-watching and spotting other, larger forms of marine wildlife. Some of the businesses offering these kinds of cruises and day tours are

Alaska Maritime Tours—(907) 235-2490.

"Danny J" Cruise Tours—(907) 235-8110.

Kachemak Bay Adventures—(907) 235-8206.

Kachemak Bay Ferry Tour—(907) 235-7847.

Rainbow Tours—(907) 235-7272.

WHERE TO STAY

ACCOMMODATIONS

Most Homer-area accommodations fall into either the $$ or $$$ price categories.

Bay View Inn
Top of the hill as you enter Homer by road. **(907) 235-8485.**

Bidarka Inn
Restaurant and lounge. Call collect for reservations. **575 Sterling Highway. (907) 235-8148.**

Heritage Hotel/Lodge
Restaurant, courtesy limo to airport. **147 E. Pioneer Avenue. (907) 235-7787.**

Lakewood Inn
Restaurant and lounge. Suites with kitchens. **984 Ocean Drive #1. (907) 235-6144.**

Land's End
Tip of Homer spit. Restaurant and lounge. **(907) 235-2525.**

BED AND BREAKFASTS
Beach House—(907) 235-5945.

B&B by the Sea—(907) 235-7886.

Brass Ring B&B—(907) 235-5450.

Brigitte's Bavarian B&B—(907) 235-6620.

Jelly Bean B&B—(907) 235-8720.

Kiana B&B—(907) 235-8824.

The Lily Pad—(907) 235-6630.

Ridgetop B&B—(907) 235-7590.

CAMPGROUNDS
Homer Spit Campground—(907) 235-8206.

Land's End RV Park—(907) 235-2525.

Oceanview RV Park—(907) 235-3951.

Rocking-J-Ranch—(907) 235-6239.

Chugach National Forest

Much of the land on the Kenai Peninsula is part of the Chugach National Forest, headquartered in Anchorage and maintaining a district office in Girdwood just off the Seward Highway leading to the Kenai Peninsula. As part of its stewardship, the Forest Service maintains an excellent system of hiking trails, 18 public-use cabins and numerous campgrounds at roadside.

The two best-known trails are Resurrection Pass and Johnson Pass, both described earlier in this chapter. Other trails are available, and information on them can be had by writing to the **Chugach National Forest, 201 E. 9th Avenue, Suite 206, Anchorage, AK 99645.**

The 18 public-use cabins can be rented for $20 a day (noon to noon) on a first-come, first-served reservation basis. The maximum you can stay at one of the three cabins along the Resurrection Pass trail is three days; the longest consecutive stay at the other cabins is a week. For a map showing the locations of these cabins, the opportunities for fishing and exploring at each and the appropriate means of access, write the Chugach National Forest at the address given earlier and inquire about cabin rentals. The map and information you receive will also note cabins available on Forest Service lands surrounding Prince William Sound.

Roadside campgrounds managed by the Forest Service are primitive with tent sites, parking spaces for RVs, perhaps a water pump, picnic tables and outhouses. There are generally no hookups or dump stations for RVs.

The U.S. Forest Service maintains an excellent system of hiking trails and public-use cabins in the Chugach National Forest. (Photo by Ernst Schneider, Alaska Division of Tourism)

The Matanuska-Susitna Valley

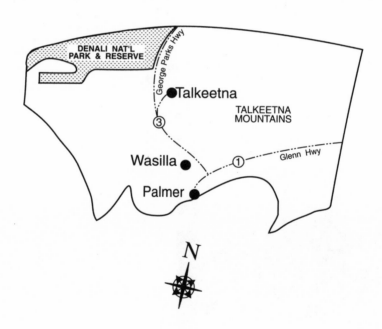

N

THE MATANUSKA–SUSITNA VALLEY

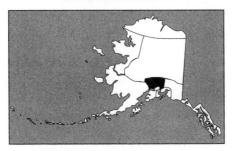

OVERVIEW

Back in the early 1930s, President Franklin Roosevelt had a couple of small problems both exacerbated by his biggest problem, the Great Depression. Taken alone, the two small problems seemed unrelated. First was the growing legion of farmers in the Midwest being done in by the Depression or the winds creating the dustbowl or a combination of both. The second, more distant, was in the territory of Alaska. Little of Alaska's food was grown in the territory; all of it had to be shipped in at considerable cost.

In what he probably thought was a masterful idea, his administration hatched a scheme to solve both of these relatively minor irritants. The federal government would select several hundred farm families from the upper Midwest, ship them to Alaska and provide free land with houses and barns for each. The best farming land that could be found was the Matanuska Valley about 45 miles northeast of Anchorage.

Although a good idea in concept, it never quite worked as envisioned.

Indeed, 205 farmers and their families were selected and moved to the land surrounding the tiny frontier town of Palmer. A lottery was held to fairly divide up the various 160-acre plots of land, and the farmers went to work clearing the land and planting crops.

Some vegetables did quite well in the Palmer area. Others were hopeless in the short growing season. And while many of the farmers got things up and running so they could at least make a minimal living, the Matanuska Valley was never able to feed Alaska as originally planned. In fact, there was at least one major detour around the production of foodstuffs.

Farmers seeking a profit quickly realized in these early years of the Colony (as the project was called) that growing the makings of moonshine produced surer profits in this time of prohibition than the production of turnips or some other vegetable. For a time, then, talk of profit was not in bushels per acre, but in terms of gallons per acre, always accompanied by a wink.

Many of the colonists brought to Alaska in the 1930s remained in or near Palmer. A few are still alive today, and their descendants are common throughout the region. With only a couple of exceptions, the farms still operating produce mostly hay for livestock kept in the region or potatoes. Few other cash crops remain.

A legacy of this era is the Matanuska-Maid Dairy in downtown Palmer, still producing milk and ice cream. Partly because of it, the state of Alaska tried in the 1980s to succeed where the federal government had failed.

In the early 1980s the state took over operation of the dairy to keep it from going under. With its demise, there would have been no dairy operation left in Alaska. And, in conjunction with an already started barley-growing operation near Delta Junction, the state had decided to create a dairy industry near Palmer. Huge tracts of state land on Point MacKenzie, across Knik Arm of Cook Inlet from both Anchorage and Palmer, were subdivided into dairy farms, and a lottery was planned to award these tracts to qualified farmers.

Then the lawyers got involved, and ultimately came a court decision noting that anyone who wanted to try being a dairy farmer could put in for the Point MacKenzie lottery, not just qualified farmers. When the land was parceled out, few qualified farmers got the prized state-sponsored leases. This, coupled with an overly ambitious state plan for paying back the leases killed the dairy industry before it started.

Those who got the leases and the loans immediately built the required houses and barns, cleared land for growing silage and began to import cows. Several times in the mid-1980s, Anchorage newspapers carried front-page photos of cows being led down a ramp from 747 jumbo jets. Milk actually began to flow to the Matanuska-Maid Dairy from the farms, though it was expensive milk. Mat-Maid was paying as much as $20 or more a hundredweight for milk at times ($11 or $12 per hundredweight is about normal in the Lower 48 these days), and the price of its products in the stores reflected these rates. Few Alaskans were willing to fork over an additional 50 cents a gallon for milk racked next to milk flown in from Seattle at lower cost.

Farmers, too, complained that they couldn't make good on their loans even with $20 milk. At least one refinancing scheme was tried to ease the repayment burden, but without much success.

State auditors then entered the picture to count the cows, inspect the barns and in general see that farmers were complying with the terms of their agreements. Some of the farmers tried to mislead the auditors and got caught. Cows counted in one field were trucked to another farmer's field when the auditors weren't looking. Two farmers, going with the letter of the law though not necessarily with its spirit, built a overly large barn on their property line—half on one farmer's property, half on the other's. The auditors didn't particularly care for that stunt either, even though the result was a more cost-efficient operation for both.

Loans came due, and most of the farms were out of business. Only a couple remain in operation today, and much of Mat-Maid's raw milk is imported from the Lower 48. Even so, Mat-Maid's milk still costs more in local stores and is not a big hit on the shelves, despite the made-in-Alaska logo. The state's grand plan for farming in the Mat-Su Valley met the same fate as the federal government's, only in a shorter time.

Though all these schemes went for naught, Palmer and the Matanuska Valley is still thought of as Alaska's breadbasket, and there are occasionally some home-grown vegetables sold in local stores that can compete in price with flown-in produce.

Where the valley really gets its farming reputation, though, is from the **Alaska State Fair** held each year in Palmer in late August and early September. The growing season is short, but the long days of almost continual sunlight do make some rather special vegetables possible. In good years, it takes a cabbage weighing upwards of 80 pounds to win a blue ribbon at the fair. Zucchini squash likewise grow to huge proportions. And like all state fairs in rural states, the usual profusion of farm animals, baked goods and crafts are all judged with many of the winners getting their pictures in the local paper.

The state fair, though, is more than just farming displays. It's a 10-day celebration ending on Labor Day of the best that Alaska has to offer. Although you do have to wonder sometimes about the zany ideas of the fair's managers. A couple years back they named the theme of the fair as Texas. Then there are demonstrations where volunteers lie in plywood boxes while dynamite is detonated all around them. Said Don Burt in 1991, after he was the dynamite victim, "I always wanted to do that."

Cabbages, Texas and dynamite aside, the last week in August is a great time for a visit to the Matanuska–Susitna Valley, which includes Palmer, Wasilla, Talkeetna and several other communities.

Silver salmon fill area streams in August, as do king salmon in June. In fact, Mat–Su Valley streams host more than twice as many returning king salmon in any given year as do the more famous streams on the Kenai Peninsula. Because these rivers have never gotten nearly the amount of hype as the streams on the Kenai, there are fewer people chasing this greater number of fish. If you think that's a suggestion that the salmon fishing in the valley is better than on the Kenai River, you're right.

As a result of this lack of hype, the valley is little known by visiting fishermen, or tourists in general. Those driving around on Alaska's road system often drive right through the valley without stopping. There is a definite name-recognition problem here, and there's a bit of a tug-of-war going on as to whether things should remain so.

Those actively supporting a larger share of the tourism pie in the valley want more people to know about the good fishing, the hiking trails, the friendly people and all the other things there are to do in and around the Mat–Su Valley. Those who like things as they are as a means of keeping down the crowds in their favorite fishing holes are less likely to be enthused about additional tourists.

There's pressure from outside the region as well. More tourism dollars spent in Palmer, Wasilla and Talkeetna means there are fewer to be spent in Anchorage or on the Kenai. The rivalry isn't bitter or vindictive, but it is there.

There is, however, one point that tends to make the rivalry mute. Tourism is really Alaska's only growth industry these days, and is likely to remain so into the foreseeable future. The Kenai River, for one, has pretty much reached its saturation point for visiting fishermen, so the opening of new areas for pursuing salmon and other species is of critical importance. With a little thought and sound planning, the Mat–Su Valley is perfectly situated to take advantage of this growth in tourism. And, until it gets the name recognition it deserves, it's a great place to visit if you want to see (in the words of Mat–Su's tourism brochure) "Alaska as you imagined it to be."

For more information on visiting the Matanuska–Susitna Valley, contact the **Matanuska–Susitna Convention and Visitors Bureau, HC01 Box 6166 J21, Palmer, AK 99645, (907) 746-5000.**

Palmer

When you stop in Palmer, the first place you should go is to the city's visitors center a block or so from the old railroad station downtown. This is one of the prettiest visitors centers in the state, an old log cabin set next to a carefully tended garden that demonstrates the potential of the region. Most who stop here spend quite a bit of time wandering through the garden before even entering the building. Anyone with any interest at all in gardening will be captivated by the lush flowers and shrubs that are the star attractions in this parklike setting.

FESTIVALS AND EVENTS

THE ALASKA STATE FAIR

Eleven big days beginning on a Friday in late August and ending on Labor Day in early September, with a wide range of Alaskan exhibits, booths, games and a carnival. Horse shows, rodeos, lumberjacking and sundry other activities have all been highlighted in recent years. This is a great way to spend several days in Alaska. (*Insider's tip*: Come early to see the giant vegetables at their best. These tend to wilt after several days on display.) Contact the **August Information Line, (907) 745-FAIR,** for details on dates and places for specific events. In months other than August call **(907) 745-4827.**

COLONY DAYS

On the third weekend in June, this celebration has a parade, a crafts show, a trade fair and other events. Contact the **Palmer Visitors Center, (907) 745-2880,** for details.

ACTIVITIES

FISHING

Though most of the valley's major salmon streams are closer to Wasilla and Talkeetna, there are several possibilities near Palmer. Local lakes in and around the town are stocked with rainbow trout, Dolly Varden and grayling. The Jim River, accessed from the Palmer Alternate Highway near the Knik River bridge, yields silver salmon in August and rainbows most of the summer. Check with the local **Alaska Department of Fish and Game** office, **(907) 745-5016,** for up-to-date fishing information in and around Palmer.

FLIGHTSEEING

Charlie and Linda Akers can take you fishing or just out to see the sights in their floatplane. This is an excellent way to grasp the magnificence of the region or to put yourself in a fishing hotspot untouched by others. **(907) 745-3477.**

GLACIERS

Two easily viewed glaciers are within a short drive of downtown Palmer. **Matanuska Glacier** is about a one-hour drive east on the Glenn Highway and you can actually walk up to the ice and explore on foot. The land in front of the glacier is private, Matanuska Glacier Park Resort, and there is a small admission charge. **Knik Glacier** access is about 10 miles from town; views of the glacier can be had by driving out Knik Road next to the Knik River bridge. For a special tour, contact **Knik Glacier Tours, (907) 745-0675**, for a thrilling airboat ride up the Knik River to the face of the glacier.

HATCHER PASS

About a 45-minute drive from downtown Palmer (east on the Glenn Highway, then left on Palmer-Fishhook Road and keep going) brings you to the old mine site at the top of the pass. The mine is now **Independence Mine State Historic Park,** and many of the buildings are open for exploration. There are beautiful views in all directions, especially when the weather's good, and there's great berry picking in August.

HIKING

The Matanuska–Susitna Valley offers more than 140 known trails for hikes of almost any length or level of difficulty. Contact the **Matanuska–Susitna Borough Parks and Recreation Division, 350 E. Dahlia, Palmer, AK 99645, (907) 745-9636,** for a list and brochures for the more popular hikes. Included in their list are canoe trails as well as hiking trails.

HISTORIC SITES

Colony Museum is in the basement of the visitors center. Open daily in the summer months. **Church of a Thousand Logs,** located at United Protestant Church (Presbyterian) on Elmwood, two blocks east of the visitors center.

HORSEBACK RIDING

Hoof & Wheel Transporters, (907) 746-5843, offer half-day, full-day and overnight trail rides in the Palmer area and near Hatcher Pass. Depending on how you want to go, they will either furnish the camping gear you need, or you can bring your own. Another operator is **J Bar D, (907) 746-3020,** offering hourly, half-day and full-day horseback adventures.

MUSK-OX FARM TOUR

Few people visiting Alaska get to see these shaggy tundra dwellers in the wild. However, the **Musk-Ox Farm** just east of Palmer on the Glenn Highway will get you close to them. Musk-oxen are raised for their wool. Qiviut, as this material is called, is the warmest wool in the world, and garments made from qiviut are available for purchase in a gift shop at the farm. Knowledgeable guides will take you around the facility pointing out the different animals and their habits. It's well worth a visit, and the cost for the tour was just $6 per person in 1993. **(907) 745-4151.**

PALMER TSUNAMI OBSERVATORY

This is headquarters for the Alaska Regional Tsunami Warning System. About a half-mile from downtown Palmer on the Palmer-Wasilla Highway, the facility monitors seismic activity throughout Alaska and the North Pacific. Public tours are every Friday from 1 to 3 P.M. **(907) 745-4212.** (During a discussion of the effects of the 1964 earthquake, which devastated downtown Anchorage about 45 miles away, one of the scientists at the center noted that Anchorage rebuilt and expanded on much of the same unstable ground. "Why do you think we're here instead of Anchorage," he said at the end of the discussion—and not in jest.)

WHITEWATER RAFTING

NOVA Riverrunners, (907) 745-5753, offers a wide variety of trips. Most popular are day adventures on the Matanuska River east of Palmer, although expeditions of several days duration are also available.

WHERE TO STAY

ACCOMMODATIONS

Fairview Motel
Across from the state fairgrounds, mile 40.5 on Glenn Highway. Restaurants nearby. **(907) 745-1505.**

Motherlode Lodge
Hatcher Pass. Restaurant and lounge. **Mile 14 on Fishhook Road. (907) 746-1464.**

Sheep Mountain Lodge
Two-hour drive east of Palmer on Glenn Highway. Hiking, horseback riding, fishing, hunting, glacier viewing, wildlife viewing, cross-country ski trails and much more. Restaurant and lounge. **(907) 745-5121.**

Valley Hotel
Downtown Palmer. Restaurant and lounge. **606 S. Alaska Street. (907) 745-3330.**

BED AND BREAKFASTS

This list is by no means complete; there are many more. Contact the **Palmer Visitors Center, (907) 745-2880,** for a complete list.

Alaskan Agate B&B Inn—(800) 770-2290.

Glacier House B&B—(907) 745-4087.

Lake Shore B&B—(907) 376-6132.

Pollen's B&B—(907) 745-8920.

Teddy Bear Corner Country Inn—(907) 745-4156.

Tern Inn—(907) 745-1984.

The Weathervane House—(907) 745-5168.

CAMPGROUNDS

Best View RV Park—Next to Mat-Su Visitors Center on Parks Highway just north of junction with Glenn Highway. **(907) 745-7400.**

The Homestead RV Park—Five miles west of town on Glenn Highway. Full hookups, valley tours, lake fishing across the road. **(907) 745-6005.**

Matanuska River Park—(public). Dump station, wooded sites. Just past the airport on Old Glenn Highway.

Mountain View RV Park—About four miles west of town on Old Glenn Highway, then turn on Smith Road. Hookups. **(907) 745-5747.**

WHERE TO EAT

$$$

Chardonet's
Across the Palmer-Wasilla Highway from the Carr's shopping center. Superb dining, excellent service, with a slightly European flair to the food. Reservations recommended, particularly on the weekends. **(907) 746-6060.**

$$

Frontier Cafe
Seafood buffet on Friday nights, Sunday brunch. **133 W. Evergreen. (907) 745-3392.**

Peking Express
Inside Carr's shopping center. Good to excellent take-out or eat-in Chinese food. **(907) 746-5757.**

Wasilla

Until the early 1970s, Wasilla was little more than a road junction 10 miles from Palmer. With the opening of the Parks Highway between Anchorage and Fairbanks in 1971, followed by the boom in oil-company and government-related employment in Anchorage generated by the building of the trans-Alaska oil pipeline in the mid-1970s, Wasilla grew at a phenomenal rate. Many of the "petroleum yuppies" who found work in Anchorage in the 1970s and early 1980s made their homes in Wasilla for a small taste of the wilderness lacking in Anchorage.

The result is a long, narrow town at roadside described as "several miles long and two blocks deep." Another result is heavy traffic mornings and evenings as commuters go to work in Anchorage or head for home.

Wasilla sits closer to the major salmon streams in the southern part of the Mat-Su Valley than does Palmer, and, as such, is the center for fishing activity on the Little Susitna, Deshka and other rivers. A number of fishing guides from both Wasilla and Palmer run their charter operations on area streams.

Wasilla is also where the "real" starting line is for the famed Iditarod Trail Sled Dog Race from Anchorage to Nome. The televised start from Anchorage ends just 10 miles out of town. Mushers and their teams are then trucked to Wasilla to be restarted in the order that they completed the first few miles out of Anchorage. Here the race really begins in earnest.

For more information on Wasilla and more extensive lists of fishing guides and accommodations than presented below, contact the **Wasilla Chamber of Commerce, (907) 376-1299.**

ACTIVITIES

DOROTHY G. PAGE WASILLA MUSEUM AND FRONTIER VILLAGE

Dorothy Page, who died in late 1989, was known as the Mother of the Iditarod. Much of what the race is today is due in large part to her efforts. Besides her work with the Iditarod, she devoted much of her time working to preserve the history of the Wasilla area. The museum, in downtown Wasilla, is actually a collection of buildings from Wasilla's early days.

FISHING

In the Wasilla area, king salmon activity is generally concentrated in June. The king run in the Little Susitna River, easily accessed from town, peaks on or about June 15 each year. There are relatively few red salmon available, except on the Yentna River (fly-out or a long boat ride), so July is usually a fairly slow month for salmon. At the end of July the silver salmon arrive and fishing stays good well into September. Listed below are several salmon guides, mostly offering day charters, that can get you into the thick of the action.

Alaska Jetboat Charters—(907) 376-4776.

Catch My Drift Charters—(907) 373-6360.

Fishtale River Guides—(907) 745-2888.

Silver Slayer Charters—(907) 376-7529.

Skwentna Roadhouse—(fly-in lodge), (907) 696-9080 or (907) 345-6447.

Trophy Catch Charters—(907) 745-4101.

IDITAROD
Iditarod Trail Headquarters is just a short distance out of downtown Wasilla on Knik-Goose Bay Road. Exhibits reflecting the race's history and honoring its winners are on display, and there is a small gift shop.

To watch the restart of the race, be downtown in mid-afternoon on the first Saturday in March. Usually the leaders will be hitting the trail about 2 P.M. Volunteers will be evident throughout town to assist you with parking and provide directions to the viewing areas. Contact the **Iditarod Trail Committee, (907) 376-5080,** for information on the race or on visiting headquarters.

Museum of Alaska Transportation and Industry
Just north of Wasilla along the Alaska Railroad is this facility featuring various items of equipment important to the history of Alaska. Airplanes, vehicles and railroad rolling stock are all on display. Contact the **Wasilla Chamber of Commerce, (907) 376–1299,** for detailed directions and information.

WHERE TO STAY

ACCOMMODATIONS

$$
Kashim Inn
Restaurant and lounge. On the Parks Highway in Wasilla. **(907) 376-5800.**

Mat-Su Resort
Motel, cabins, restaurant and lounge. Floatplane dock. On Wasilla Lake. **(907) 376-3228.**

BED & BREAKFASTS
This list is only partially complete. For additional B&B information and reservations, contact the **Mat-Su Valley Bed & Breakfast Association, (907) 376-5868.**

Ede Den B&B Antiques—(907) 376-2162.

Lakeshore B&B—(907) 376-1380.

Snowbird Inn—(907) 376-7048.

Wasilla Lake B&B—(907) 376-5985.

CAMPGROUNDS
Green Ridge Camper Park—(907) 376-5899.

Nancy Lake Resort—(40 miles north), (907) 495-6227.

Susitna Landing—(public, no phone). Drive 17.2 miles from Wasilla on Knik-Goose Bay Road, turn right at campground/boat launch sign for 12 miles on gravel road.

WHERE TO EAT

$$
Country Kitchen
American food, great for families. **(907) 376-5800.**

Mat-Su Resort
BBQ ribs, steaks and seafood. Part of resort complex that overlooks Wasilla Lake. **(907) 376-3228.**

Windbreak Cafe
American food. South of town on Parks Highway. **(907) 376-4484.**

Talkeetna

On Alaska's road system, Talkeetna's one of the best places available to check out the "frontier" spirit of the largest state. Most who live here are fiercely independent and like the semi-isolation of being 14 miles off the main highway on the Talkeetna Spur Road.

These folks could have been on the main road. When the Parks Highway was constructed, the original plan was to route it through Talkeetna. "No thanks," chorused the townspeople, and they raised such a fuss that the route was altered to pass several miles west of town. Those who get to Talkeetna have to want to go to Talkeetna; there's no passing through en route to somewhere else.

This small town dates back to the construction of the Alaska Railroad in the early part of the century and even before. There was and is a fair amount of mining done in the region, and Talkeetna grew up as a supply point for the mines.

Airplanes, specifically bush planes and bush pilots, have been a major part of the Talkeetna scene since the early 1930s. Flying supplies in to miners was quickly recognized as much more efficient than hauling by horse-drawn wagon or sled, and Talkeetna offered access to a wealth of prime hunting and fishing territory with no other means of reasonable access.

Those activities aside, Talkeetna is an even more important aerodrome because of its proximity to Mount McKinley. Virtually everyone who attempts to climb the mountain flies out of Talkeetna to a base camp on Kahiltna Glacier. When they finish on the mountain, they are flown back to Talkeetna. The National Park Service maintains an office in Talkeetna for serving the ever-growing number of climbers and for tourists who want a flightseeing trip into Denali National Park and near Mount McKinley. Additional visitors information on Talkeetna is available from the **Talkeetna Chamber of Commerce, P.O. Box 334, Talkeetna, AK 99676, (907) 733-2330.**

FESTIVALS AND EVENTS

MOOSE DROPPING FESTIVAL

This annual celebration of the walnut-sized droppings of Alaska's largest land mammal is a fund-raiser for the Talkeetna Historical Society that is usually on the second Saturday in July. And there's always somebody, somewhere who refuses to understand. ...

In 1991, a perfectly serious caller from an animal-rights group back East called the Talkeetna Chamber of Commerce and demanded to know, with righteous indignation, just how high the moose were before they were dropped. The lady in Talkeetna who answered the phone came right back to him and said, "It depends on if we're dropping them on gravel or on concrete." The caller didn't even laugh when several minutes later he finally figured it out.

Contact the chamber at the above address and phone number for more information on this great midsummer party.

TALKEETNA BACHELORS BALL AND WILDERNESS WOMAN COMPETITION

What do you do when you're one of several lonely men in the middle of nowhere and there isn't an eligible woman in sight? You form the Talkeetna Bachelor's Society, charge dues, and blow the whole treasury for a party whenever one of the members gets married and is no longer eligible for membership. But to attract suitable candidates to increase the odds that some of the members will ultimately meet just the right female you gotta have a plan, even if it sometimes seems to get a little out of hand.

Thus was born this early winter party in Talkeetna. It starts with the wilderness woman competition. Prospective females (some have come from as far away as Chicago) compete in a variety of events like wood chopping, fire building, serving a harried trapper his beer and sandwich, snowshoe racing and other exciting events pertinent to life in the Alaska bush.

After the day's competition ends, there's the bachelors ball, where some of these backwoodsmen actually take showers and dress in a tuxedo. Arguably, wearing a tuxedo with mukluks on your feet does somewhat spoil the effect. At the ball, the competitors from the day's wilderness woman competition and other belles who prefer formal balls to wood chopping, bid for dates with members of the society. Money raised goes into the treasury to help support the bachelor party thrown for the next unlucky member to get hitched. Without question, a good time is had by all—and there have actually been a couple of marriages to come out of all this revelry.

Contact the chamber, **(907) 733-2330**, for information on exact dates and times.

ACTIVITIES

CLIMBING MOUNT MCKINLEY

Virtually everyone who climbs North America's highest peak sets forth from Talkeetna. From late April through mid-June, much of the activity in town is dedicated to shuttling climbers and their gear to and from the base camp area about 7,000 feet above sea level on Kahiltna Glacier. From there, most parties take the heavily traveled West Buttress route to the summit. All climbers are required to check in at the Park Service office in Talkeetna and are shown a short film detailing some of the hazards on the mountain. The film is available in several foreign languages, as McKinley treks are becoming quite popular all over the world.

Technically, climbing Mount McKinley is not all that difficult. The constantly changing weather, however, makes it among the more dangerous climbs in North America. Almost every year several climbers are killed in their efforts to conquer McKinley, and daring helicopter rescues of injured or ill climbers are frequently featured on local news programs. At least one National Park Service ranger skilled in mountain climbing and high-altitude rescue is on the mountain at all times during the climbing season.

For information about climbing Mount McKinley, write to **Denali National Park and Preserve, P.O. Box 9, Denali Park, AK 99755.** The summer phone number is **(907) 683-1266,** the winter phone number is **(907) 683-2294.**

FISHING

King salmon action really heats up on Talkeetna-area streams around July 1. That's when the fish swimming up from the Palmer-Wasilla area reach local streams. Clear Creek, just upstream on the Talkeetna River from town is a good bet as are several other tributaries. To get to one of these places, though, you'll either need to have your own riverboat or purchase a seat on a commercial riverboat operated from

Talkeetna. Try **Mahay's Riverboat Service, (907) 733-2223,** if you want a long-time operator in the region who handles both drop-offs and guided fishing. Another good bet is **Talkeetna Riverboat Service, (907) 733-2281,** for the same kinds of services.

Besides five species of salmon at differing times during the summer, there are opportunities for native rainbow trout and grayling.

FLIGHTSEEING

Talkeetna has long been famous for its bush pilots, and still is today. The pilots who haul climbers on and off the mountain also carry thousands of people out over Denali National Park and close to Mount McKinley. This is a tremendous way to view Denali National Park, and really the only way to get even a momentary glimpse of most of this remote wilderness. Many trips also include a landing on a glacier and the opportunity to leave the plane and walk around for a short time. Operators in Talkeetna who can take you up to see the sights or fly you in for a trek up the mountain include

Doug Geeting Aviation—1-800-770-2366.

Hudson Air Service, Inc.—(907)733-2321.

K-2 Aviation—(907) 733-2291.

MUSEUM OF NORTHERN ADVENTURE

Twenty-four life-size scenes of historic Alaskan events and characters. Main Street. **(907) 733-3999.**

RAFTING

Talkeetna-area rivers offer wonderful opportunities for day trips and longer rafting adventures in the heart of the wilderness. Operators include:

Denali Floats—(907) 733-2384.

Denali River Guides—(907) 733-2697.

Jacques Adventure Company—(907) 337-9604.

———— WHERE TO STAY ————

ACCOMMODATIONS
$$–$$$
Latitude 62 Lodge/Motel
Restaurant and lounge. Player piano. Dogsled and snow-machine rides available in winter. **(907) 733-2262.**

Paradise Lodge
Fishing, canoeing, horseback riding, sleigh rides, dog mushing and more. **(907) 733-1471.**

Swiss-Alaska Inn
Restaurant and lounge. Near boat launch ramp on east side of town. **(907) 733-2424.**

Talkeetna Motel
Restaurant and lounge. **(907) 733-2323.**

Talkeetna Roadhouse
Restaurant and motel. **Main Street. (907) 733-1351.**

BED AND BREAKFASTS
Alaska Log Cabin B&B—(907) 733-2668.

Bays B&B—(907) 733-1342.

Chase-on-the-Susitna Remote B&B—(907) 733-3028.

River Beauty B&B—(907) 733-2741.

CAMPGROUNDS

The two area campgrounds are not full-service RV parks. Both are suitable for either tents or parking a self-contained RV.

Talkeetna River Park is at the end of the Talkeetna Spur Road, and camping sites are available near the **boat launch facility** on the east side of town.

──── ADDITIONAL INFORMATION ────

The valley's three major communities have been described in some detail here. Yet there is so much more, including smaller towns such as Big Lake, Sutton, Chickaloon, Willow and others. These are spread out all along the road system in the valley, which is larger than several of the New England states combined. There are, as well, a host of backcountry lodges on the Yentna River, the Skwentna River, Alexander Creek and other streams and lakes. Contact the **Mat-Su Visitors Center, (907) 746-5000,** for information on these facilities and their locations.

Almost everyone who climbs Mount McKinley, North America's highest peak, sets forth from Talkeetna. (Photo by Ron Dalby)

The Copper River Basin

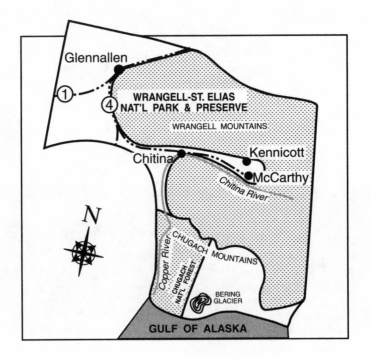

THE COPPER RIVER BASIN

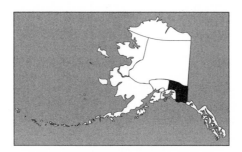

OVERVIEW

East of the Matanuska–Susitna Valley, north and east of Valdez and southeast of Fairbanks, lies one of Alaska's most magical and accessible wilderness areas. There are few towns even though a couple of major roads crisscross the region. The largest national park in the United States dominates the area, but relatively few people know about it, much less bother to visit. The fishing is tremendous; huge runs of king, red and silver salmon, native rainbow trout, lake trout and grayling populate the streams and lakes. Massive river gorges and canyons cut through the mountains. Glaciers melt into raging rivers. Wildlife—grizzlies, black bears, caribou, moose, Dall sheep and Rocky Mountain goats to name some of the larger mammals—roam the tundra, forests, cliffs and muskeg.

Almost everybody who drives to Alaska passes through the Copper River Basin at least once. Anyone who drives from Anchorage to Valdez clips the southwestern corner. If you fly into Alaska in an airliner, it's visible out the right-side windows of the airplane for almost an hour. The second-highest mountain in the United States, Mount St. Elias anchors the eastern edge on the Canadian border; three other massive peaks, Mounts Sanford, Drum and Wrangell challenge climbers—some say these peaks are even more challenging than Mount McKinley. And there's an almost constant venting of volcanic steam from near the top of Mount Wrangell.

In the late 1870s, Army Lieutenant Frederick Schwatka led an expedition through the region, noting that he found isolated bands of Indians,

143

mostly starving. He reported and described the inland course of the powerful Copper River for the first time. Little happened immediately after his visit. It wasn't until gold fever gripped the land in the wake of the Klondike gold rush that fortune seekers in any number began to penetrate the area. Although they did find some gold, what really set things in motion was the discovery of huge copper deposits high in the Wrangell Mountains near Skolai Pass.

That somebody would mine this copper was a foregone conclusion; the deposits were just too rich to ignore. But before the mines could be developed, a transportation system to get the ore to a deep-water port had to be put in place. Only a railroad could possibly handle the volume.

Two companies immediately swung into action, starting their lines from Valdez, already an operational seaport. However, the copper mines could only support one railroad, and tempers flared in both companies in Keystone Canyon just a few miles out of Valdez. A wild-west-style shootout occurred and both railroads went out of business.

Iron Mike Henry, the man who had built the White Pass and Yukon Railway from Skagway to Whitehorse, entered and announced plans to start in Cordova and follow the path of the Copper River to what is today Chitina, then turn east to the mine site near the foot of Kennicott Glacier. Most people thought this railroad couldn't be built. Following the path of the Copper River meant blasting a railroad bed out of almost sheer cliffs at riverside for much of the route. It meant bridging the Copper River near the base of Miles Glacier outside of Cordova.

Iron Mike succeeded; the bridge alone cost $1 million, a frightful sum in early twentieth-century America. Picks, shovels and dynamite did the rest, and in a remarkably short time the Copper River and Northwestern Railroad was operating trains from Cordova to Kennicott. The first reliable access into the Copper River became operational in 1911. It would operate for a mere 27 years, but that was enough.

The mine at Kennicott was built by the Guggenheim-Morgan syndicate from New York, and was, quite possibly, their most ambitious project in North America. Most of the ore came from four separate sites, 6,000 feet or more above sea level, and far above the railroad terminus at about 2,000 feet. A huge tram was constructed to haul the ore in big buckets from the mine sites to the stamp mill at trackside. A small city, Kennecott—spelled with an *e* not an *i*—was constructed to house the staff for the mine; small communities also sprouted near each of the actual mine sites with barracks and service buildings as necessary to assist in extracting the ore.

At the mill site, the city included barracks, houses for senior staff members and their families, a school, a community center and other buildings pertinent to a town. The railroad carried in the people and equipment and carried the ore to tidewater in Cordova.

In 1938, the price of copper fell, and the high-grade ore was played out at the mine sites. Rather than try to hang on until either prices rose or new mine sites could be found, the owners closed the mine. The last train out of the town of Kennecott was in November 1938.

More than half a century later, Kennecott remains much as it was when abandoned in 1938. The blacksmith's tools are still laid out around the forge. Papers are scattered throughout the administrative offices. The hospital, though a creek periodically runs through it these days, still smells like a hospital. This is a historic site of the first magnitude in Alaska, yet it is only in the last couple of years that serious actions have been taken to begin preserving it. Weather—and souvenir hunters— have taken a heavy toll over the years. Thankfully, because of the remoteness of the site, souvenir hunters have been relatively few.

At the time of the railroad, the overland trail from Valdez was expanded into one of Alaska's first major roads, the Richardson High- way linking the port city of Valdez with Fairbanks in the Interior, then Alaska's largest city. It never developed into much of a freight route, because the Alaska Railroad from Seward to Fairbanks was built at about the same time. No road would parallel this latter railroad, however, until the early 1970s. Extensions off the Richardson Highway would eventu- ally link the road with Denali National Park (the still-gravel Denali Highway starting from the north edge of the Copper River Basin in Paxon and running to Cantwell near the park entrance), and the Glenn High- way connecting the Richardson Highway with Palmer and Anchorage. Later still, the Glenn Highway would be extended to connect with Tok on the Alaska Highway near the Canadian border (the Tok Cutoff). Thus, in an unusual twist for Alaska's wilderness regions, the Copper River Basin is comfortably accessible on what are today excellent roads.

Towns, though, are still few and far between. The largest is Glennallen, grown up on the Glenn Highway just west of its junction with the Richardson Highway. Kennecott itself is a ghost town, and nearby McCarthy has but a few full-time residents. Chitina, more or less between Glennallen and McCarthy, still boasts a handful of full-time residents. That's about it save for a few hardy souls at Gakona, where the Glenn Highway splits from the Richardson and leads to Tok; Copper Center on the Richardson Highway south of Glennallen; and a few other isolated pockets of population. If you want a taste of Alaska's wilderness that's relatively accessible from the road, this is the place to look.

Contact the **Greater Copper Valley Chamber of Commerce, P.O. Box 469, Glennallen, AK 99588, (907) 822-5555,** for details and informa- tion about visiting the Copper River basin.

Wrangell-St. Elias
National Park

Total acreage makes this the largest national park under the U.S. flag—it's six times bigger than Yellowstone National Park. Nine of the 16 highest peaks in the United States are within its boundaries. Four major mountain ranges converge in the park, the Wrangells, Chugach, St. Elias and the Alaska Range. The largest subpolar ice field on the continent, the Bagley Ice Field, gives birth to Tana, Miles, Hubbard and Guyot glaciers. Malaspina Glacier flowing out of the St. Elias Range and reaching tidewater between Icy Bay and Yakutat is, alone, a mass with an area larger than that of Rhode Island.

The western boundary of the park is the Canadian border, though it doesn't exactly end there. The St. Elias Mountains on the Canadian side of the border are part of Canada's Kluane National Park. Collectively, these two parks combined protect as wilderness a region larger than the state of Missouri. Those who drive to Alaska via the Alaska Highway will skirt the northeastern boundary of Kluane National Park as they drive between Haines Junction and Burwash Landing beginning about 100 miles northwest of Whitehorse.

As noted, Wrangell–St. Elias is a wilderness park. There are no accommodations or services within the park boundaries. Tent camping is allowed anywhere within the park, though please observe private property postings. Considerable acreage within the park is private property, either Native lands or private holdings that were titled before the park was created in 1980.

Two roads, the Nabesna Road and the Chitina-McCarthy Road, touch the park, the former on its northern boundary and the latter a state-owned route extending westward into the center of the park. Much of the land at roadside on both routes is private property, though there is hiking access into the park if you wish to start from your vehicle.

Contact park headquarters at **Wrangell–St. Elias National Park and Preserve, P.O. Box 29, Glennallen, AK 99588, (907) 822-5235,** for details and information about visiting the park. There are also ranger stations maintained in **Nabesna (P.O. Box 885, Slana, AK 99586, (907) 822-5238), Chitina (P.O. Box 110, Chitina, AK 99566, (907) 823-2205)** and **Yakutat (P.O. Box 137, Yakutat, AK 99689, (907) 784-3295).**

ACTIVITIES

BIRD-WATCHING

The Bureau of Land Management, in conjunction with the Alaska Department of Fish and Game and with Wrangell–St. Elias National Park, publishes a field checklist entitled "Birds of the Copper River Basin and Surrounding Areas." Virtually all of the more than 200 species of birds listed can be found within the boundaries of the park. Copies can be obtained from the park headquarters address listed above or from the **Bureau of Land Management, Glennallen District Office, P.O. Box 147, Glennallen, AK 99588.**

Here is a sampling from the list under the heading of "Eagles and Hawks."

Northern Goshawk
Sharp-shinned Hawk
Red-tailed Hawk
Swainson's Hawk
Rough-legged Hawk
Golden Eagle
Bald Eagle
Northern Harrier
Osprey
Gyrfalcon
Peregrine Falcon
American Kestrel
Merlin

Other categories on the field checklist include Loons and Grebes, Herons, Waterfowl, Cranes and Rails, Sandpipers and Plovers, Auks, Owls and Goatsuckers, Woodpeckers, and many more. Wrangell–St. Elias National Park is a great place to spend some time if you want to add to your life list.

CROSS-COUNTRY SKIING

Moving over the ground in Alaska's wilderness is almost always easier on the snow when the rivers and lakes are frozen. March, April and even May (in the high country) are the best months, after the severe cold from the dead of winter eases. There's also plenty of daylight in these months, unlike the midwinter months of December and January. As with hiking described below, this is wilderness country and there are no options other than what you can carry yourself—on your back or by towing a light sled. Be prepared, and make certain that someone knows where you're going and when you expect to be back.

HIKING

Very few prepared and marked trails exist within **Wrangell–St. Elias National Park.** Hikers are pretty much on their own, selecting routes and destinations after carefully studying maps. River crossings can be exceedingly dangerous, particularly on the large glacier-fed streams roaring out of the mountains. Weather can also be a hazard as it is apt to change violently with little warning. Wild animals can be dangerous, particularly grizzly bears when surprised or moose if you chance to get between a cow and calf. Give warning of your presence by making plenty of noise as you hike, and stay together as a group whenever possible. Statistically, almost all bear attacks occur on people hiking alone or individuals temporarily separated from a group.

You are essentially on your own when you strike out overland in Wrangell–St. Elias National Park. There are no facilities off the roads, and patrols of any given portion of the park are few and far between. You must carry all your own food and gear and be prepared to wait out hazardous weather conditions. Be certain that you leave word with someone where you are going and when you will be back. Check in at park headquarters or one of the ranger stations before departing, and be sure to stop briefly and let them know you have returned. Be as specific as you can about your route of travel and the number of days you expect to be gone when you give your itinerary.

RAFTING/KAYAKING

Both the Copper and Chitina rivers offer excellent opportunities for rafters and kayakers—either shorter day trips or extensive expeditions. Either plan and execute your own adventure, or go with an established company. Businesses that should be able to help include

Glennallen Sporting Goods—(907) 822-3780.

Ram River Outfitters—(907) 822-5252.

Rivers Unlimited—(907) 822-3535.

St. Elias Alpine Guides—(907) 277-6867.

Ultima Thule Outfitters—(907) 344-1898.

WHERE TO STAY

ACCOMMODATIONS

As noted earlier, there are no overnight accommodations on National Park Service lands. However, there are a couple of businesses operating in Kennicott and McCarthy on private lands within the borders of the park.

$$$

Kennicott Glacier Lodge

On the actual site of Kennecott, this facility is reached either by flying into McCarthy or by driving to the end of the Chitina–McCarthy Road and taking the hand tram across the river into McCarthy. From McCarthy, a local bus service can run you the five miles to Kennecott. Packages for just the room or including the room and meals are available. The lodge is surprisingly inexpensive for its remoteness, and the owner, Rich Kirkwood, is a great host. **(907) 258-2350.**

McCarthy Lodge

In McCarthy on the main street in town. Restored building. **(907) 333-5402.**

$$

McCarthy Wilderness Bed and Breakfast

Get to McCarthy as described above and stay in town. Explore Kennecott mines by day. **(907) 277-6867.**

McCarty Road gift shop. (Photo by Ron Dalby)

Glennallen/Gakona/ Copper Center

The largest community in the Copper River basin is Glennallen. At mile 115 of the Richardson Highway (between Valdez and Fairbanks) turn east for 1.5 miles on the Glenn Highway to reach Glennallen. Fewer than 1,000 people call the town home.

The region's major airport, Gulkana, is about two miles north of the junction of the Glenn and Richardson highways. Limited scheduled air service is available from Anchorage. Most people arrive by vehicle.

KACM Radio, 790 AM, airs a very popular program called Caribou Clatter twice daily. These are messages read over the air to bush dwellers in remote cabins who have no other contact with the outside world on a day-to-day basis. Instructions for appointments in town, birth announcements, the timing of supply planes, arrivals and departures are all broadcast over the air. Anyone who wants to get a feel for life in the Alaska bush should tune in to these broadcasts, one in the morning and one in the evening. Messages are limited to a few words and are read unedited. Glennallen is not the only town broadcasting such messages. However, as the other towns like Fairbanks and Anchorage become much more urbanized, some of the distinctive "bush" tone of their radio messages decreases. Caribou Clatter is still the best and "bushiest" of the radio message services in Alaska.

ACTIVITIES

FISHING

Close to town, fishing is pretty much on your own in a number of creeks and lakes. Some of the lakes are stocked by the Alaska Department of Fish and Game. Off the road system, it's fly-in only for fishing. Several air services at the Gulkana and Gakona airports can get you out away from the crowds to various lakes and streams.

North of town on the Gulkana River (crosses the Richardson Highway near Gakona) there's excellent fishing for king and red salmon in July if the water's clear and not high and muddy from recent rains. Rainbows and grayling are also available in the Gulkana River. Bank fishing is available near the bridge and at Sourdough, a few miles farther north on the Richardson Highway. Best bait for kings is normally a glob of salmon roe with some sort of attractor such as Spin 'n Glo. Day charter operators in Gakona and at streamside at Sourdough can take you out for a day's fishing. Inquire locally in Gakona.

KLUTINA LAKE

Got a hankering to do a little four-wheeling into the backcountry? It's pretty tough in most places in Alaska, but there is one spot a few miles from Glennallen that should warm the hearts of most off-roaders.

Twelve miles south of Glennallen on the Richardson Highway, turn east on Brenwick–Craig Road. About a quarter-mile in there'll be a sign warning you of rough conditions ahead. It's 25 miles or so to the end of the trail at Klutina Lake, and those are 25 spectacular miles looking down into the canyon created by the Klutina

149

River flowing out of the lake. Lots of good camping areas lie near the lake outlet and along the river in the last few miles before reaching the lake. Fishing is excellent around the first of July with king salmon, red salmon, lake trout, grayling, Dolly Varden and whitefish all available. You may want a small boat to use on the lake. If boating, watch the weather carefully; this is a huge lake, and just a little wind will quickly raise big whitecaps. Do not, under any circumstances, attempt to float out on the Klutina River unless you are a skilled whitewater rafter with the appropriate equipment. This is a very rugged river with major stretches of class IV and class V whitewater.

This road is not recommended for RVs of any description, though 4-by-4 pickups with campers can probably make it in and out if they're careful. Allow four hours one way from the turnoff on the Richardson

Highway to Klutina Lake; more time may be required if the road is wet and muddy. Also, there is considerable private property at roadside along the trail. It is generally posted with highly visible signs and warnings. Stay off the posted land and do your camping on the BLM lands that are public property.

LAKE LOUISE

Thirty-two miles east of Glennallen on the Glenn Highway going towards Anchorage, a side road leads 19 miles to a number of facilities on Lake Louise. Fishing for lake trout and grayling are the primary summer activities. In winter there is considerable cross-country skiing and snow-machine activity on established trails. Several lodges, RV parking and a state campground are on the lake.

WHERE TO STAY

ACCOMMODATIONS
$$–$$$
Caribou Hotel
Downtown Glennallen. Restaurant and gift shop. Reservations recommended in the summer. **(907) 822-3302.**

Copper Center Lodge
Historic roadhouse 14 miles south of Glennallen on the Richardson Highway in Copper Center. Restaurant and lounge. **(907) 822-3245.**

Gakona Junction Village
Restaurant, fishing guides and hookups for RVs. At the junction of the Richardson Highway and Tok Cutoff about 11 miles north of Glennallen. **(907) 822-3664** or **1-800-962-1933.**

BED AND BREAKFASTS
Carol's B&B—(Glennallen), (907) 822-3594.

Klutina B&B—(Copper Center), (907) 822-5858.

CAMPGROUNDS
Bishop's RV Park—P.O. Box 367, Glennallen, AK 99588.

Klutina River Campground—(Copper Center), **(907) 822-3311.**

Northern Lights Wilderness Park—(Copper Center), **(907) 822-3199.**

Gakona RV Wilderness Campsite—(Gakona), **(907) 822-3550.**

Tazlina River RV Park—(west of Glennallen), **(907) 822-3034.**

Tolsona Lake Resort—(west of Glennallen), **(907) 822-3433.**

Tolsona Wilderness Campground—(west of Glennallen), **(907) 822-3865.**

Chitina

About 30 miles south of Glennallen on the Richardson Highway, turn east on the Edgarton Highway, which leads 27 miles to Chitina. A popular Alaska bumper sticker asks: "Where the Hell is Chitina?" and you'll see why after you get there.

There's not much there, yet thousands and thousands of Alaskans flock to this tiny settlement every June and July. The reason is the **Copper River Dip Net Fishery** for salmon. Resident Alaskans can take up to 30 salmon per family by swinging a long-handled net through the murky waters of the river and hoping it snares an unwary salmon. When the fish are running thick and heavy, the action is unbelievable. Camping is at a premium during these times, and there isn't very much to begin with, anyway.

Just past Chitina, where the road crosses the Copper River, look down to your right and you'll see hundreds of RVs and tents established on gravel river bars and in the trees on the far side of the river. Downstream from Chitina on a rather flaky road that leads to O'Brien Creek, there are hundreds more RVs and tents at the height of the dipping season. Salmon fever brings these people out, even though this is tough, hard work. If you're not a resident of Alaska, you'll have to be content to sit and watch, but this is a fine spectator activity.

If you elect to camp with the dip netters on the river bars, be alert for the river rising in response to heavy rains or rapidly melting glaciers. Quite often the popular gravel bars near the bridge are underwater, forcing people to find other places to park or set up tents.

A good bet for area camping, if you can get space, is **Liberty Falls State Recreation Site** about 4 miles before you reach Chitina. A splendid waterfall and a few wooded sites make this a very pleasant place to stay, and one that is far removed from the strong winds that seem to be forever blowing along the river.

After you cross the Copper River Bridge at Chitina, the road becomes the Chitina-McCarthy Road and leads another 60 rugged miles to the **Kennicott River.** Here you'll have to park your vehicle and pull yourself across the river on a hand tram if you want to visit McCarthy or the ghost town and mine that is Kennecott. **Wrangell–St. Elias National Park** occupies most of the land on both sides of the road.

Along the road to McCarthy, though, there are some places worth investigating for fishing. Ten miles in is **Silver Lake.** A small private campground there offers boat launching facilities and rental boats and canoes. The rainbow trout fishing is excellent, from a boat or from the dock by the campground. Fish to five pounds or more are quite common. This is probably Alaska's best roadside fishery for rainbow trout. (*Author's note*: As Silver Lake and neighboring Van Lake are stocked by the Alaska Department of Fish and Game, it's perfectly acceptable to keep the rainbows you catch up to the allowable bag limit. The last time my son and I were there, we rented a canoe and fished from about 6 P.M. to midnight and came back with a stringer of 17 'bows weighing a total of 41 pounds.)

Several other creeks and lakes at roadside offer opportunities for trout, grayling and Dolly Varden. Accommodations at Kennicott and McCarthy were covered previously in the Wrangell–St. Elias National Park section of this chapter. Camping at the end of the road is simply a matter of finding a space to park your RV or pitch a tent. Similar opportunities for camping can be found near stream crossings on the way in. There is one other private campground on the road besides Silver Lake, **Nelson's Lakeside Campground,** 12 miles after crossing the bridge at Chitina.

Prince William Sound

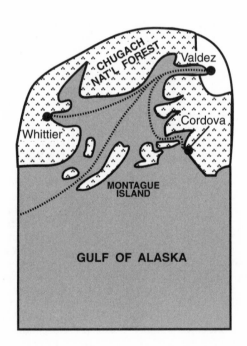

‒ PRINCE WILLIAM SOUND ‒

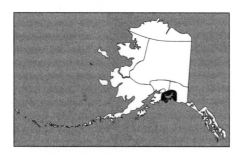

OVERVIEW

Imagine an inland sea dotted with emerald green islands, its coastline broken with deep, jagged fjords. Animals large and small drift in and out of the shadows of the rain forest. Offshore, denizens from the smallest plankton to the largest whales live out their lives in a wilderness of sparkling water.

But this is not a tropical paradise, because at the head of many fjords lie huge glaciers, massive rivers of ancient, slow-moving ice. This is Prince William Sound, or, to many Alaskans, simply the Sound.

Alaska's most valuable commodity, oil, moves across its surface in monstrous oil tankers; visitors flock to the region from across Alaska, the nation and the world. Normally these two opposites are in harmony, though this pattern was shattered for a while when the now-infamous *Exxon Valdez* wandered off course and struck a favorite fishing reef in March 1989.

For a time, tourism was interrupted as the vast resources of Exxon poured into Prince William Sound to clean up the mess made by 11 million barrels of oil. Today, little of the oil can be seen, though its presence in the Sound is still felt through declines in the populations of certain fish, sea mammals and sea birds. Yet, for the most part, even the populations of the most affected species seem to be recovering. Every visitor who ventures into the Sound by boat can expect to see large numbers of sea otters, seals, sea lions and rookeries teeming with new generations of sea birds. With luck, they will also see whales in the sea

153

and bears on the shore—the amount of luck necessary to see these creatures is about the same as it was before the oil spill.

Will the Sound ever be the same again? Unfortunately, no. Is the Sound still worth visiting? Emphatically, yes. Other than the movement of glaciers, a picture taken today will look more or less identical to a picture of the same scene taken in the years before the oil spill. There are a few more restrictions on fishing—cutthroat trout on the western side of the Sound have apparently suffered from the oil spill, and fishing is closed for them as of this writing. Cutthroat fishing is still open and good on the eastern side of the Sound, though.

Mostly, however, the change in the Sound is people, more specifically the attitudes of people who live and work on the Sound. Having almost lost this jewel, those to whom it matters the most, whether oil companies or kayakers, are more than ever determined to protect it from further harm. This deeply held sentiment affects almost everything one sees and does in Prince William Sound.

Whatever your Alaskan plans, be sure you include Prince William Sound on your itinerary. Without stopping here, however briefly, your visit to Alaska would be incomplete.

HISTORY

Prince William Sound is Alaska's original melting pot. Here, and only here, did most of the original inhabitants of Alaska—Eskimos, Athabaskans and Tlingets—meet and coexist. The land mostly resembles southeastern Alaska, the domain of the Tlingets. But it abuts the lands settled by Eskimos and Athabaskans, the latter coming seaward from the Interior and the former moving slowly along Alaska's coastal fringe.

The Sound boasts a plethora of names all related to its exploration: Valdez has a Spanish or Portuguese ring to it, Tatitlik and Chenega reflect a Native heritage, Bligh Island was named for Captain Cook's favorite lieutenant, who later earned himself a passel of trouble while commanding the ill-fated HMS *Bounty* on a voyage to the South Pacific.

Yet despite the region's lush beauty and rich resources, none of those visiting in the 1700s and most of the 1800s had much of an impact. Even the Russians, who ruled Alaska for more than 100 years, showed little interest in Prince William Sound, other than minor installations dedicated to the harvest of sea otter pelts.

It was only well after the United States gained title to Alaska that activities centered on resource extraction in or near the Sound formed the towns now best known in the area. Valdez came into being as a shipping/ travel point to Interior Alaska during the time of the gold rushes at the end of the 1800s. Cordova was first settled as a fish cannery site in 1889. Whittier arose as an ice-free port with railroad access during World War II; many of its residents still live in the multistory barracks built to house soldiers during the period. Until a few years ago it was a standard Alaskan joke that the whole town of Whittier lived in the same building; actually, the barracks was divided into separate apartments when it was taken over by the civilians.

The early years of Western civilization in Prince William Sound had more than their share of excitement. In the first years of this century, two businesses attempted to build a railroad from Valdez into the Interior. Their not-so-friendly competition ended in a shootout at Keystone Canyon about 10 miles from present-day Valdez. The result was that no Valdez-based railroad was ever built. Instead, the Copper River and Northwestern Railroad started at tidewater in Cordova and followed the Copper River into the Interior, terminating at the copper mines of Kennecott. The railroad lasted until the copper mines closed in late 1938.

And the excitement continues, though gunfights are relatively rare these days. In Cordova, the great debate today centers on whether the town should be connected to the Alaska road system. In good fishing years, the vote usually goes 51 to 49 percent against the road. In bad fishing years, the numbers are reversed. In 1991, Governor Walter Hickel decided to build a rudimentary road on the old railroad grade of the Copper River and Northwestern. Everybody involved, including some groups who actually want a road, filed some sort of lawsuit against the state after or during the first summer's work on the project. The state of Alaska spent about $250,000 on road work, mostly clearing brush on the railroad bed, and more than half a million dollars defending against various litigants. In 1992, the litigants combined these numbers as proof that the governor spent three times as much as the $250,000 from the road maintenance funds that he budgeted for upgrading the railroad bed in the summer of 1991. You figure it out.

By the time you read this it might be possible to drive to Cordova, but don't hold your breath. Plan to fly to Cordova or take the Alaska Marine Highway from Valdez or Whittier.

Besides the earlier turbulent history, the major event shaping the land in the Sound and today's living patterns was the 1964 Alaska earthquake. Wave action generated by the quake virtually obliterated Old Valdez, and the town that exists today (sometimes called New Valdez) was built about three miles from the original town site.

In Cordova, the land rose several feet, dramatically affecting the Copper River delta, a huge wetland used for breeding by crowds of waterfowl every summer. Because of the rise in the land, these wetlands are drier now and the number of breeding birds has declined, though there are still a lot of them.

Because of the date of the earthquake, Good Friday, and the date of the *Exxon Valdez* oil spill, also Good Friday, Prince William Sound residents should be forgiven for any outward displays of nervousness when it comes time to celebrate the resurrection each year.

Valdez

GETTING THERE

Of all the communities bordering Prince William Sound, Valdez is the only one accessible by road. It's about 300 miles from Anchorage (north and east on the Glenn Highway to Glennallen, then south on the Richardson Highway to Valdez) and about 360 miles from Fairbanks (south on the Richardson Highway).

Valdez is a great destination for RVers or for those in cars wanting a hotel room. Both public and private parks for RVs and tents are available; there are many more camping spaces in Valdez than in either Anchorage or Fairbanks. Several hotels, though none in the luxury class, are available for those seeking rooms. Valdez also supports a thriving bed and breakfast industry.

Visitors can also fly into Valdez on either Alaska Airlines (planes are from its ERA Aviation affiliate) or MarkAir. Be aware,

however, that the weather in Valdez is frequently bad enough that flights can be delayed or canceled, sometimes for several days running. Numbers for airlines in Valdez are:

Alaska Airlines (ERA): **(907) 835-2636**
1-800-426-0333
MarkAir: **(907) 835-5147**
1-800-478-0800

Rental cars are available at the airport, and reservations can be made in advance through a travel agent.

Visitors can also reach Valdez via an Alaska Marine Highway ferry from either Cordova or Whittier. The M/V *Bartlett* makes several trips weekly in the summer. Call the **Alaska Marine Highway** offices in Valdez at **(907) 835-2400** or the ticket agency at **(907) 835-4436.**

FESTIVALS AND EVENTS

Appropriately enough, fishing derbies highlight the summer season in Valdez. The Sound as a whole, which includes Port Valdez (the large bay headed by the city of Valdez), boasts huge numbers of halibut, pink salmon and silver salmon. Derbies, with large cash prizes, are held for each of these species of fish.

The **halibut derby** runs throughout the summer with weekly prizes and an overall prize for the largest fish. Tickets are available from commercial outlets all over town and from most of the charter boat operators. Prizes are awarded strictly according to the weight of an individual fish. As a general rule, it will take at least a 200-pound halibut to claim the overall prize for the derby. Halibut in the range of 150 pounds are common weekly winners.

Next in line chronologically is the **pink salmon derby,** two frantic days of fishing on or near the July 4th weekend. Pink fishing can be done from shore or boat. As for all fishing derbies, you must buy your derby ticket in advance of your actual fishing. Good places for shore-based fishing for pinks include the ferry dock in downtown Valdez or Allison Point near the Alyeska pipeline terminal across the bay from Valdez. Because of the large number of RVs parked at the Allison Point pullout during July and August, the area is known locally as Winnebago Point. Expect the winner of the pink salmon derby to haul in a fish of about 10 pounds. The absolute favorite lure for pink salmon fishermen is a Pixie, a pounded silver spoon with a colored plastic insert. Green and pink seem to be favorite colors for the inserts.

Valdez's longest-running contest, the **silver salmon derby,** takes place during three weeks in August. Though shore-bound anglers have some success from Allison Point, most silver fishing is done from boats. Troll whole or cut-plug herring at varying depths until fish are found, then troll at that depth. Again, buy a derby ticket before fishing, and there must be at least two derby tickets on a boat for a fish to count—the fish must be caught by a ticket holder and observed by another. Seventeen-plus pounds of fighting silver salmon are generally required for your fish to be in the running for a prize.

Outside the fishing derbies, the most popular scheduled events are the annual **Valdez Winter Carnival** and **Gold Rush Days.** The latter event generally coincides

with the first week of the silver salmon derby; the winter carnival is held in mid-March. Both activities involve most of the residents in the town, and both are lots of fun.

A last event of note, though with a somewhat more narrow range of audience and participants, is the **Extreme Skiing Competition** held in early April at the summit of Thompson Pass, about 25 miles from Valdez. If plunging off of 3,000-foot cliffs with a couple of boards strapped to your feet, or watching others do it, qualifies as your idea of fun, this one's for you. It's definitely breathtaking, for both the doers and the watchers.

Call the **Valdez Convention and Visitors Bureau, (907) 835-2984,** for exact dates and additional details on all these events.

OUTDOOR ACTIVITIES

CRUISING

Valdez's most popular attraction may be the day-long cruises which include close-up views of one or more tidewater glaciers (usually Columbia Glacier) and a look at a variety of marine mammals. Most trips leave fairly early in the morning and stay out eight hours or more. Depending on the tour you select, prices range from $50 per person to $75 or slightly more.

Variations of these cruises include trips with a lunch stop on Growler Island and the option of a cruise that includes an overnight stay on the island. Prices go up accordingly for these trips.

The most-experienced cruise operator in Valdez is Stan Stephens Charters. Stephens and his family have been taking visitors on Prince William Sound cruises for nearly 30 years. The original boat, the relatively small *Vince Peedee,* has been replaced by a fleet of sleek new tour boats offering comfortable seats, snack bars and other amenities. Large picture windows and outdoor seating are available for passengers depending on the weather. Most hotel desks and campground managers

can arrange for tickets with Stan Stephens Charters or with any of the other sightseeing boats operating out of Valdez. Call **1-800-478-1297** for reservations and information on Stan Stephens Charters.

Longer cruises involving one or more overnights on board with all meals and comfortable berths are available as well. A good example is the *Natchik* run by Ken Valentine. Ken and his crew can take you out for a day's halibut fishing or up to six people on extended overnight cruises and fishing expeditions throughout the Sound. Call Ken at **(907) 835-5042** for more information and reservations.

An unusual experience can be had through **Phantom Mountain Adventures, (907) 835-2608.** They'll take your party for an overnight stay at Ellemar Lodge with lots of fishing and a side trip to Shoup Glacier. This is a much smaller boat, but a fast one. There's plenty of fishing and lots to see and do on this trip.

FISHING

It's often a toss-up as to which is most popular in Valdez, cruising to see the sights or testing your skill against the many fish available in Prince William Sound. As with cruising, an entire segment of the travel industry has grown up in Valdez to assist visitors in their fishing. From May through July, halibut day charters are the biggest draw; halibut compete with silver salmon for anglers in August. Few people do charter fishing for pinks; they're too easy to catch from the shore without going to the expense of hiring a boat. And because Port Valdez is usually pretty calm, those desiring to fish for pinks from the water need little more than a rowboat. If you do go boating on your own, keep a close watch on the tides and an eye on the weather.

Typical halibut charters start early in the morning and last about 12 hours or until everybody aboard catches a limit of two fish per person. Depending on the area where a skipper likes to fish, the boat ride to the fishing grounds can last from one to four hours with an equal amount of time required for your return. Halibut fishermen are generally asked to bring their own lunch and snacks; tackle and bait are provided. The best way to select a halibut charter is to walk the docks about 6 P.M. when the boats get in. Deckhands and fishermen will be cleaning their catch at stations provided on the docks, and a few minutes' observation and conversation

Passengers take in the views aboard the Alaska State Ferry. (Photo courtesy of the Alaska Division of Tourism)

should give you a good idea of which skippers are successful and who had a good time. Often, during peak periods, the boats make two 12-hour runs daily, one during the day and an all-nighter. The boat is in harbor just long enough to refuel and get a new crew before heading out again. Expect to pay $125 to $150 per person for a day-long halibut charter.

Silver salmon charters are usually of shorter duration and lower cost—about $75 to $100 per person. Tackle may or may not be provided depending on the operator. Most of the silver salmon fishing is done in or near Port Valdez, so the boat ride to the fishing grounds takes less time. Trolling is the preferred fishing method for silvers; herring is usually the favored bait. As with halibut charters, visit the docks in the late afternoon or evening to determine which boats are most successful and which parties had the most fun.

Charter fishing skippers in Valdez include

Capt. Jim's Great Alaska Charter Company—M/V *Sea Ruby* and M/V *Sea Gypsy*, **1-800-478-2280.** (Note: Capt. Jim's diesel-powered steel boats are quite noisy; it helps to bring along a set of ear plugs or other hearing protection.)

Edkath Charters—*Playtime*, **(907) 835-4346.**

Glacier Angler Charters—M/V *No Alibi*, **(907) 835-4734.**

C.R. Goodhand's Fishing Charters—**(907) 835-4333.**

Lil Fox Charters—M/V *Lil Fox* and M/V *Glacier Fox*, **(907) 835-2624.**

Patty Anne Charters—**(907) 835-2544.**

Something Fishy—**(907) 835-5732.**

FLIGHTSEEING

Weather permitting, there's no better way to see the massive glaciers and narrow fjords of Prince William Sound than from a light aircraft or helicopter. For flightseeing adventures from amphibious airplanes contact **Ketchum Air Service, (907) 835-3789.**

Helicopter flightseeing, which can offer even closer views under certain circumstances, is available from **ERA Helicopters, (907) 835-2595.** Helicopters are almost always more expensive than airplanes.

HIKING

Two trails for day hiking are available in or near Valdez. The first of these, **Soloman Gulch,** with two rather steep inclines, leads 1.3 miles from the fish hatchery on Dayville Road. Allow about three hours for a leisurely roundtrip. Soloman Lake at the end of the trail supplies about 80 percent of Valdez's electrical power.

The second trail is called **Goat Trail,** and follows the route of the original road through Keystone Canyon leading to Valdez. The trailhead is at Horsetail Falls, about 13.5 miles from Valdez on the Richardson Highway. Total one-way distance is about 5 miles.

Besides these trails, Valdez has an excellent bike path running out of the city alongside the Richardson Highway for several miles. Opportunities for viewing waterfowl, spawning pink salmon and occasionally a black bear are available along this route. A great after-dinner walk to help settle a good meal.

RIVER RAFTING

The Lowe River running through Keystone Canyon offers some of the most thrilling rafting in Alaska. Trips are available from **Keystone Raft & Kayak Adventures, (907) 835-2606.** Keystone also offers longer trips on various other rivers. Call for details.

——— INDOOR ATTRACTIONS ———

ALYESKA PIPELINE TERMINAL TOUR

Spend a couple of hours marveling at this huge facility that ships 25 percent of the oil used in the United States. There are several tours daily; call the **Valdez Visitors and Convention Bureau, (907) 835-2984,** for details.

VALDEZ MUSEUM

This is one of Alaska's best museums and it's located in the heart of downtown Valdez—just walk down Egan Drive and you'll see it. Several vestiges of Old Valdez (the town destroyed by the 1964 earthquake) are on display. Have a drink at Truck Egan's bar, saved from the old city and transported to New Valdez. Plan to spend a couple of hours. Admission is free, although the museum asks for donations of $1 per person if you enjoyed the exhibits.

——— WHERE TO STAY ———

ACCOMMODATIONS

(Valdez has no luxury hotels, and no really cheap lodgings in hotel accommodations. Prices are slightly higher than similar Anchorage-area hotels, generally falling into the $$$ range. There are hotels other than those listed here; these are representative.)

$$$
Totem Inn

As you approach the town by vehicle, the Totem is the first hotel you'll see, on the left. Clean, comfortable rooms, restaurant and bar. The restaurant is probably Valdez's favorite breakfast stop. Short walk to boat harbor and cruise or charter boats. **(907) 835-4443.**

Village Inn

Entering Valdez, this facility is immediately on your right. One hundred rooms, meeting facilities and health spa. Restaurant and bar in separate building next door. **(907) 835-4445.**

Westmark Valdez

Part of a chain of hotels in Yukon and Alaska, the Westmark Valdez is situated at the edge of the small boat harbor. You can linger over dinner in the restaurant or drinks in the lounge and watch the boats come and

go. Usually the most expensive hotel in town, though only by a few dollars. During the summer, the Westmark also operates a two-story annex on Egan Drive to handle additional guests. There is no restaurant or lounge at the annex site. **(907) 835-4391.**

BED AND BREAKFASTS

(Because of a critical lack of rental housing in Valdez during the *Exxon Valdez* oil spill in 1989, the bed and breakfast industry boomed. Most of the businesses formed then are still in operation and even more have been added since. This is probably the best thing that has happened for tourism in Valdez in decades. Popular as it was, Valdez frequently suffered a shortage of bed space during the height of the travel season before the bed and breakfast boom. Now, though Valdez can still be crowded, there's generally somewhere for every visitor to sleep.)

This rather extensive list of Valdez-area bed and breakfasts is by no means complete, but it does provide some idea of the wide variety of accommodations. Besides the B&Bs listed here, there's a referral service available to help if you just want to make a single phone call. Bonnie Stripe at Prince William Sound reservations, **(907) 835-3717,** provides B&B referrals as well as reservations services for charter and cruise operators in Valdez.

Alpine Mountain Inn—P.O. Box 1838, Valdez, AK 99686, (907) 835-2624.

Arctic Tern B&B—P.O. Box 1542, Valdez, AK 99686, (907) 835-5290.

Barra's Sunshine Inn—P.O. Box 1676, Valdez, AK 99686, (907) 835-2776.

Best of All B&B—P.O. Box 1578, Valdez, AK 99686, (907) 835-4524.

Birch Tree B&B—P.O. Box 2500, Valdez, AK 99686, (907) 835-4254.

Blueberry Mary's B&B—P.O. Box 1244, Valdez, AK 99686, (907) 835-5015.

The Boat House Bed and Sourdough Breakfast—P.O. Box 1815, Valdez, AK 99686, (907) 835-4407.

Casa de LaBellezza—P.O. Box 294, Valdez, AK 99686, (907) 835-4489.

Chalet Alpine View—P.O. Box 1888, Valdez, AK 99686, (907) 835-5223.

Colonial Inn B&B—P.O. Box 654, Valdez, AK 99686, (907) 835-4929.

Cooper's Cottage B&B—P.O. Box 563, Valdez, AK 99686, (907) 835-4810.

Copper Kettle B&B—P.O. Box 1133, Valdez, AK 99686, (907) 835-4627.

Downtown B&B Inn—P.O. Box 184, Valdez, AK 99686, (907) 835-2791.

Easy Living B&B—P.O. Box 2435, Valdez, AK 99686, (907) 835-4208.

Forget-Me-Not B&B—P.O. Box 1153, Valdez, AK 99686, (907) 835-2717.

France Inn B&B—P.O. Box 1295, Valdez, AK 99686, (907) 835-4295.

Frosty's B&B—P.O. Box 954, Valdez, AK 99686, (907) 835-4679.

Gussie's Lowe Street Inn—P.O. Box 64, Valdez, AK 99686, (907) 835-4448.

Kiska's B&B—P.O. Box 961, Valdez, AK 99686, (907) 835-4326.

The Mayne's Inn—631 S. Moraine Dr., Valdez, AK 99686, (907) 835-2388.

Northern Comfort B&B—P.O. Box 1135, Valdez, AK 99686, (907) 835-4308.

Orca House—P.O. Box 1821, Valdez, AK 99686, (907) 835-2814.

Pat's Place—733 Copper Dr., Valdez, AK 99686, (907) 835-5078.

Pine Tree Inn—P.O. Box 2090, Valdez, AK 99686, (907) 835-2779.

Porcupine Lodge B&B—P.O. Box 2530, Valdez, AK 99686, (907) 835-5150.

Puffin Inn—P.O. Box 1430, Valdez, AK 99686, (907) 835-5448.

Snowtree Inn—P.O. Box 2195, Valdez, AK 99686, (907) 835-4399.

Starr's Country Inn—P.O. Box 2197, Valdez, AK 99686, (907) 835-2917.

Wendy's B&B—P.O. Box 629, Valdez, AK 99686, (907) 835-4770.

Wildwood B&B—P.O. Box 875, Valdez, AK 99686, (907) 835-5038.

CAMPGROUNDS
Airport Campground
Operated by the city of Valdez, this facility is off the end of the runway. About $5 a night gets you a fairly private site screened by brush and trees, a picnic table and use of pit toilets. Water is available from a pump. Most sites have built-up pads for tents, necessary in the wet climate in this area. Pull-through sites available for larger rigs. About five miles from downtown. Keep a clean

camp as there are lots of black bears in the area.

Allison Point

Though not really a campground, this is one of the most popular RV parking places in the Valdez area. Those parked here can step from their rigs and cast for pinks in July and August and silvers in August. Starting in 1992, the city was charging $5 a night for parking, much to the disgust of long-time users; there was never previously a charge for parking at Allison Point. The only facilities are a couple of portable outhouses and a dumpster for trash. Though conditions can get tight during the height of the season, most people at Allison Point have a lot of fun during their stay; the atmosphere is fairly laid back, and there are a lot of fish to catch when the pinks are in.

Bear Paw Camper Park

Across the street from the boat harbor, this private facility offers the best RV parking available for those going out in cruise or charter boats. Cost is about $20 per night

per rig depending on the number of people in your party and hookups desired. Not particularly appropriate for tent campers. Can be noisy when the fishing fleet is in port and there are parties in the harbor. Very crowded at the height of the summer with limited space between rigs. Call **(907) 835-2530** for reservations and information.

Eagle's Rest RV Park

On the right as you pull into town, this private facility offers full hookups for RVs of any size. Not particularly suitable for tent campers. Within comfortable walking distance of most Valdez facilities. About $20 a night depending on number of people and hookups desired.

Sea Otter RV Park

You'll have to look a little for this one, but some of the sites offer superb views of the channel leading to the small boat harbor. Sea otters are frequently seen from the shore and hookups are available. Call **(907) 835-2787** for information and reservations. About $20 a night depending on number of people and hookups desired.

—————— WHERE TO EAT ——————

(Valdez offers none of the all-too-common, nationwide, fast-food emporiums. It also has no restaurants suitable for listing under the heading of fine dining. T-shirts, shorts, jeans or whatever are all appropriate dress at any time.)

$$–$$$
The Pipeline Club

Serves the biggest and, some say, best steaks in town. Full-service bar. On Egan Drive downtown. **(907) 835-4332.**

Wheelhouse

The dining room in the Westmark Hotel is probably the most lavish in Valdez. Good steaks and Alaska seafoods in season. Overlooks the small boat harbor. **(907) 835-4391.**

$–$$
Alaska Halibut House

At the corner of Fairbanks and Meals, the Halibut House is Valdez's answer to fast-food restaurants. Eat in or take out seafood (mostly fried) and burgers. **(907) 835-2788.**

Cafe Valdez

This one's a little different. Generally open weekdays for lunch, but not always for dinner. Deli sandwiches and daily specials depending on the mood of the chef. (Thursday's special is always a Reuben, but menu varies on other days of the week.) Relaxed and informal. **310 Egan Drive. (907) 835-5455.**

Mike's Palace

Without a doubt the most popular dinner spot in town. There's almost always a line in the evenings during the summer. Besides pizza, there are Mexican dishes and American standbys. Desserts can be very good. North Harbor Drive across from the small boat harbor. **(907) 835-2365.**

Totem

Probably Valdez's favorite breakfast stop. Wide range of omelets. Predictably American fare for lunch and dinner. Part of the Totem Inn as you come into town.

Limit of Halibut, Valdez, Alaska. (Photo by Ron Dalby)

Cordova

GETTING THERE

Someday, as was mentioned earlier, you may be able to drive to Cordova. In the meantime, access is pretty limited—a Boeing 737 from Alaska Airlines or the Alaska Marine Highway's M/V *Bartlett*.

A northbound Alaska Airlines jet originating in Seattle stops in Cordova daily. A southbound airliner, originating in Anchorage, does the same. The northbound flight is an up and down trip, stopping in Ketchikan, Juneau and Yakutat before landing at Cordova. Cordova is the first stop southbound from Anchorage. Locally,

Alaska Airlines's jets are known as "salmon-thirty-salmons," because they haul a lot of freshly caught fish from Cordova to restaurants in Seattle.

Alaska Airlines: **1-800-426-0333**

The Alaska Marine Highway's M/V *Bartlett* calls several times weekly in Cordova during the summer months. Board with or without your vehicle in either Whittier or Valdez.

FESTIVALS AND EVENTS

Cordova's major annual fling, and a midwinter event attended by Alaskans from all over, is the **Iceworm Festival** held in mid-February. Nine big days, with most of the best events during the last big weekend. It has parade, various contests including a survival-suit race (jumping into the partly frozen harbor and swimming to a

life raft wearing a complete cold-water survival suit) and a host of parties. Be prepared to laugh and have a good time; you'll have ample opportunities for both. Contact the **Cordova Chamber of Commerce, (907) 424-7260,** for specific dates and details. The Iceworm Festival is one of Alaska's best winter parties.

ACTIVITIES

BIRD-WATCHING

The **Copper River Delta,** just a few miles east of Cordova proper, is literally a duck factory. Breeding waterfowl congregate here every summer, including trumpeter swans and geese as well as the ducks and a host of other species. Easily accessed by road, the area can be watched from the car or you can get out and slog around in the marsh for closer views. Other wildlife you might see include brown bears, fox and Sitka black-tailed deer. An excellent place to add to your life list if you're a

serious birder. Many of the streams lacing the delta are filled with silver salmon in August and Dolly Varden and cutthroat trout at almost any time of the year.

CORDOVA MUSEUM

This dandy facility in downtown Cordova gives you a glimpse of the past in the southeastern corner of Prince William Sound. There are lots of interesting things to look over, including Cordova's original telephone switchboard. Contact the museum at **(907) 424-6665** for operating hours.

FISHING

Though Cordova's economy is based on commercial fishing, there is all but unlimited opportunity for freshwater or saltwater sportfishing. The most sought-after species are halibut, silver salmon, cutthroat trout and Dolly Varden. The Eyak River on the edge of town offers excellent opportunities for Dollies and silver salmon. Other streams a little farther east of town have the same or even better fishing. Prince William Charters, listed above, can get you offshore for halibut or saltwater fishing for silver salmon or can put you ashore on various cutthroat streams.

Two other businesses serving sport fishermen in Cordova are **Alaska Wilderness Outfitting Co., (907) 424-5552,** and **Cordova Charters, (907) 424-5895.**

WHERE TO STAY

ACCOMMODATIONS

$$–$$$
Cordova Hotel
Nothing fancy, just serviceable rooms in downtown Cordova on First Street. Includes a bar. **(907) 424-3388.**

Prince William Motel
Again, nothing fancy, but downtown Cordova. **(907) 424-3201.**

The Reluctant Fisherman Inn
The best located and most modern hotel in Cordova, the Reluctant sits atop a small bluff overlooking the small boat harbor. Restaurant and lounge. **(907) 424-3272.**

WHERE TO EAT

$$–$$$
The Club Cafe
Behind the Club Bar in downtown Cordova. Great breakfasts and standard lunch and dinner fare. Occasional specials such as fresh razor clams. **(907) 424-3405.**

The Powder House
A short distance on the only road leading out of town, which goes to the airport.

Can be lively. Overlooks Eyak Lake and has large deck area for relaxing in good weather. **(907) 424-3529.**

The Reluctant Fisherman
Clean, comfortable restaurant, part of the Reluctant Fisherman Inn. **(907) 424-7446.**

Whittier

GETTING THERE

If ever the old adage "Getting there is half the fun" applies, it is to Whittier. One does not drive to Whittier or fly to Whittier. You first drive to Portage and board an Alaska Railroad train, either as a walk-on passenger or by driving your car onto a flatcar. Then it's about a 30-minute train ride through (literally) the mountains, most of it in the darkest tunnels imaginable, to Whittier. If you drive your car aboard, you ride to Whittier seated in your car; only walk-on passengers get to ride in railroad passenger cars.

The train runs back and forth several times daily during the summer months, usually about every 90 minutes to two hours. Other than the train, your only option is the

Alaska Marine Highway ferry, the M/V *Bartlett*, from either Valdez or Cordova. If you take the ferry, arrange your schedule so you'll at least have the opportunity to take the train either into or out of Whittier. This is one of those rides it would be a shame to miss. You don't know what dark really is until you're halfway through a tunnel that's several miles long.

There is no regularly scheduled air service of any kind to Whittier.

In 1992, an idea of blasting a road through to Whittier was making the rounds in Alaska, though no formal action had yet been taken at this writing. If the road goes, it will be much like the railroad, mostly underground.

FESTIVALS AND EVENTS

The major event of the summer season is the July 4th salmon bake held for residents and visitors alike. Lots of food. For

more information on this or anything else going on in Whittier, call the city offices at **(907) 472-2337.**

ACTIVITIES

CRUISING

Unless mountain climbing is your bag, there's really no place to go in Whittier except to sea on Prince William Sound. But these voyages are worthwhile in every sense of the word.

For those who can only devote a day to the Whittier area, you can hardly go wrong with the 26 Glacier Cruise. For about $120 per person, you are whisked deep into College Fjord on the M/V *Klondike*, a twin-hulled powerboat that is probably the fastest cruiser in Prince William Sound.

This trip is a photographer's dream with wildlife onshore and offshore, and more glaciers in a single voyage than any other trip in Alaska. Despite its speed, this is one of the most stable boats afloat.

The cost cited above is for the boat trip only. **Phillip's Cruises,** based in Anchorage, can make reservations for the cruise and also arrange for transportation to Whittier for an additional fee. Call them at **(907) 276-8023** or **1-800-544-0529** for details.

For extended cruises of a few days to a week or more, two Whittier-based operators can help. Alaska's **Freedom Charter and Sales** operates the *Mariah*, a 32-foot sailboat for $125 per person per day. You'll sail through the Sound, stopping occasionally to go ashore and explore. Fishing tackle is provided for halibut and salmon. Call **(907) 472-2376** for details.

Sound Water Adventures (SWA) offers day or overnight trips aboard the *Sound Runner*. Another specialty is the dropping off and picking up of kayakers planning to paddle at their own pace through parts of the Sound. Starting in 1992, SWA claims to have "Alaska's first beachable, wheelchair accessible tour boat." Up to 1,200 pounds of people and gear per trip. **(907) 472-2455.**

FISHING

Several operators in Whittier can take you out for a day's fishing for salmon, halibut or other bottom fish. Call the city of **Whittier** at **(907) 472-2337** for details.

—— WHERE TO STAY/WHERE TO EAT ——

$$–$$$

Accommodations in Whittier are limited; this is, after all, a pretty small town. Both inns have restaurants and bars on the premises offering fairly standard fare. Try the **Anchor Inn, (907) 472-2354,** or the **Sportsman Inn, (907) 472-2461.** Facilities and services are similar at both, as are the prices.

Columbia Glacier from Prince William Sound. (Photo by Ron Dalby)

The Great Interior

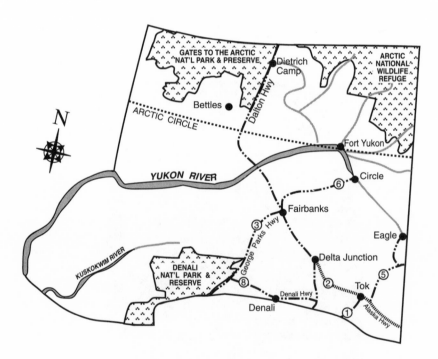

THE GREAT INTERIOR

OVERVIEW

In a word: GOLD! The precious yellow metal, more than anything else, is responsible for the contemporary development of Alaska's vast Interior. Without the gold, this would likely have remained a little-developed and relatively unpopulated region.

Whenever people connect Alaska to gold, they immediately think of the Klondike gold rush of the late 1890s. In fact, there were two major, active gold-mining areas in Interior Alaska well before gold was discovered near Dawson in 1896. Miners were very active in the Forty Mile area north of present-day Tok, and there was considerable gold being brought out of the Central area north of Fairbanks near the Yukon River. Both areas are still producing gold today.

But the timing of these two earlier gold strikes in the 1870s and 1880s wasn't quite right for a major gold rush, and though good quantities of gold were and are available, it was nothing like the quantity close to the surface near Dawson. Thus the Alaska gold rush of 1898, which occurred during a major economic depression in the United States, was actually in Canada. However, the Klondike goldfields are just a few short miles east of the Alaska-Canada border.

Most of those who rushed to the Klondike were U.S. citizens, so Dawson quickly came to be a Canadian city populated by people from the United States. Only local law enforcement and other government agencies were decidedly Canadian. By the time the real rush was on, most of the good ground had been staked; fortune seekers in Dawson from 1898 on had to be looking elsewhere for productive ground that they could call their own.

Felix Pedro had lost out in Dawson by arriving too late. But he did a little figuring before setting out to prospect in Alaska. If, as indeed was the case, there were good quantities of gold near Circle and in the Forty Mile country, both of which are on the north side of a low range of mountains between the Yukon and Tanana rivers, there should be gold available on the south side of those same mountains. Or so Pedro thought, and he wasn't alone with that idea. At the turn of the century, Pedro bought a burro and struck out overland from Circle, south toward the Chena and Tanana rivers.

He found gold once, then lost it when he couldn't find his way back to it. By August 1901, he was a bit disgusted with himself but not really discouraged; he knew the gold was there. Pedro was preparing to head for Circle, about 100 miles away for supplies, when he saw the smoke from a riverboat some miles away near the Chena River. With a little luck, he figured he might get enough supplies there to save him a trip to Circle.

And he was right. The *Lavalle Young* was then in the process of unloading E. T. Barnette, a few other people, and a large supply of trade goods on the bank of the Chena River. Barnette had wanted to go much farther up the Tanana River to build a trading post where he had inside information about a trail to the Interior being pushed through. Unable to get any farther on the Tanana, the skipper sailed a couple of miles up the Chena and unceremoniously dumped Barnette and his party on the bank, in line with the agreement the two men had made if the boat was unable to penetrate the upper reaches of the Tanana River.

Barnette happily made his first sale to Pedro who soon disappeared into the woods north of the Chena River. After building cabins and storage buildings, Barnette and his wife mushed outside in early winter to take a ship from Valdez to the southern states. Leaving his brother-in-law in charge of the fledgling trading post, Barnette gave strict orders to sell trade goods and supplies only for cash; he didn't want to be grubstaking a lot of indigent, would-be gold miners.

In one of the most fortunate acts of civil disobedience in the North, Barnette's brother-in-law disobeyed his orders when a broke Felix Pedro showed up to buy more supplies for the summer of 1902. Living off these borrowed supplies in July 1902, Pedro struck gold about 14 miles north of present-day Fairbanks.

Barnette, meanwhile, back in Saint Michael at the mouth of the Yukon, had just decided to name his new trading post "Fairbanks" for political reasons. He heard of Pedro's strike and rushed to the scene. Wise in the ways of the North, Barnette and his brother-in-law quickly staked all the good ground they could find in their own names and in the names of all their friends and relatives. The few others who arrived that summer of 1902 did exactly the same thing. It came to be, even before the real rush to Fairbanks started, that a few men held title to most of the productive ground.

But that didn't stop miners from rushing to Fairbanks from Dawson and Nome over the winter. Fairbanks boomed and from then on would be the population center for Interior Alaska.

Were it not for gold, the site of Fairbanks had little chance of being picked as the place for what would be Alaska's largest city for the next four decades. It gets frightfully cold in Fairbanks and the surrounding area during the winter. Weeks of 40-below zero are common, and temperatures of 65-below zero are routine at times during these cold snaps. The summer temperatures reach 90 degrees or more. Interior Alaska is both the hottest and the coldest part of Alaska.

Wherever a gold rush creates a town, it creates an economic decline when the easy-to-find gold is depleted. From its earliest days, Fairbanks has had just this kind of boom-and-bust economy. The initial bust was followed by a smaller boom in gold mining when heavy dredges were brought in during the 1920s to sift the precious dust from area streams; afterwards things declined again. During World War II, Fairbanks boomed again as the end of the road for the Alaska Highway project and as a stopover for pilots delivering lend-lease aircraft to Russia via the Siberian route. In the 1950s and early 1960s, Fairbanks declined again. In the late 1960s, discovery of oil on the North Slope of Alaska generated another boom that lasted through the construction of the trans-Alaska pipeline and until the mid-1980s when the price of oil declined.

Today, Fairbanks's major industries are government and serving as a supply center for Alaska's Interior. Though things are not nearly as bad as in earlier busts, the economy is far from strong these days. There is, too, the potential for another oil boom in the Arctic National Wildlife Refuge little more than 100 miles from the Prudhoe Bay wellhead. However, with a democratic administration in Washington as of January 1993, the odds of this oil field being developed in the immediate future are fairly low.

Gold is still being extracted north of Fairbanks near Central and Circle, from the Livengood area northwest of town and from Eureka west of Livengood. However, increasingly strict water-quality standards and other environmental laws are making it tougher and tougher to earn a profit mining gold.

But Fairbanks and its people are tough, too, sometimes tougher than the law. In late 1992, Fairbanks successfully challenged a federal mandate requiring the sale of oxygenated gasoline in all area gas stations.

People there didn't like it because this gas was more expensive, it didn't work very well in snow machines and other gas-powered recreation equipment and it was seen as another attempt by an unsympathetic government in Washington, D.C., to regulate something the lawmakers knew nothing about. The challenge in court, however, was somewhat more sophisticated. The oxygenated gas mandate was discontinued for Fairbanks simply because lawyers pointed out that its use had never been tested in arctic conditions. For now, Fairbanks is the only city required to dispense oxygenated gas under federal air pollution guidelines that is legally exempt from the requirement. Look for this battle to surface again in the years ahead.

Though Fairbanks is the hub of Alaska's Interior, it isn't the only place to visit in this vast part of the state. Highway travelers will almost certainly become familiar with Tok, Delta Junction, Nenana and of course Denali National Park. Then, too, there's the bush, never more than a few minutes' flying time away from any town in Alaska's Interior.

Nome Creek gold dredge near Fairbanks. (Photo by Ron Dalby)

Dawson City, Yukon

Though Dawson is technically in Canada and seems at first glance outside the scope of an Alaskan guidebook, its omission would be a serious error. Contemporary Alaskan history begins with Dawson and the Klondike gold rush in the late 1890s, when the character of today's Alaska, and particularly Interior Alaska, began to take shape. Also, Dawson is so close to the Alaska border that its character is as much Alaskan as Canadian.

By road, Dawson is easily accessed by driving north on the gravel Taylor Highway from Tok, crossing into Canada at Boundary then driving an additional few miles down to the bank of the Yukon River. There is no bridge at Dawson, but a free ferry will get you and your vehicle across the river and into town.

On the Alaska side of the river there's a very nice Yukon Territorial Campground at the water's edge. A government campground, this park has no RV hookups. Those wanting hookups will find several RV parks in or near Dawson.

Staying at the park on the riverbank, though, does provide something you won't find in town. After you set up camp here, take a short walk downstream along the river's edge. Shortly you'll find yourself in the graveyard of the sternwheelers that used to ply the North's mightiest river. Several boats, gradually being disintegrated by the elements, were parked here at the end of their last season of work on the

river and abandoned. The growth of a road system in Yukon and Alaska spelled their demise. No longer did goods have to be barged upstream from the mouth of the river. Freight could be trucked to closer destinations, and, where necessary, moved to riverfront communities by a system of modern tugs and barges working shorter trips. The grand era of the river steamers, which actually lasted into the early 1960s, ended with the highway system. (Alaska's lone congressman, Don Young of Fort Yukon, is a qualified river pilot from the last days of the sternwheelers.)

In Dawson itself, there's a fully restored sternwheeler sitting high and dry on the riverbank, and tours of it are run several times daily in the summer months.

As a town, Dawson is sort of a living history project. Downtown buildings are required to be built or refurbished in the style of the late 1890s. Boardwalks are still in use in lieu of concrete sidewalks, and recreations of nightlife during the gold rush are part of the local scene. If you want just a taste of the way things were during the gold rush and a glimpse at where contemporary Alaska got its start, Dawson should be on your list of places to visit during an Alaska vacation.

In planning your visit to Dawson, be sure to contact the **Klondike Visitors Association, P.O. Box 389, Dawson City, Yukon, Canada Y0B 1G0,** or call **(403) 993-5575.**

FESTIVALS AND EVENTS

CANADA DAY

July 1st is Canada's equivalent of Independence Day in the United States. And like small-town Alaska, small-town Canada seems to do a much better job of celebrating than the larger cities. Any town in Yukon, for that matter, is a good place to be on July 1st, for parades, games and just a general good time.

173

DISCOVERY DAYS

Several days in mid-August celebrate the finding of gold on the Klondike in 1896. The one-hundredth anniversary of the discovery in 1996 should be an extra-special event if your schedule brings you this way.

YUKON QUEST

This 1,000-mile sled dog race between Whitehorse and Fairbanks commemorates those who rushed to Fairbanks for gold in the winter of 1902–3. Though not as well known as the longer-running Iditarod, most mushers consider this race much more grueling and a better test of skills. There are fewer checkpoints along the way compared to the Iditarod, which means much more gear must be carried. And, since it's run earlier in the winter than the Iditarod, the weather tends to be more severe. When the mushers reach Dawson, they are required to take a 24-hour layover to rest themselves and their teams. Dawson wakes briefly from its winter slumber to greet the mushers and provide some trailside recreation. Great winter party.

For information on this and the other events noted here, contact the Klondike Visitors Centers at the address and telephone number given previously.

— ACTIVITIES —

DIAMOND TOOTH GERTIE'S

Saloon, dance hall and gambling casino, Gertie's does a pretty good job of recreating gold rush revelry. Gambling is legal here, and there are plenty of tables with various games to test your luck. The floor show is great, too.

MIDNIGHT SUN

Though Dawson itself is just barely below the Arctic Circle, you can see the midnight sun on June 21 and 22, weather permitting, from the top of Midnight Dome, the mountain rising behind the town. A road leads to the top of the hill. This is one of the most accessible places in Yukon and Alaska for watching the sun that never sets.

MUSEUM

Dawson City Museum, Old Territorial Administration Building on Fifth Avenue. Historic train collection, city life gallery. **(403) 993-5291.**

PALACE GRAND THEATRE

Melodramas and light sketches are performed by professional actors much as was done at the turn of the century. It's a great way to spend an evening, so get your tickets early.

TOURS

Gold City Tours, (403) 993-5175, can take you through downtown Dawson and its historic buildings and on out to the Klondike goldfields.

WALKING TOUR

Stroll through gold rush history as you peer into restored shops and buildings, all part of the northern edge of Klondike Goldrush Historic Park. Maps and brochures to aid your interpretation of the buildings are available at the visitors center in the old Northern Commercial Co. building at the corner of Front and King streets.

Recommended Reading:
Klondike Park: From Seattle to Dawson City, Archie Satterfield, Fulcrum, 1993.

WHERE TO STAY

ACCOMMODATIONS

(*Author's note:* Dawson operates little more than three months a year, therefore most things are relatively expensive. And, because everything is operating at capacity during the short summer season, don't expect to find any bargains.)

$$$

Downtown Hotel
    2nd and Queen streets. Saloon and restaurant. **(403) 993-5076.**

Eldorado Hotel
    3rd and Princess. Lounge and restaurant. **(403) 993-5451.**

Klondike Kate's
    3rd and King streets. TV in every cabin. **(403) 993-5491.**

Triple JJJ Hotel
    5th and Queen streets, next to Diamond Tooth Gertie's. Lounge and restaurant. **(403) 993-5323.**

Westmark Inn
    5th and Harpter streets. Part of chain in Alaska and Yukon. Restaurant and lounge. **1-800-544-0970 from the U.S.; 1-800-999-2570** in Canada.

BED AND BREAKFASTS
Dawson City B&B—(403) 993-5649.

5th Avenue B&B—(403) 993-5941.

White Ram Manor B&B—(403) 993-5772.

CAMPGROUNDS
Dawson City RV Park and Campground
    Hookups and dump station, showers, car wash and gold panning. **(403) 993-5142.**

Gold Rush Campground RV Park
    5th and York downtown. Hookups, store and laundromat. **(403) 993-5247.**

Guggie Ville
    On Bonanza Creek a couple of minutes from the city center. Hookups, gold panning and gift shop. **(403) 993-5226.**

Gaslight Follies Building, Dawson City, Yukon Territory, Canada. (© 1993 Alissa Crandall)

Tok

From Dawson City, Yukon, the obvious overland route to Alaska leads you down the Taylor Highway, through the mining town of Chicken, to Tok. Along the way, there's a turnoff for Eagle on the banks of the Yukon River in Alaska.

This is a gravel road, and not necessarily the best one in Alaska, either. It's only about 150 miles from Dawson to Tok, so take your time. After you get to Tok, there are faster roads to drive on if you're in a hurry.

Whether you drive into Alaska via the Taylor Highway from Dawson or the Alaska Highway from Whitehorse, Tok is the first Alaska town most people remember reaching. It's an important road junction. From there you can go northwest to Fairbanks, south to Valdez and Anchorage, north to Dawson, or southeast to Whitehorse. As you'll quickly learn driving about in Alaska, having four options at a single junction is a big deal. In fact, Tok is the only such road junction in Alaska.

Most who visit Tok only do so as an overnight stop en route to somewhere else. That's unfortunate, because there are several things to see and do in the area, and for those just arriving in Alaska by vehicle, this is the first chance to get a feel for the "Last Frontier."

Tok doesn't have its own visitors center, as such. However, the chamber of commerce operates a small building next door to the Alaska Public Lands Information Center. For information on visiting Tok and the surrounding area, contact the **Alaska Public Lands Information Center, P.O. Box 359, Tok, AK 99780, (907) 883-5667.**

Directly across the road from the Public Lands Information Center is the office for the U.S. Fish and Wildlife Service, managers of the nearby Tetlin National Wildlife Refuge. Contact them by writing **Tetlin National Wildlife Refuge, P.O. Box 155, Tok, AK 99780,** or call **(907) 883-5312.**

ACTIVITIES

ARTS AND NATIVE CRAFTS

Native crafts are available at several outlets in Tok and at the Native-operated gift shop at Northway Junction southeast of Tok on the Alaska Highway. Birch baskets, beaded moccasins, boots and necklaces are the most common items available. **Snowshoe Fine Arts and Gifts, (907) 883-4511,** offering a variety of works by Alaskan artists, including bronzes by noted Alaskan artist Frank Entsminger, is a good place to stop for something authentically Alaskan.

BIKE TRAIL

A 13-mile bike trail winds through and around Tok, with access available at several points in town.

FISHING

Fishing in the Tok area is mostly fly-in for freshwater species such as grayling, northern pike and lake trout. Inquire at the Tok airstrip for flying services that can put you in a fishing hotspot.

MUKLUK LAND

Museum, northern lights video, dogsled rides, Native dancers and more. **(907) 883-2571.**

SLED DOGS

For years, Tok has been known as the "Sled Dog Capital of Alaska." A number of residents are actively engaged in breeding or training dogs. Visitors looking for either a pet or a racing sled dog will have a number of options in Tok.

—————— WHERE TO STAY ——————

ACCOMMODATIONS
$$–$$$
Snowshoe Motel
Across from the Public Lands Information Center and part of a complex with Snowshoe Fine Arts and Gifts. **(907) 883-4511.**

Tok Lodge
Along the Alaska Highway. Restaurant, lounge and package liquor store. **(907) 883-2852.**

Westmark Tok
Part of a chain in Alaska and Yukon. Restaurant and lounge. Junction of Alaska and Glenn highways. **1-800-544-0970** from the United States, **1-800-999-2570** from Canada.

Young's Motel
On the Alaska Highway. Restaurant. **(907) 883-4411.**

CAMPGROUNDS
As you might guess, Tok offers a multitude of RV parks because of its status as the first major road junction travelers reach when entering Alaska. If you arrive late in the day or evening, you may have to hunt around a bit before you find a vacancy.

The Bull Shooter RV Park
Mile 1313.3 on Alaska Highway. Part of a complex with sporting goods store of the same name. Hookups. **(907) 883-5625.**

Rita's Campground RV Park
Mile 1315.7 on Alaska Highway. Hookups, fireplaces with free wood, gift shop. **(907) 883-4342.**

Sourdough Campground
One of the oldest and best RV parks in Tok. About two miles south of town on the Tok Cutoff toward Anchorage. Restaurant (breakfast only) and gift shop. **(907) 883-5543.**

Tok RV Village
Mile 1313.4 on Alaska Highway. Full or partial hookups, handicap accessible, and gift shop. Accepts reservations. **(907) 883-5877.**

—————— WHERE TO EAT ——————

$$
Sourdough Pancake Breakfast
Sourdough RV Park, two miles south of town on Tok Cutoff. Specializes in sourdough hotcakes and reindeer sausage. Serves breakfast only until 11 A.M. **(907) 883-5543.**

Tok Gateway Salmon Bake
Barbecued king salmon, halibut, reindeer sausage, ribs and buffalo burgers. RV parking on site (no hookups). **(907) 883-5555.**

Delta Junction

Folks in Delta will quickly and pridefully tell you that their town is the official end of the Alaska Highway, not Fairbanks as most outsiders seem to think. The reason for this is that the road from Delta to Fairbanks, officially the Richardson Highway, is the final leg of the route running from Valdez to Fairbanks (via Delta Junction), and had been in operation long before anyone ever thought of building the Alaska Highway.

Next to Palmer, the area around Delta is Alaska's largest farming region, this because of a state-sponsored program that was at least somewhat more successful than the dairy farm fiasco in the Mat–Su Valley. The crops are primarily grains and potatoes, and crop levels are determined mostly by in-state demand for the items. No one has yet been able to find much of an outside market for these items owing to the high cost of transporting them overseas. (An unused grain elevator at tidewater in Valdez, built as part of the Delta farming project, is mute testimony to the lack of an international market.)

Contact or stop by the **Delta Visitors Information Center** at the highway junction in town, or call **(907) 895-9941.**

FESTIVALS AND EVENTS

BUFFALO WALLOW
Four-day square dance event held over Memorial Day weekend at the end of May.

JULY 4TH
Independence Day is big in Delta, with a buffalo barbecue and all the usual events.

DELTANA FAIR
A kind of mini state fair held the first Friday, Saturday and Sunday of August.

ACTIVITIES

BUFFALO VIEWING
American bison were transplanted into the Delta area during the 1920s. The herd today numbers about 500 or a little more. It began to thrive particularly when the state-sponsored farming project took root in Delta. Farmers, though, are not too impressed by the beasts. The best place to observe the animals is at mile 241 of the Richardson Highway, about 25 miles south of town. A viewpoint is there, and you will probably need binoculars. Keep an eye out for moose also.

FISHING
The Delta-Clearwater River, about 13 miles east of town, offers excellent opportunities for grayling and whitefish. Silver salmon are available in October, just before freeze-up. Quartz Lake, access road about 10 miles northwest on the Richardson Highway, offers good to excellent fishing for stocked rainbows and landlocked silver salmon. State campgrounds are available at both locations.

RIKA'S ROADHOUSE

A popular Alaska Highway stop for most major tour companies, Rika's is a restored roadhouse with a gift shop and restaurant set amidst a 10-acre park on the banks of the Tanana River. Admission is free, tours are available. The staff is in period costumes from the turn of the century. The roadhouse is nine miles northeast of Delta on the Richardson Highway.

———— WHERE TO STAY ————

ACCOMMODATIONS
$$

Alaska 7 Motel
Four miles northwest of Delta. **(907) 895-4848.**

Cherokee Lodge
Mile 1412.5 on Alaska Highway, about 10 miles southeast of Delta. Restaurant and lounge. **(907) 895-4814.**

Kelly's Country Inn Motel
Downtown Delta. **(907) 895-4667.**

Miner's House and Hide-A-Way
Five miles northwest of Delta. Restaurant. **(907) 895-1084.**

CAMPGROUNDS
Bergstad's Travel and Trailer Court
Mile 1420.9 on Alaska Highway (1 mile southeast of Delta). **(907) 895-4856.**

Smith's Green Acres RV Park
Two miles northwest of Delta on Richardson Highway. **(907) 895-4369.**

Rika's Roadhouse, Mile 1431 on the Alaska Highway. (© 1993 Alissa Crandall)

Fairbanks

Fairbanksans call their town the Golden Heart City of Alaska, and, indeed, the state's second-largest community sits near the geographic center of Alaska. There may be other, subtler meanings. Fairbanks is the major transshipment point for goods going into more remote locations in Alaska, thus it can be considered the hub of the Interior. Also, it's a reference to the friendly people you're likely to meet in Fairbanks.

Two large military bases, Fort Wainwright at the southeastern edge of town, and Eileson Air Force Base about 20 miles to the southeast, are part of the town's character, much more so than military bases in other areas tend to be part of their local communities. You rarely see any local business put off limits to soldiers by military authorities, and local folks tend to include the Army and the Air Force in community functions whenever possible.

Another group living in the region for much of the year are students at the University of Alaska on the northwest side of town. Like the military, relatively few of these young men and women are from Fairbanks, though most of them are from Alaska. The Fairbanks campus is the head-

quarters for the statewide University of Alaska system.

All these elements, plus the long-time residents of Fairbanks, tend to make Fairbanks quite diverse in skills, talents and attitudes. Most Fairbanksans are proud of that diversity, and proud to stand up for their own small part of that diversity—city council meetings aren't always calm, cool and collected.

The frontier—or the wilderness—is never very far away from Fairbanks. To the south loom the massive peaks of the Alaska Range; north are the less tall but no less magnificent mountains of the Brooks Range. Denali National Park to the south straddles the Alaska Range, and Gates of the Arctic National Park to the north covers the central Brooks Range. Fairbanks is the closest major city to both places.

For additional information on visiting Fairbanks, contact the **Fairbanks Visitors and Convention Bureau, 550 1st Avenue, Fairbanks, AK 99701, (907) 456-5774 or 1-800-327-5774.** Ask them to send you a *Fairbanks Visitor's Guide*, a book in itself that offers much more complete listings of facilities and activities than is possible here.

FESTIVALS AND EVENTS

SUMMER SOLSTICE

The longest day of the year in Fairbanks generates some special activities. Among these is a baseball game that starts at 10:45 P.M. without lights and generally lasts until midnight or later. The Fairbanks Goldpanners, the local semi pro team, always puts on a good show, and has graduated some top-flight players into the major leagues. The Yukon 800, a boat race of outboard-powered skiffs on the Tanana

and Yukon rivers kicks off on the same day (June 21) with the winners coming in the next day, having gone all the way downstream to Galena and back.

FAIRBANKS SUMMER ARTS FESTIVAL

This is two weeks of workshops, classes, concerts and performances in late July and early August. Almost all performing and visual arts are involved.

GOLDEN DAYS

The nine-day bash in mid-July celebrates Felix Pedro's discovery of gold north of Fairbanks and is highlighted by all sorts of activities including a parade, pancake breakfasts, a dance, canoe and raft races and outdoor concerts. It's a great time to visit Fairbanks.

WORLD ESKIMO-INDIAN OLYMPICS

Usually toward the end of the Golden Days celebration, the Olympics include such traditional contests as ear pulls, knuckle walks, high kicks and many other activities.

———— ACTIVITIES ————

ALASKALAND PIONEER PARK

Historic buildings, shops, playgrounds and entertainment are all available at this park alongside Airport Way. There's a **Native Village Museum** as well as the displays of buildings demonstrating the white person's early presence in the Fairbanks area. The **Palace Grand Theatre** presents its Golden Heart Review seven nights a week at 8 P.M. **(907) 459-1087.**

ALASKA WILDLIFE PARK

Bears, caribou, fox and other Alaskan animals live in natural settings. A petting zoo is available for children. Closed Tuesdays. College Road, 1 mile east of intersection with University Avenue.

CHENA HOT SPRINGS

Large pool filled with water from a natural hot spring about 58 miles from Fairbanks at the end of Chena Hot Springs Road. Hotel, RV parking and restaurant on site. **(907) 452-7867.**

CREAMER'S FIELD

This is both a state historic site and a wildlife refuge within the city limits. Spring officially returns to Fairbanks when the geese arrive at Creamer's Field around the middle of April. Sandhill cranes use the facility throughout the summer, and geese and other waterfowl gather before flying south in the fall. The historic site is the large dairy that operated on these grounds

for many years. The buildings are still standing and can be explored on a tour. **(907) 452-1531.**

FISHING

Freshwater streams and lakes in the Fairbanks area offer a host of opportunities to try your luck for grayling, northern pike, lake trout and stocked rainbow trout. The Chena River, running through town, traditionally has been Alaska's largest grayling fishery, but bag limits are severely restricted now because of a fall-off in the number of fish. The Chatinika River north of town on the Steese Highway offers opportunities for grayling. Minto Flats just northwest of Fairbanks is the favorite hole for northern pike. Though you can drive to the flats and take a boat, it's almost always easier to go in with one of the local flying services; you'll have a line in the water 20 minutes after you take off from Fairbanks.

If stocked rainbows are your goal, head 20 miles southeast to the Chena Lakes Recreation Area. Lots of fish are here, and swimming beaches are available for the hot Interior days.

GOLD DREDGE NUMBER 8

North of town on the Old Steese Highway, this is a **National Mechanical Engineering Historic Landmark** (isn't that a mouthful?), with the only gold dredge in Alaska open to the public. Collection of mammoth tusks on display. Gold panning at your leisure; you keep anything you find. **(907) 457-6058.**

GOLFING

The **Fairbanks Golf and Country Club** offers a nine-hole course at the corner of Farmers Loop and Ballantine Road. **(907) 479-6555.** On Fort Wainwright, the nine-hole **Chena Bend Golf Course** is available to duffers. **(907) 355-6749.**

THE MALEMUTE SALOON

Whoop it up just as they did in the old days, and over the same bar they used in the old days. Ten miles west of town on the Parks Highway at Esther. **(907) 479-2500.** Entertainment includes readings of Robert Service poetry, vaudeville-type acts, and singing along with a honky-tonk piano.

RIVERBOAT DISCOVERY

Many call this the finest attraction in Fairbanks. The standard cruise aboard a sternwheeler on the Chena and Tanana rivers lasts about three hours and includes a stop at a traditional Native fish camp where local Native culture is highlighted. There's also a dog-mushing demonstration by Mary Shields, the first woman to enter the Iditarod. **(907) 479-6673.**

SANTA CLAUS HOUSE

This is a huge roadside gift shop in North Pole Alaska, about 10 miles before you get to Fairbanks.

SLED DOG RACING

The Alaska Dog Mushers Association is headquartered in Fairbanks. Two major races dominate its schedule. The **Yukon Quest**, a distance race between Whitehorse and Fairbanks in February, and the **Open North American Championship** in March. The latter is a sprint race run in four heats over four days. ADMA also maintains the Dog Mushing Museum with the world's most comprehensive exhibits on the sport. **(907) 457-MUSH.**

TANANA VALLEY FARMERS MARKET

On College Road at the entrance to the fairgrounds, locally grown produce is available for purchase seasonally from July through September. There are also flowers and shrubs for planting in your own garden.

THE UNIVERSITY OF ALASKA MUSEUM

One of the finest museums in Alaska, this facility features cultural and natural history displays from across Alaska and across the ages. A mummified Stepp bison, dug from the permafrost a few years back, is one of the highlights. Admission is $4 for adults. Family rates and discounts for seniors and military are available. **(907) 474-7505.**

——— WHERE TO STAY ———

ACCOMMODATIONS

$$–$$$

Captain Bartlett Inn
Airport Road, near Alaskaland. Restaurant and lounge. **(907) 452-1888.**

Cripple Creek Resort
Esther, 10 miles west of Fairbanks on Parks Highway. Part of a complex that includes the Malemute Saloon. **(907) 479-2500.**

Regency Fairbanks
95 **10th Avenue.** Restaurant and lounge. **(907) 452-3200.**

Sophie Station Hotel
1717 **University Avenue.** Restaurant and lounge. **(907) 479-3650.**

Westmark Fairbanks
813 **Noble Street.** Restaurant, coffee shop and lounge. **(907) 456-7722.**

BED AND BREAKFASTS

Fairbanks boasts a thriving B&B industry with more than 50 facilities operating in all parts of the community. The list here is just a sampling; a Fairbanks Visitors Guide from the Fairbanks CVB will provide you with many more options.

1940s Age Old B&B—(907) 451-7526.

Ah, Rose Marie B&B—(907) 456-2040.

Alaska Wild Iris Inn—(907) 474-IRIS.

Arctic Rose B&B—(907) 479-8246.

Borealis B&B—(907) 479-5666.

Chena River B&B—(907) 479-2532.

Chokecherry Inn—(907) 474-9381.

Hall's With a View—(907) 479-6120.

Little Fox Inn—(907) 457-6539.

Ravenswood B&B—(907) 457-6613.

Two River B&B—(907) 488-9038.

CAMPGROUNDS

Alaskaland
Airport Way. Self-contained RVs only. Dump station and water fill available. (907) 459-1087.

Chena Lakes State Recreation Area
Seventeen miles from town on Richardson Highway. (907) 488-1655.

Fairbanks International Airport Fly In Campground
At the airport with tiedowns for light planes. (907) 474-2506.

Norlite Campground
1660 Peger Road. (907) 474-0206.

River's Edge RV Park and Campground
4140 Boat Street. Day tours to Denali and city tours available from campground. Close to Alaskaland and the Riverboat Discovery. (907) 474-0286.

Tanana Valley Campground
1800 College Road. Part of the fairgrounds complex. (907) 456-7956.

WHERE TO EAT

$$$$

Bear & Seal
Westmark Hotel, 813 Noble Street. Superb food in a quiet setting. (907) 456-7722.

$$$

Clinkerdagger Bickerstaff & Pett's
24 College Road. (on edge of shopping center). Favorite gathering place in the Fairbanks area. (907) 452-2756.

Club 11
Eleven miles out on Richardson Highway. Steaks, prime rib and seafood. (907) 488-6611.

El Sombrero
The town's favorite Mexican restaurant. (907) 456-5269.

Pike's Landing
4438 Airport Way. Overlooking the Chena River. (907) 479-6500.

Pump House
Chena Pump Road out past the University. Old water pumping station on the river. (907) 479-8452.

Tiki Cove
427 1st Avenue, top of the Polaris Hotel. Oriental cuisine. (907) 452-1484.

Two Rivers Lodge

Mile 21 Chena Hot Springs Road. Excellent steaks and seafood. Try the Cajun barbecued ribs if they're available. (907) 488-6815.

$$

Alaska Salmon Bake

Next to Alaskaland on Airport Way. Barbecued salmon and ribs, fried halibut. The original salmon bake in Alaska. (907) 452-7274.

Food Factory

Noisy but great food and plenty of it. Three locations—36 College Road, (907) 452-3313; 1705 S. Cushman, (907) 452-6348; and 101 Santa Claus Lane (North Pole), (907) 488-3638.

Fox Roadhouse

Mile 11 Old Steese Highway. Steaks, prime rib and seafood. Popular with long-timers in the Fairbanks area. (907) 457-7461.

Ivory Jack's

2581 Goldstream Road. Good food and extensive display of carved and scrimshawed ivory on the walls. (907) 455-6666.

Outhouse Race held in Chatinika. (Photo by Ron Dalby)

Denali National Park

Formerly Mount McKinley National Park, Alaska's oldest and best-known park draws more visitors than all the rest of the national parks in Alaska combined. Yes, it can get crowded here, particularly in July. The best way to beat the crowds is by visiting in early June, late August or early September.

Denali can be reached by vehicle from either Anchorage (about a five-hour drive) or Fairbanks (a two-and-a-half-hour drive) via the Parks Highway, or by regularly scheduled passenger service on the Alaska Railroad. There's one train daily from both Anchorage and Fairbanks.

The train trip, in particular, is quite a spectacular way of reaching the park. It does more or less parallel the Parks Highway, but freed of the need to concentrate on driving or on your location, you can gaze out the windows as Mount McKinley and the Alaska Range loom ever closer. Complete food service and a lounge car are available on the train. It is a splendid way of relaxing and taking in the scenery. Contact the **Alaska Railroad, 1-800-544-0552,** for details on departures and fares.

A lengthy round of choices awaits you once you arrive at Denali National Park. The big draw, and the most used attraction for most visitors, is the bus trip on the Park Road to either Wonder Lake or the Eileson Visitors Center. Two means of accomplishing this exist. The National Park Service manages a fleet of **shuttle buses,** mostly old school buses, that leave the information center two or three times an hour for the trip along the road. You must obtain tokens for boarding these buses ($3 per person) at the information center. The tokens specify which bus you can get on to depart. From there, however, the tokens are relatively meaningless; you can disembark and reboard alternate buses almost at will once you are in the park. In that sense,

these tokens are most valuable—if you wish to get out and hike for a time, you do; then just get on the next bus going whichever direction you want to go.

The disadvantage to the Park Service buses is that they are fairly crowded and not particularly comfortable. If you ride one of these all the way to Wonder Lake and back, you'll be sitting in a hard seat designed for schoolchildren for nine or ten hours. The privately run buses, on the other hand, offer much more comfortable seats.

Costs for a trip on these private buses is about $50 per person, and it usually includes a sack lunch. The primary disadvantage is that once you're on one of these buses, it's the bus you stay with. There's no getting off for a hike in the tundra other than for a few brief moments at rest stops. Generally, the Park Service buses host a younger crowd and families with small children; the private buses cater to a more conservative and older crowd.

Whichever bus you take, it will be an experience you'll remember for the rest of your life. Almost certainly in the course of your tour, you will see moose, caribou, Dall sheep and a host of smaller mammals and birds. Grizzly bears are seen on almost every trip, and with a large piece of luck you may even see a wolf. No other national park in the United States can offer you this range of wildlife.

Proper etiquette on the buses requires that you sing out loudly upon spotting an animal, because everybody else will want to see it, too. Generally the driver will stop the bus so all can get a good look and take photographs, particularly if the animal in question is close to the road. You will not be allowed off the bus for a better camera angle or whatever, so be sure, to share viewing opportunities out your window with others on the bus. You'll want them to do the same for you when they spot the next animal.

During the course of your trek into the park, the bus will make several rest stops at outhouse facilities. The Park Service buses will also stop at a number of predesignated spots to drop off and pick up passengers. Though there will be little opportunity to get off and stretch at pick-up/drop-off stops, take advantage of every rest stop to get out and walk around. The high tundra of Denali is a fascinating place, and probably unlike any other terrain you will ever encounter.

About 60 miles into the park the bus will make a lengthy stop at the **Eileson Visitors Center.** Most of the private buses and some of the Park Service buses turn around at this point. The majority of the Park Service buses, however, continue to Wonder Lake, another 20 miles distant, after the stop at Eileson.

What are your chances of seeing **Mount McKinley** during the bus trip? So-so. The mountain is only visible about one day in three during the summer months.

Backpacking in Denali National Park. (Photo by Jennifer Dalby)

Most of the time it is hidden in the clouds. However, if you watch carefully to the southwest as you're riding along in the bus, you might get an occasional brief glimpse of Mount McKinley through gaps in the clouds.

The good news about the mountain being hidden by clouds is that the animals are more likely to be active in marginal or bad weather. On sunny warm days, when the mountain is constantly visible, the animals are more lethargic and less easily seen.

And, though the bus trip is the most popular Denali option, it is but one of many. One of the hardest questions most people have to answer is where they are going to stay at Denali. If you spend all day on a bus, you're almost certainly going to need overnight accommodations the night before or the night after—if not both.

RV drivers and campers can find themselves in a real bind. There are only about 200 campsites in the park itself, and most of these are claimed early. If you want a campsite in the park, go straight to the **Riley Creek Visitors Center** and register upon arrival and hope for the best. The ideal time to arrive for a campground is midmorning when those who have campsites begin checking out. If you're next in line when a campsite opens up, it's yours. Be prepared to hang around the visitors center for several hours waiting for a campsite.

The **Alaska Public Lands Information Centers** in Anchorage and Fairbanks do have a limited number of campsite reservations that can be made in advance. You must visit these offices in person 7 to 21 days in advance of your projected stay in the campground and be prepared to pay in full for your campsite at time of registration. This is a relatively new wrinkle in campgrounds allocations at Denali and is subject to change. Most Alaskans fervently hope that it works. For the past several years campgrounds have been only first-come, first-served, and most people just gave up any hope of ever getting a campsite in Denali. Contact the APLI Center in Anchorage at **(907) 271-2737** for directions to the office, and in Fairbanks at **(907) 451-7352**. These

are the only places you can make a campground reservation for Denali.

(*Author's note*: Denali's lack of campsites is cause for considerable grumbling in Alaska. Admittedly, it is a wilderness park. However, most people seem to believe that in an expanse of land larger than the state of Maryland space could be found for more than 200 campsites. On a summer day, as many as 5,000 people visit Denali Park. At two people per campsite, only 400 of them (8 percent) can find a place to camp within the park.)

In the 1980s, private industry moved to narrow the gap between demand and available accommodations in Denali National Park. There are now a couple of private RV parks just outside the gate as well as several hotels and lodges. Though there is still barely enough space to park RVs, particularly in July, there's not nearly as many rigs looking for a wide shoulder along the Parks Highway to spend the night these days.

Those looking for more substantial lodging will find it both hard to get a reservation at the last minute and fairly expensive. Later in this section there are detailed lists of hotels, lodges and campgrounds. In this one instance, the book tries to cover every possibility in a congested area simply because it's hard to find overnight accommodations in Denali on short notice. Also, there is no organized visitors bureau involving the Denali Park businesses, so there is no single source you can write to for more information.

Beyond the big items of a bus trip and a place to stay, Denali offers a host of other activities. There's whitewater rafting on the Nenana River at the eastern edge of the park, guided interpretive walks with Park Service naturalists, sled dog demonstrations near Park Headquarters (rangers patrol the park via dog team in the winter months) and much, much more. For detailed information, contact **Denali National Park and Preserve, P.O. Box 9, Denali Park, AK 99755**. In winter call **(907) 683-2294**; in summer call **(907) 683-1266**.

WHERE TO STAY

ACCOMMODATIONS

$$$$

Camp Denali
On private land near the end of the Park Road. Three-, four-, five- and seven-day packages available. Includes all meals and lodging and a number of activities. Winter: **(603) 675-2248;** summer: **(907) 683-2290.**

Denali Backcountry Lodge
Full-service lodge with one- to four-night packages including all meals and transportation into the park. Winter: **(907) 783-1342;** summer: **(907) 683-2594.**

Denali National Park Hotel
The only hotel on national park property within the boundaries of Denali National Park. One hundred rooms, restaurant, lounge and gift shop. **(907) 276-7234.**

Denali Wilderness Lodge
Fly-in lodge in the Alaska Range, 12 minutes by air from Denali National Park. **1-800-541-9779.**

Kantishna Roadhouse
Ninety-five miles into the park at the old mining settlement of Kantishna. Spectacular views, varied activities, and Maggie Kelley, a charming host. Overnight packages include all meals and transportation into the park. **1-800-942-7420.**

$$$

McKinley Chalet Resort and Mt. McKinley Village Lodge
Both are part of the recent buildup just outside the park entrance, and both are splendid facilities with restaurants, lounges and gift shops. Denali Park Hotels, a company that also runs the Denali National Park Hotel, handles these facilities. **(907) 276-7234.**

Mount McKinley Motor Lodge
One mile north of the park entrance. **(907) 683-2567.**

$$

Backwoods Lodge
Thirty miles south of Cantwell; approximately 50 miles south of the park entrance. **(907) 768-2232.**

Denali Grizzly Bear Cabins
Mile 231 on Parks Highway on Nenana River. Winter: **(907) 457-2924;** summer: **(907) 683-2696.**

Denali River Cabins
Mile 231 on Parks Highway. Train station pickup if needed. **(907) 683-2594.**

Denali River View Inn
Mile 238 on Parks Highway. Winter: **(206) 384-1078;** summer: **(907) 683-2663.**

Denali Suites
Fifteen miles north of the park entrance near Healy. **Mile 248.8 on Parks Highway. (907) 683-2848.**

McKinley/Denali Cabins
Mile 238.5 on Parks Highway. Closest to the park entrance. **(907) 683-2733.**

Sourdough Cabins
One mile north of the park entrance. All services within walking distance. **(907) 683-2773.**

Waugaman Village
Motel units in Healy, about 15 miles north of the park entrance. **Mile 248.7 on Parks Highway. (907) 683-2737.**

$

Denali Hostel
A bunk for $22. **(907) 683-1295.**

BED AND BREAKFASTS
Dome Home B&B (Healy)—**(907) 683-1239.**

Grandview B&B (Healy)—**(907) 683-2468.**

Healy Heights B&B—**(907) 683-2639.**

Homestead B&B (Healy)—**(907) 683-2575.**

CAMPGROUNDS

The first six campgrounds listed are within Denali National Park and managed by the Park Service. Fees were $12 a night in 1993.

Riley Creek: 102 spaces, RVs and tents.
Savage River: 33 spaces, RVs and tents.
Sanctuary River: 7 spaces, tents only.
Teklanika River: 50 spaces, RVs and tents.
Igloo Creek: 7 spaces, tents only.
Wonder Lake: 28 spaces, tents only.

Denali Grizzly Bear Campground

RV and tent sites. Hookups. **Mile 231.1 on Parks Highway** along the Nenana River. **(907) 683-2696.**

Denali Riverside RV Park

Mile 231.1 on Parks Highway, on Nenana River just south of the park entrance. RV and tent sites. **(907) 683-2500.**

Denali RV Park

New for 1993. **Mile 245.1 on Parks Highway,** about eight minutes from the park entrance. **(907) 683-1500.**

McKinley KOA Campground

In Healy, 12 miles north of the park entrance. **(907) 683-2379.**

Waugaman Village

30 RV hookups, laundry facilities. **Mile 248.7 on Parks Highway,** 11 miles north of the park entrance. **(907) 683-2737.**

Majestic 20,320-foot Mount McKinley as seen from Denali National Park. (Photo by Ron Dalby)

Gates of the Arctic
National Park

This massive national park straddles the mountains of the central Brooks Range for hundreds of miles. The most obvious means of access is to take a commercial flight from Fairbanks to Bettles, and from there charter a bush plane to take you into the park. Try **Bettles Air Service, (907) 692-5111,** for a carrier to take you into the park.

The Dalton Highway (Pipeline Haul Road) just touches the eastern boundary of the park near the small communities of Wiseman and Coldfoot. Overland access on foot from the road is possible, but is rarely attempted.

The only facility within the park is **Peace of Selby Wilderness.** This organization offers lakeside log cabins as a base for fishing, hiking and rafting expeditions into the park. Both full-service lodge packages and camp/tent rental are available. Fly-in only. **(907) 672-3206.**

Of all the stupendous scenery in Alaska, nothing even comes close to the Brooks Range during its brief summer and early (mid-August) fall. This is truly the remote wilderness envisioned by many: high mountains, tumbling streams, raging rivers and endless untrammeled vistas. The National Park Service fully intends

that this park should remain so. No development is permitted within the park, and operators taking people into its vast reaches are severely restricted as to where they can and cannot go.

Hikers and rafters vacationing on their own must be self-sufficient. Leave word in the Park Service office in Bettles on your proposed route and return date along with notification of which carrier is transporting you in and out of the park.

Whatever your intent in this wilderness, a firearm and ammunition are highly recommended in case a survival situation develops. Do not under any circumstances carry a firearm that you are unfamiliar with. It is less dangerous for you and your party to be unarmed than to be armed and not know what you are doing.

For a Park Service brochure on Gates of the Arctic National Park and a list of operators permitted to operate within the park, contact the **Alaska Public Lands Information Center, 350 Cushman St., #1A, Fairbanks, AK 99701, (907) 452-7286.** When inquiring about Gates of the Arctic, ask for every pertinent piece of literature available from that office regarding backcountry travel in the wilderness.

― GATES OF THE ARCTIC OUTFITTERS ―

BEC's Alaska Adventures
Gates of the Arctic backpacking treks. **(907) 457-8907.**

Alatna Lodge and Wilderness Cabins
Native land inholdings within the park. Wildlife viewing. **(907) 479-6354.** Seasonal service in July and August only.

Arctic Treks
Backpacking/rafting trips in Gates of the Arctic. **(907) 455-6502.**

Brooks Range Adventures
Guided backpacking, rafting, kayaking and wildlife adventures. **(907) 479-8203.**

Brooks Range Wilderness Trips

Explore by canoe and raft. Professionally guided small-group adventures. **(907) 488-6787.**

Gates of the Arctic Wilderness Adventure

Guided backpacking and rafting. **(907) 474-8600.**

Quest Expeditions

Five- to 14-day trips in northern Alaska, including Gates of the Arctic. **(907) 688-4848.**

Sourdough Outfitters

Backpacking, fishing, rafting, canoeing and more. Based in Bettles. **(907) 692-5252.**

Be sure to wear your bug repellent in the Gates of the Arctic National Park. Note the mosquitoes covering their vests. (Photo by Ron Dalby)

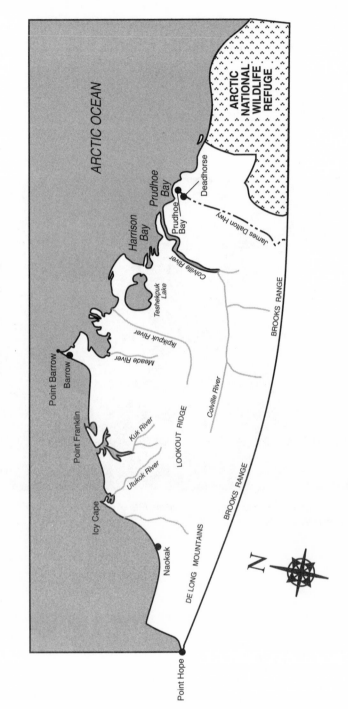

The Arctic

ARCTIC OCEAN

ARCTIC NATIONAL WILDLIFE REFUGE

Prudhoe Bay

Deadhorse

Prudhoe Bay

James Dalton Hwy

Harrison Bay

Coville River

Teshekpuk Lake

Ikpikpuk River

Meade River

BROOKS RANGE

Point Barrow

Barrow

Point Franklin

Kuk River

LOOKOUT RIDGE

Colville River

Utukok River

Icy Cape

BROOKS RANGE

Naokak

DE LONG MOUNTAINS

Point Hope

N

THE ARCTIC

OVERVIEW

By most definitions, the Arctic describes that region of the globe north of the Arctic Circle, which is a line circumventing the globe north of which there is at least one 24-hour period when the sun never sets. However, in this book some land within the Arctic Circle is described in two other sections: Western Alaska and Interior Alaska. The reasons have to do with both climate and physical geography.

South of the Brooks Range but north of the Arctic Circle in central Alaska, the climate, terrain and means of access are most like the Interior. Only north of the Brooks Range does one move into a land devoid of trees and, significantly, a Native culture that is Eskimo instead of Indian.

In western Alaska, the climate north to the edge of the Brooks Range is slightly more maritime, and trees can be found, though not along the coastline itself. Indigenous peoples in western Alaska are Eskimo as opposed to the Indians of the Interior, and the dividing line in this book between western Alaska and Interior Alaska more or less follows the distinction between Indian and Eskimo cultures. North of this book's western and Interior regions is the Arctic as outlined here; its Native peoples are exclusively Eskimo.

Alaska's Arctic north of the Brooks Range is almost a land unto itself. There are no trees and only in river valleys do shrubs exceed the height of a man. Geologically, this was the last portion of the Alaskan landmass to butt against the North American continent. From the air, much of the

193

region appears as a kaleidoscope of small lakes and polygons, the latter a distinctive feature of land whose surface is frozen most of the year and only thaws to a depth of a couple feet for a brief period in summer.

Despite the harshness of the environment, there is life here, a lot of it. Caribou are often the most visible, and the largest herds of these animals in North America call Alaska's Arctic home. Caribou herds are migratory, almost in constant motion; were they to remain rooted in a single place for any length of time, they would quickly devastate their own food supply.

Where there are caribou, there are usually wolves, and packs can be found on the fringes of the herds, moving in to eliminate a weak or injured animal or acting on opportunity if an animal gets separated from the herd. The theory that wolves prey on only the injured and the sick is a myth. Certainly they do cull these animals from the herd as the easiest of all possible prey, but when wolves are hungry they have to eat, whether or not a disabled animal is available.

This myth about wolves is just one of many perpetuated about the Arctic, but one story that is true is the proliferation of mosquitoes during the short summer. Some years back a biologist in Fairbanks calculated that the biomass of mosquitoes on the North Slope of Alaska outweighed the biomass of all the caribou, upward of half a million animals weighing an average of more than 200 pounds apiece. That is, without a doubt, an unbelievable number of mosquitoes. Obviously, wilderness travelers in the region must be alert to mosquito problems.

Besides the caribou, moose numbers are high and increasing in the Arctic. Mostly these animals are found in the dense stands of alder along creeks and riverbanks, but occasionally they can be found on the more open tundra.

Grizzly bears, too, are common in the Arctic, though it does take a fairly large territory to support a single bear. And, of course, there are polar bears along the north coast of Alaska. These animals spend most of the summer months out on the ice pack, and only a few come ashore in the winter, mostly females seeking dens to give birth to cubs.

Smaller mammals and birds are everywhere. Marmots, foxes, arctic hares and arctic ground squirrels can be seen on almost any day. Birds include a variety of raptors, breeding waterfowl in summer and count- less other species.

It's a land friendly to adapted wildlife because man has yet to fully adapt to the land and likely never will. Scattered bands of Eskimos did adapt to the land, though thriving is an inappropriate word when describing their living conditions in centuries gone by. Starvation was common, and in that subsistence era people of the land rarely knew where or when the next meal would appear.

Today the few villages in the region fare much better for a food supply. If the caribou don't appear, it's possible to use an airplane to find them. If wild food is completely unavailable, airplanes can bring in groceries to the few villages dotting the landscape or to individuals living alone in remote areas.

Other than short journeys on foot close to home and snow machines in winter (few people use dog teams these days), airplanes are really the only means of getting around in the Arctic. There are no roads and only a few boats in the villages. But even airplanes have their limitations. Fueling sites are few and far between, often hundreds of miles apart. At certain times of the year, a light plane may require skis, wheels and/or floats in combination just to fly from Barrow to Fairbanks.

Unless you're packing a tent on your back or in a kayak or raft, there are very few places to stay. There's a hotel in Barrow and one in Prudhoe Bay, not much else. In the state of Alaska's Vacation Planner, the Far North listing, which includes Nome, Kotzebue and Gates of the Arctic National Park, has only three pages of data—which contrasts with, for example, 14 pages for the Interior.

Barrow and Prudhoe Bay also have a restaurant or two, though the prices may scare you. Remember, everything served up here is flown in from either Anchorage or Fairbanks. Everything you use on a wilderness trek in this region is also flown in. When you pay the bill for that kind of service, you'll marvel at how relatively cheap restaurant prices are in this land.

Pack ice in the fall. The Beaufort Sea on the northern coast of Alaska. (Photo by Ron Dalby)

Barrow

There's a tendency to call Alaska's largest Eskimo village Point Barrow, and that is wrong. Barrow is the town; Point Barrow is the northernmost edge of a sand spit that marks the point farthest north on the North American continent. It's a short distance north of the town.

Barrow is the seat of government for the 88,000-square-mile North Slope Borough, by acreage the largest municipality in the world. That works out to about three square miles per person in this thinly populated region.

April and May are the traditional whaling months in Barrow, and whaling captains and their crews sail on open leads far out into the polar ice pack in search of humpback whales. Today a quota system severely limits kills and strikes. But, because of the whale's place in the traditional diet of North Slope Eskimos, whaling crews do their utmost to fill their allowable bag limits every year. Whales killed are shared throughout the community involved, another deeply rooted Eskimo tradition.

Most who visit Barrow do so as part of an overnight package tour from either Anchorage or Fairbanks. One price takes care of your airfare, a hotel room and several tours, and may include a stop at Prudhoe Bay either coming or going. Some tours overnight at Prudhoe and stop at Barrow for a short time on the first day of the trip.

In answer to the most frequent question about Barrow, the sun rises on May 10 and does not set again until August 2. There are an equal number of days in winter when the sun never rises.

———— WHERE TO STAY/TOURS ————

$$$
Arctic Safari Tours

Sheila Taranto will rent you a car or take you on a local tour in an honest-to-gosh limo, the latter seldom if ever seen before in Barrow. A local resident, she's thoroughly familiar with the area. Great fun. Sheila can also help with local lodging and other activities. **(907) 852-4444.**

Tundra Tours/Top of the World Hotel

"Don't you dare stop until you reach the top," is the motto expressed in their advertising. Barrow packages include a sampling of the native culture, airfare and lodging. **(907) 852-3900.**

Prudhoe Bay

Prudhoe Bay and neighboring Deadhorse, the latter is where the airport is located, are collectively a company town. The only reason they exist is to get oil out of the ground and send it down the trans-Alaska pipeline to tidewater at Valdez. With only a couple of exceptions, nobody lives here. They come here to work a week or several weeks of 12-hour days, then fly home to Anchorage or Fairbanks or even the Lower 48 for a break of equal time. Huge dormitory and dining complexes house the workers, and virtually every piece of equipment in sight is dedicated to producing oil.

The scenery is, in a word, flat. On the clearest days, the peaks of the Brooks Range are just barely visible to the south. The ice pack stays against the shore all year long except for a brief break in August or September.

All this aside, Prudhoe Bay is an increasingly popular destination for visitors. They come to see the oil fields and watch the people who work there bring the oil out of the ground. Fly-in packages that combine a stop in Barrow either coming or going are popular, but, increasingly, a fly-bus package over three days is becoming the way to visit Prudhoe Bay.

The basic fly-bus package brings travelers from Fairbanks to Prudhoe Bay over the Dalton Highway with an overnight stop along the way in Coldfoot. After touring the oil fields and spending the night at Prudhoe, passengers are flown back to either Fairbanks or Anchorage on the third day. It also works in reverse; fly to Prudhoe the first day and take the bus to Fairbanks on the second and third days.

These fly-bus packages open a whole new world of opportunity for Prudhoe travel. Very, very few visitors get to see the spectacular scenery in the Brooks Range up close, such as out the window of a bus. **Princess Cruises and Tours, 2815 2nd Avenue, #400, Seattle, WA 98121, (206)728-4202,** is a good operator to contact if you're interested in one of these fly-bus packages to Prudhoe Bay.

WHERE TO STAY

$$$
North Star Inn
Restaurant, entertainment center and health club. Packages with airfare available. **(907) 659-3160.**

Arctic National
Wildlife Refuge

If myths persist about the Arctic in general, myths about ANWR have grown all out of proportion in the past decade as the nation as a whole debates the idea of drilling for oil in this vast region.

To begin with, ANWR is roughly as large as the state of West Virginia, more than 20,000 square miles. The coastal plain of ANWR, the only area of interest to oil companies, is barely 5 percent of this total land space. None of the spectacular river valleys or mountain ranges are part of the coastal plain.

Caribou do use the coastal plain as a calving ground, but not exclusively. The Alaska Department of Fish and Game notes that these animals often go for years without visiting the coastal plain during the calving season.

Finally, this small stretch of Alaska's shoreline is far from the last remaining undisturbed Arctic coastal plain. There are, in fact, several hundred more miles of untouched coastal plain stretching west from Prudhoe Bay to Barrow and beyond. And that's just in Alaska. Canada's north coast has extensive stretches of coastal plain as well.

Most of the reporters in the Lower-48 press who write about ANWR and the debate over oil exploration know little of what they are writing about, and that includes people on both sides of the issue. More than anything else, this lack of knowledge tends to muddy the issue for everyone.

ANWR is spectacular in almost any way you describe it. The vastness, ruggedness and remoteness of the land are worth preserving, and will likely endure for centuries because the region is essentially uninhabitable for people.

Significantly, drilling for oil in ANWR wouldn't change the part of the refuge most wilderness enthusiasts visit—the mountains and the canyons on the north side of the Brooks Range. To be sure, flying in or out you might briefly notice some activity along the coastal plain from the window of your airplane, but that, in almost all cases, is miles and miles removed from where people venture.

What you will see from an airplane, drilling or no drilling, is wilderness stretching to the limits of your vision—and sometimes those limits can exceed 200 miles in the incredibly clear northern air. You will see wild, untamable rivers flowing from the mountains to the sea. Bands of caribou will undulate across the tundra beneath your wings. With luck, you might even see a small herd of shaggy musk oxen. Nothing beneath you is domesticated; all is wild.

For the most part, those who visit ANWR are those who most appreciate these vistas: hunters seeking the pure white Dall sheep of the mountains, photographers searching for unspoiled landscapes to put before their lenses and wilderness enthusiasts hiking or rafting through the nation's northernmost wildlife refuge.

Though you can put together your own adventure in ANWR, the logistics are daunting. It's far better to find a company specializing in the type of adventure you seek, and contract with them for your adventure. Many of these kinds of companies will tailor an itinerary to your wishes.

Almost all of the outfitters listed under Gates of the Arctic National Park in the previous chapter also run trips in ANWR. These people can arrange everything for you; all you need do is show up at the appointed time with your personal gear.

A Special
Arctic Adventure

Most who visit the Arctic's wilderness do so as part of tour assembled by an outfitter. But there is one trip that you can put together yourself that gets you some of the best the Arctic has to offer. From Fairbanks it will cost about $4,000 for two people to assemble and execute this trip, but you will remember it all your life.

From Fairbanks, take a scheduled flight to Bettles. In Bettles, charter an aircraft to take you to a small lake near Easter Creek on the north side of Gates of the Arctic National Park. Either blow up a rubber raft or assemble a folding kayak on the banks of Easter Creek and start downstream. Easter Creek will shortly flow into the Killik River, which flows north to the Colville River, the major drainage on Alaska's North Slope. Continue downstream on the Colville to Umiat, a small settlement with an airport. Total time, a week or so, depending on far you want to go in a single day.

The best time for this trip is in late August. Hundreds of thousands of caribou are migrating across the lower Killik River then. In addition, you'll almost certainly see Dall sheep on the mountains, grizzlies on the tundra and huge moose in the willows at riverside. Late August is good, too, because relatively few mosquitoes will be left and the fall colors will be coming out.

If you like to fish, grayling and possibly arctic char should be available in both rivers. All in all, this is a package that offers all of the best that is available in the Arctic's wilderness.

Once you reach Umiat, you can either be flown to Prudhoe Bay by Umiat Air Service to connect with a commercial jet to Anchorage or Fairbanks, or you can have the operator who flew you in from Bettles pick you up at Umiat and return you to Bettles.

One word of caution: Don't float downstream beyond Umiat. There's no other place to get off the river after you pass Umiat.

Appendix A

AGENCY ADDRESSES AND TELEPHONE NUMBERS

Alaska Marine Highway System
P.O. Box 25535
Juneau, AK 99802-5535
1-800-642-0066

Alaska Department of Fish and Game
P.O. Box 25526
Juneau, AK 99802-5526
(907) 465-4112

Alaska Division of Tourism
P.O. Box 110801
Juneau, AK 99811-0801
(907) 465-2010

Alaska Public Lands Information Center
605 W. 4th Avenue, #105
Anchorage, AK 99501-5162
(907) 271-2737

Alaska Public Lands Information Center
250 Cushman Street, #1A
Fairbanks, AK 99701
(907) 451-7352

Alaska Public Lands Information Center
P.O. Box 359
Tok, AK 99780-0359
(907) 883-5667

Alaska Railroad Corp.
Passenger Service Department
P.O. Box 107500
Anchorage, AK 99510-7500
1-800-544-0552

Alaska's Southwest
3300 Arctic Blvd., Suite 203
Anchorage, AK 99503
(907) 562-7380

Alaska State Chamber of Commerce
217 2nd Avenue
Juneau, AK 99801
(907) 586-2323

Alaska State Parks
P.O. Box 107001
Anchorage, AK 99510-7001
(907) 762-2261

Anchorage Chamber of Commerce
441 W. 5th Avenue, Suite 300
Anchorage, AK 99501
(907) 272-7588

Anchorage Convention & Visitors Bureau
1600 A Street, #200
Anchorage, AK 99501-5162
(907) 276-4118

Anchorage Visitor Information Center
4th Avenue and F Street
Anchorage, AK 99501
(907) 274-3531

Anchor Point Chamber of Commerce
P.O. Box 610
Anchor Point, AK 99556
(907) 235-2600

Bethel Chamber of Commerce
P.O. Box 329
Bethel, AK 99559
(907) 543-2911

Bethel Visitors Center
P.O. Box 388
Bethel, AK 99559
(907) 543-2098

Big Lake Chamber of Commerce
P.O. Box 520067
Big Lake, AK 99652
(907) 892-6109

Bureau of Land Management
222 W. 7th Avenue, #13
Anchorage, AK 99513
(907) 271-5555

Chugiak-Eagle River Chamber
of Commerce
P.O. Box 770353
Eagle River, AK 99577
(907) 694-4702

Cordova Chamber of Commerce
P.O. Box 99
Cordova, AK 99574-0099
(907) 424-7260

Cordova Visitors Center
P.O. Box 391
Cordova, AK 99574
(907) 424-7443

Delta Junction Visitor Information Center
P.O. Box 987
Delta Junction, AK 99737
(907) 895-5068 (winter)
(907) 895-9941 (summer)

Denali Visitor Information Center
P.O. Box 987
Cantwell, AK 99729
(907) 768-2420

Dillingham Chamber of Commerce
P.O. Box 348
Dillingham, AK 99576
(907) 842-5115

Fairbanks Chamber of Commerce
2nd Avenue
Fairbanks, AK 99709
(907) 452-4105

Fairbanks Convention & Visitors Bureau
550 1st Avenue
Fairbanks, AK 99701-4790
1-800-327-5774

Golden Circle Highway Visitors Association
P.O. Box 518
Haines, AK 99827
1-800-458-3579

Greater Copper Basin Chamber of Commerce
P.O. Box 469
Glennallen, AK 99588
(907) 822-5555

Gustavus Visitors Association
P.O. Box 167
Gustavus, AK 99826
(907) 697-2358

Haines Visitors Bureau
P.O. Box 518
Haines, AK 99827-0518
1-800-458-3579

Homer Chamber of Commerce
P.O. Box 541
Homer, AK 99603
(907) 235-7740 (winter)
(907) 235-5300 (summer)

Houston Chamber of Commerce
P.O. Box 940356
Houston, AK 99694
(907) 892-6129

Hyder Community Association
P.O. Box 149
Hyder, AK 99923
FAX: (604) 636-9148

Juneau Chamber of Commerce
217 2nd Street, Suite 201
Juneau, AK 99801
(907) 586-2323

Juneau Convention & Visitors Bureau
369 S. Franklin, #201
Juneau, AK 99801
(907) 586-1737

Juneau Visitor Information Center
Davis Log Cabin
134 3rd Street
Juneau, AK 99801
(907) 586-2201

Kenai Bicentennial Visitors & Convention
Bureau
P.O. Box 1991
Kenai, AK 99611-6935
(907) 283-1991

Kenai Peninsula Tourism Marketing Council
110 S. Willow Street, #106
Kenai, AK 99611
(907) 283-3850

Kenai Peninsula Visitor Information Center
P.O. Box 236
Soldotna, AK 99669
(907) 283-7989

Ketchikan Visitors Bureau
131 Front Street
Ketchikan, AK 99901-6413
(907) 225-6166

King Salmon Visitors Center
P.O. Box 298
King Salmon, AK 99613
(907) 246-4250

Kodiak Chamber of Commerce
P.O. Box 1485
Kodiak, AK 99615
(907) 486-5557

Kodiak Island Visitor Information Center
100 Marine Way
Kodiak, AK 99615
(907) 486-4070

Mat-Su Visitors Center
HC 01 Box 6166 J-21
Palmer, AK 99645
(907) 746-5000

Nenana Chamber of Commerce
P.O. Box 70
Nenana, AK 99760
(907) 832-5441 (winter)
(907) 832-9953 (summer)

Ninilchik Chamber of Commerce
P.O. Box 164
Ninilchik, AK 99639
(907) 567-3395

Nome Convention & Visitors Bureau
P.O. Box 251
Nome, AK 99762-0251
(907) 443-5535

North Pole Chamber of Commerce
P.O. Box 55071
North Pole, AK 99705
(907) 488-2242

Palmer Chamber of Commerce
P.O. Box 45
Palmer, AK 99645
(907) 745-2880

Petersburg Chamber of Commerce
P.O. Box 649
Petersburg, AK 99833
(907) 772-3646

Prince William Sound Tourism Coalition
P.O. Box 243044
Anchorage, AK 99524-3044
(907) 338-1213

Seldovia Chamber of Commerce
Drawer F
Seldovia, AK 99663
(907) 234-7643

Seward Chamber of Commerce
P.O. Box 749
Seward, AK 99664
(907) 224-3046

Sitka Chamber of Commerce
P.O. Box 638
Sitka, AK 99835
(907) 747-8604

Sitka Convention & Visitors Bureau
P.O. Box 1226
Sitka, AK 99835
(907) 747-5940

Skagway Convention & Visitors Bureau
P.O. Box 415
Skagway, AK 99840-0415
(907) 983-2854

Soldotna Chamber of Commerce
P.O. Box 236
Soldotna, AK 99669
(907) 262-9814

Southeast Alaska Tourism Council
369 S. Franklin Street, Suite 205
Juneau, AK 99801
(907) 586-4777

Sutton Chamber of Commerce
P.O. Box 24
Sutton, AK 99674
(907) 745-4527

Talkeetna Chamber of Commerce
P.O. Box 334
Talkeetna, AK 99676
(907) 733-2330

Tok Chamber of Commerce
P.O. Box 389
Tok, AK 99780
(907) 883-5887 (winter)
(907) 883-5775 (summer)

Unalaska/Dutch Harbor Chamber of Commerce
P.O. Box 833
Dutch Harbor, AK 99692
(907) 581-2190

Unalaska Visitors Center
The Henry Swanson House
P.O. Box 89
Unalaska, AK 99685
(907) 581-1483

USDA Forest Service Information Center
Centennial Hall
101 Egan Drive
Juneau, AK 99801
(907) 586-8751

U.S. Fish & Wildlife Service
1011 E. Tudor Road
Anchorage, AK 99503
(907) 786-3487

Valdez Visitor Information Center
P.O. Box 1603
Valdez, AK 99686
(907) 835-4636

Wasilla Chamber of Commerce
1801 Parks Highway, #C18
Wasilla, AK 99654
(907) 376-1299

White Mountain Visitor Information Center
c/o City Hall
White Mountain, AK 99784
(907) 638-3411

City of Whittier
P.O. Box 608
Whittier, AK 99693
(907) 472-2337

Willow Chamber of Commerce
P.O. Box 286
Willow, AK 99688
(907) 495-6823

Wrangell Chamber of Commerce
P.O. Box 49
Wrangell, AK 99929
(907) 874-3901

Wrangell Visitors Bureau
P.O. Box 1078
Wrangell, AK 99929
(907) 874-3779

Appendix B

NEWSPAPERS

Alaska Business Monthly
P.O. Box 241288
Anchorage, AK 99524-1288
1-800-770-4373

Alaska Commercial Fisherman
3709 Spenard Road, #200
Anchorage, AK 99503
(907) 562-4684

Alaska Journal of Commerce
P.O. Box 91419
Anchorage, AK 99509-1419
(907) 249-1900

Alaska Travel News
P.O. Box 202622
Anchorage, AK 99520
(907) 278-5891

Alaska Traveler
P.O. Box 201894
Anchorage, AK 99520
(907) 272-7500

The Alaskan Southeaster
P.O. Box 240667
Douglas, AK 99824
(907) 364-3700

Alaskan Viewpoint
HCR 64, Box 453
Seward, AK 99664
(907) 288-3168

Aleutian Eagle
3709 Spenard Road, #200
Anchorage, AK 99503
(907) 562-4684

Anchorage Daily News
P.O. Box 149001
Anchorage, AK 99514-9001
(907) 257-4200

Aniak Paper
P.O. Box 116
Aniak, AK 99557
(907) 675-4418

Arctic Sounder
P.O. Box 290
Kotzebue, AK 99752
(907) 442-2716

Barrow Sun
3709 Spenard Road, #200
Anchorage, AK 99503
(907) 562-4684

Bristol Bay News
3709 Spenard Road, #200
Anchorage, AK 99503
(907) 562-4684

Bristol Baytimes & Dutch Harbor Fisherman
P.O. Box 1129
Dillingham, AK 99576
(907) 842-5572

Capital City Weekly
8365 Old Dairy Road
Juneau, AK 99801
(907) 789-4145

Chilkat Valley News
P.O. Box 630
Haines, AK 99827
(907) 766-2688

Chugiak-Eagle River Star
16941 N. Eagle River Loop
Eagle River, AK 99577
(907) 694-2727

Copper River Country Journal
P.O. Box 336
Glennallen, AK 99588
(907) 822-5233

Cordova Times
Box 200
Cordova, AK 99574
(907) 424-7181

Daily Sitka Sentinel
P.O. Box 799
Sitka, AK 99835
(907) 747-3219

Delta Paper
P.O. Box 988
Delta Junction, AK 99737
(907) 895-4310

Fairbanks Daily News-Miner
P.O. Box 70710
Fairbanks, AK 99707
(907) 456-6661

Frontiersman
1261 Seward Meridian
Wasilla, AK 99654
(907) 373-5225

Haines Sentinel
P.O. Box 630
Haines, AK 99827
(907) 766-2688

Homer News
3483 Landings Street
Homer, AK 99603
(907) 235-7767

Island News
P.O. Box 19430
Thorne Bay, AK 99919
(907) 828-3377

Juneau Empire
3100 Channel Drive
Juneau, AK 99801-7814
(907) 586-3740

Ketchikan Daily News
P.O. Box 7900
Ketchikan, AK 99901
(907) 225-3157

Kodiak Daily Mirror
1419 Selig Street
Kodiak, AK 99615
(907) 486-3227

Mukluk News
P.O. Box 90
Tok, AK 99780
(907) 883-2571

Nome Nugget
P.O. Box 610
Nome, AK 99762
(907) 443-5235

North Pole Independent
P.O. Box 55757
Fairbanks, AK 99705
(907) 488-0669

Peninsula Clarion
P.O. Box 3009
Kenai, AK 99611
(907) 283-7551

Petersburg Pilot
P.O. Box 930
Petersburg, AK 99833
(907) 772-9393

Senior Voice
325 E. 3rd Avenue, Suite 300
Anchorage, AK 99501
(907) 277-0787

Seward Phoenix Log
P.O. Box 89
Seward, AK 99664
(907) 224-8070

Skagway News
P.O. Box 1898
Skagway, AK 99840
(907) 983-2354

Tundra Drums
P.O. Box 868
Bethel, AK 99559
(907) 543-3500

Tundra Times
P.O. Box 104480
Anchorage, AK 99510-4480
(907) 274-2512

Valdez Pioneer
P.O. Box 367
Valdez, AK 99686
(907) 835-3881

Valdez Vanguard
P.O. Box 98
Valdez, AK 99686
(907) 835-2211

Valley Courier
P.O. Box 28
Healy, AK 99743
(907) 683-1254

Valley Sun
1261 Seward Meridian
Wasilla, AK 99654
(907) 376-5225

Village Voice
P.O. Box 1615
Bethel, AK 99559
(907) 543-2938

Wrangell Sentinel
P.O. Box 798
Wrangell, AK 99929
(907) 874-2301

Appendix C

CLIMATE CHART

AVERAGE TEMPERATURES (Fahrenheit), PRECIPITATION AND DAYLIGHT HOURS

		ANCH.	BARROW	BETHEL	COLD BAY	FAIRBKS	HOMER	JUNEAU	KETCH.	KING SALMON	KODIAK	NOME	VALDEZ		
JANUARY	Temperature	14.8	−13.7	6.6	28.4	−10.3	22.7	23.1	34.2	15.0	32.3	6.5	22.6	Temperature	JANUARY
	Precipitation	0.80	0.20	0.81	2.71	0.55	2.23	3.98	14.01	1.11	9.52	0.88	5.63	Precipitation	
	Daylight Hours	6:25	0	6:31	7:41	5:07	6:49	7:07	7:43	7:03	7:16	5:16	6:25	Daylight Hours	
FEBRUARY	Temperature	18.5	−19.2	7.3	27.5	−4.1	25.3	28.2	36.4	15.1	30.5	3.5	24.3	Temperature	FEBRUARY
	Precipitation	0.86	0.18	0.71	2.30	0.41	1.78	3.66	12.36	0.82	5.67	0.56	5.08	Precipitation	
	Daylight Hours	9:04	6.58	9:07	9:43	8:31	9:15	9:23	9:41	9:22	9:28	8:34	9:04	Daylight Hours	
MARCH	Temperature	24.7	−15.4	12.3	29.5	10.0	28.3	32.0	38.6	21.7	34.4	8.3	30.3	Temperature	MARCH
	Precipitation	0.63	0.15	0.80	2.19	0.37	1.57	3.24	12.22	1.06	5.16	0.63	4.06	Precipitation	
	Daylight Hours	11:44	11:32	11:41	11:48	11:41	11:45	11:46	11:48	11:46	11:46	11:41	11:44	Daylight Hours	
APRIL	Temperature	35.2	−2.2	24.7	33.0	30.0	35.3	39.2	43.0	30.8	37.6	17.3	37.0	Temperature	APRIL
	Precipitation	0.63	0.20	0.65	1.90	0.28	1.27	2.83	11.93	1.07	4.47	0.67	2.89	Precipitation	
	Daylight Hours	14:42	16:31	14:39	14:08	15:10	14:32	14:24	14:08	14:26	14:21	15:08	14:41	Daylight Hours	
MAY	Temperature	46.5	18.9	40.2	39.5	48.3	42.6	46.7	49.2	42.3	43.6	35.5	45.3	Temperature	MAY
	Precipitation	0.63	0.16	0.83	2.40	0.57	1.07	3.46	9.06	1.25	6.65	0.58	2.74	Precipitation	
	Daylight Hours	17:27	24:00	17:21	16:11	18:39	17:04	16:47	16:12	16:51	16:39	18:29	17:26	Daylight Hours	
JUNE	Temperature	54.4	33.7	51.5	45.5	59.5	49.1	53.0	54.7	50.0	49.6	45.7	52.0	Temperature	JUNE
	Precipitation	1.02	0.36	1.29	2.13	1.29	1.00	3.02	7.36	1.54	5.72	1.14	2.64	Precipitation	
	Daylight Hours	19:18	24:00	19:07	17:23	21:39	18:41	18:15	17:26	18:21	18:04	21:21	19:16	Daylight Hours	
JULY	Temperature	58.1	39.0	54.7	50.3	61.7	53.0	55.9	58.0	54.5	54.5	50.8	55.0	Temperature	JULY
	Precipitation	1.96	0.87	2.18	2.50	1.84	1.63	4.09	7.80	2.10	3.80	2.18	3.77	Precipitation	
	Daylight Hours	18:27	24:00	18:21	16:51	20:11	17:57	17:36	16:54	17:41	17:26	20:00	18:26	Daylight Hours	
AUGUST	Temperature	56.1	37.9	52.7	51.4	56.3	52.8	54.8	58.7	53.8	55.2	49.8	53.6	Temperature	AUGUST
	Precipitation	2.31	0.97	3.65	3.71	1.82	2.56	5.10	10.60	2.96	4.03	3.20	5.73	Precipitation	
	Daylight Hours	15:51	19:03	15:47	15:01	16:35	15:36	15:25	15:02	15:28	15:20	16:31	15:51	Daylight Hours	
SEPTEMBER	Temperature	48.0	30.6	45.1	47.5	45.0	47.2	49.3	54.0	47.0	50.2	42.3	47.3	Temperature	SEPTEMBER
	Precipitation	2.51	0.64	2.58	4.06	1.02	2.96	6.25	13.61	2.75	7.18	2.59	7.99	Precipitation	
	Daylight Hours	12:57	13:31	12:56	12:45	13:06	12:53	12:51	12:46	12:52	12:50	13:05	12:57	Daylight Hours	
OCTOBER	Temperature	34.7	14.5	30.5	39.7	25.2	37.8	41.9	47.0	32.6	41.2	28.3	38.1	Temperature	OCTOBER
	Precipitation	1.86	0.51	1.48	4.45	0.81	3.41	7.64	22.55	1.98	7.85	1.38	8.23	Precipitation	
	Daylight Hours	10:07	8:51	10:09	10:31	9:47	10:14	10:20	10:31	10:18	10:22	9:48	10:07	Daylight Hours	
NOVEMBER	Temperature	21.8	−0.7	17.4	34.4	3.8	28.8	32.8	40.4	22.9	35.0	16.6	27.8	Temperature	NOVEMBER
	Precipitation	1.08	0.27	0.98	4.33	0.67	2.74	5.13	17.90	1.45	6.89	1.02	6.09	Precipitation	
	Daylight Hours	7:18	2:37	7:23	8:23	6:19	7:38	7:52	8:22	7:49	7:59	6:25	7:19	Daylight Hours	
DECEMBER	Temperature	15.2	−11.8	6.9	30.1	−8.1	23.3	27.2	36.0	14.7	32.1	6.2	22.5	Temperature	DECEMBER
	Precipitation	1.06	0.17	0.95	3.16	0.73	2.71	4.48	15.82	1.19	7.39	0.82	6.65	Precipitation	
	Snowfall (mean)	14.0	7.1	9.0	9.7	12.5	11.7	32.2	9.2	7.8	9.9	8.7	62.9	Snowfall (mean)	
	Daylight Hours	5:32	0	5:41	7:10	3:49	6:03	6:25	7:08	6:20	6:35	4:00	5:33	Daylight Hours	
ANNUAL	Temperature	35.7	9.3	29.1	38.1	26.5	37.2	40.3	45.9	33.4	41.3	25.6	38.0	Temperature	ANNUAL
	Precipitation	15.37	4.67	16.90	35.84	10.37	24.93	53.15	155.22	19.28	74.33	15.64	61.50	Precipitation	

209

Index

211

— T —